SMALL GROUP DECISION MAKING:
COMMUNICATION AND THE GROUP PROCESS

McGRAW-HILL SERIES IN SPEECH

Glen E. Mills, Consulting Editor in General Speech
John J. O'Neill, Consulting Editor in Speech Pathology

Aly and Aly: *A Rhetoric of Public Speaking*
Armstrong and Brandes: *The Oral Interpretation of Literature*
Baird: *American Public Addresses*
Baird: *Argumentation, Discussion, and Debate*
Baird, Knower, and Becker: *Essentials of General
 Speech Communication*
Baird, Knower, and Becker: *General Speech Communication*
Carrell and Tiffany: *Phonetics*
Fisher: *Small Group Decision Making: Communication
 and the Group Process*
Gibson: *A Reader in Speech Communication*
Hahn, Lomas, Hargis, and Vandraegen: *Basic Voice Training
 for Speech*
Hasling: *The Message, the Speaker, the Audience*
Henning: *Improving Oral Communication*
Kaplan: *Anatomy and Physiology of Speech*
Kruger: *Modern Debate*
Mortensen: *Communication: The Study of Human Interaction*
Myers and Myers: *The Dynamics of Human Communication: A
 Laboratory Approach*
Ogilvie: *Speech in the Elementary School*
Ogilvie and Rees: *Communication Skills: Voice and Pronunciation*
Powers: *Fundamentals of Speech*
Reid: *Speaking Well*
Reid: *Teaching Speech*
Robinson and Becker: *Effective Speech for the Teacher*
Wells: *Cleft Palate and Its Associated Speech Disorders*

Small Group Decision Making: Communication and the Group Process

B. Aubrey Fisher, Ph. D.

Associate Professor of Communication
University of Utah

McGraw-Hill Book Company

New York   St. Louis   San Francisco   Düsseldorf   Johannesburg
Kuala Lumpur   London   Mexico   Montreal   New Delhi   Panama
Paris   São Paulo   Singapore   Sydney   Tokyo   Toronto

This book was set in Times Roman by Black Dot, Inc.
The editors were Stephen D. Dragin and John M. Morriss;
the designer was Barbara Ellwood;
and the production supervisor was Thomas J. LoPinto.
The drawings were done by Textart Services, Inc.
Kingsport Press, Inc., was the printer and binder.

Library of Congress Cataloging in Publication Data

Fisher, B   Aubrey, date
  Small group decision making.

  (McGraw-Hill series in speech)
  Bibliography: p.
  1. Small groups. 2. Decision-making.
  3. Communication. I. Title.
  HM133.F55   301.18'5   73-17221
  ISBN 0-07-021090-X

SMALL GROUP DECISION MAKING:
COMMUNICATION AND THE GROUP PROCESS

1 2 3 4 5 6 7 8 9 0 KPKP 7 9 8 7 6 5 4

Contents

Preface

Small Group Decision Making: Communication and the Group Process emphasizes two perspectives within the group context—decision making and communication. While groups serve a multitude of purposes in our society, probably the most typical of all real-life groups is the group that performs some form of decision-making task. This book considers knowledge gained from studying all facets of group life—including training groups, family groups, and therapy groups—but the principal interest of this book is the group that makes decisions in face-to-face interaction.

Communication is often defined as merely the transmitting and receiving of messages. While this purely structural concept of communication is certainly important, the present volume emphasizes the process of communication. Communication is considered *the* organizing element of the group. Through communication human beings process information, test ideas, exchange opinions, and achieve consensus on decisions. Through communication human beings develop interpersonal relationships and form "groups" from aggregates of individuals. Thus, communication is the crux of the task and social dimensions of all groups.

This book is intended for university students studying group discussion. The students' primary interest may lie in group formation, in task performance, in social systems, in decision making, in social conflict, or in a variety of areas. The common point of departure, however, is communication which organizes people into an active social system for the purpose of performing some task—notably decision making. Therefore, this book may be used in a variety of courses in a variety of university departments at different levels in an undergraduate curriculum.

No book springs full-blown from a single person's mind. This book is certainly no exception. While I assume full responsibility for my own biases and idiosyncrasies contained herein, this volume is also the product of many influences, direct and indirect. Unfortunately, any attempt to list comprehensively all those influences in order to express my appreciation will be inevitably incomplete.

My interest in small group communication began during my years as a graduate student at the University of Minnesota where an atmosphere of cooperative scholarship prevails. For that atmosphere I shall be eternally grateful. I must also acknowledge Glen Mills, without whose encouragement and gentle prodding this book would yet be unwritten.

It is also my enviably good fortune to be associated with the department of communication at the University of Utah. A vibrant spirit of free inquiry, superb fellowship, and scholarly excitement charges the very air we breathe. The uninhibited dialogue and argumentative exchanges—second to none—stimulate us all.

And to Irene—wife, secretary, companion, lover, and friend—an inadequate but nonetheless sincere "Thank you!"

B. Aubrey Fisher

Introduction

A lone human being surely has the capacity to make decisions on his own without the help of other small group members. But individual decision making is not the focus of this book. Rather, the focus is on decision making performed in the social context of a small group by all group members functioning as a unified social system. Chapters 2 and 3 explain how group decision making differs inherently from individual decision making both in the process of making decisions and in the nature of the decision-making task. Thus, the *group* is considered a decision-making system.

Although there are obvious similarities among different types of groups, no comprehensive treatment of the group context used as a setting to modify overtly and purposively the behaviors or personalities of the members is included. Similarities between some types of groups and group decision making are noted throughout the book in order to further our understanding of group decision making. Furthermore, for our purposes group members make decisions for and by themselves. That is, the consideration of an audience, implicitly or explicitly present, is absent from the book. Chapter 1 describes the rationale for omitting consideration of public discussions and manipulative uses of the group context.

Effective decision making is considered a natural consequence of the members' abilities to analyze and understand the process of group decision making. But people cannot acquire such an ability without active participation in group decision making. While some people may argue that one cannot effectively experience any phenomenon without thoroughly studying it from the impartial and objective perspective of the observer, others argue just as vehemently that there is no substitute for experience. Both sides of this hackneyed controversy between the values of education and experience are probably at once both right and wrong. Knowledge of anything without experiencing it is as sterile as experiencing it without any knowledge. It is strongly urged that the student of group decision making incorporate his understanding of group decision making gained from reading this book and others with actual participation in groups engaged in decision-making tasks. Combining understanding with experience leads to the most fruitful results and maximizes the effectiveness of group decision making.

Too often overlooked in the study of group decision making is the process of communication—the most vitally essential ingredient of any social system. Communication is the organizing element of a social system. To highlight the study of group communication, the group is defined in a face-to-face setting which absolutely requires verbal and oral communication as the principal mode of interaction.

The initial chapter of the book does not include the italicized definitions characteristic of many textbooks. As each concept is discussed, it is defined at that point in the book although the definition is rarely set off in italics for "handy memorization." Defining a concept is easy. Understanding it is much more difficult but infinitely more valuable. If anyone is compelled by some inexplicable urge to memorize definitions, the Appendix includes a "Reader's Guide to Jargon" giving thumbnail definitions for most specialized terms used in the book.

Chapters 2 and 3 provide a general overview of the group as a social system. This general overview emphasizes the progressive development of a group through time as a cumulative process which incorporates elements of both structure and action and emphasizes communicative behaviors as the core of the group process. Not every collection of individuals is a group. But over time, an aggregate develops "groupness." The basic process of group development emphasizing group communication is the subject of Chapters 2 and 3.

Chapters 4, 5, and 6 view the group process from the viewpoint of its socioemotional dimension. This viewpoint illustrates those aspects of the interpersonal relationships of the small group—that is, how members get along with each other in a social setting. Chapter 7 emphasizes the task dimension of the group process—that is, how aspects of getting the job done illustrate the group process.

Social interrelationships among group members and accomplishing the decision-making task are inseparably interdependent. The two basic dimensions of the group process, explicated in Chapter 3, are separated only for the purposes of analysis. But such a separation is purely arbitrary and actually impossible in realistic practice. While all chapters maintain the interdependence of the task and socioemotional dimensions of the group process, Chapters 8 and 9 illustrate how group communication binds the two dimensions of the group process interdependently together. These two chapters view the group process from the most basic perspective of its central organizing element—communication. The final chapter, Chapter 10, includes elements which were omitted from or didn't quite "fit" in the first nine chapters and attempts to draw together the elements of the book into a coherent whole.

Along with "A Reader's Guide to Jargon," The Appendix includes "Anatomy of a Decision," illustrating the four phases of group decision making described in Chapter 7. This illustration, drawing from the verbal interaction of an actual group engaged in decision making, provides actual sequences of interaction from each phase of the group process as a verbal picture of what group decision making "really looks like."

"Analysis of Small Group Interaction" in the Appendix provides a brief introduction to observing individuals who are communicating in an actual group. Any student of group communication should have some "feel" for observing and analyzing a group in the process of interacting with each other. The Appendix is not intended to make anyone an expert observer. Expertise can come only from experience and much more training. But it is hoped that the reader will nevertheless secure the "feeling" of observation and analysis of real-life group communication.

All chapters of this book emphasize an understanding of how a group is structured, how it functions, and how it evolves. Understanding is the key to effective participation in group decision making. Central to that understanding and effective participation is group communication. One must always remember that however members of a small group may differ from one another as human beings with somewhat unique personalities, they are all communicating individuals. And that facet of members' participation—their communicative acts—provides the key to effective group decision making. The reader should also keep in mind that no one can really teach effective communication; it can only be learned. It is hoped that the truth of that seemingly nonsensical statement will be apparent later.

SMALL GROUP DECISION MAKING:
COMMUNICATION AND THE GROUP PROCESS

Chapter 1

The Group Context

Robert Stroud, better known as the "birdman of Alcatraz," was truly an amazing individual. Without previous background or professional training in ornithology, he became an expert on birds and bird diseases while a prisoner in solitary confinement. For most of us the most amazing part of Stroud's story is not his self-developed expertise in ornithology but the fact that he could endure so many years of solitude. We cannot even imagine the interminable tedium of loneliness—no one to talk with day after day, no one to laugh with or argue with or just sit in silence with year after year. Most of us would probably prefer death to an indefinite sentence of absolutely solitary confinement.

One of the techniques associated with brainwashing involves social isolation. The prisoner is separated from all other prisoners and cut off from all communication with his family, friends, or even the author of a book. It is not surprising that the prisoner often develops an interpersonal bond akin to friendship with his jailer. Satisfying the compelling need for companionship is preferable to insanity. The feeling of being absolutely and totally alone is simply intolerable for a normal human being.

The human is indeed a social animal. Few of us could exist as a social hermit, and we generally consider those few hermits who do exist to be crazy. This is not to say, however, that humans crave to live in huge metropolitan communities, although a glance at any of our overcrowded and smog-ridden megalopolises would seem to indicate that many do. But the individual can feel just as alone in a large city as in solitary confinement. Humans have developed a need for intimate social relationships. In other words, humans have developed a need to belong— typically to a small group.

The small group is the oldest and most common of all social organizations. Nations and entire civilizations have come and gone, but the small group has continued throughout all recorded history. We belong to family groups of close friends, groups of associates at work, recreational groups, ad infinitum. While our membership in some small groups may involve only interpersonal friendship and serves no purpose other than the gratification of social needs, our membership in many small groups serves a much broader purpose. Work groups in an office or factory exist in order to perform some task within the larger social organization. Political action groups attempt to work collectively toward the solution of social problems.

Groups generally exist to accomplish some purpose. Group members perform some task which requires cooperative effort for the group to be productive. The goal of the group is, to some extent, the goal of each individual member. Without such task groups the larger society would shrivel and die. After all, what is a society other than the sum of coordinated and interconnected small groups existing within it? Thus groups not only have purposes, but they carry out purposes and even shape the purposes of the larger society of which they are a part.

We are concerned with small groups existing for a definite purpose. For the moment, let us not quibble about how small a small group must be. Certainly the group must be small enough so that every member is able to know and communicate with every other member. We are also concerned with communication. A group, however large or small, cannot and does not exist without communication among its members. Communication and only communication binds individual human beings together into group membership. Communication and only communication allows group members to fulfill the group purposes.

Communication, for our purposes, inherently includes speech or oral communication. Of course, people communicate nonverbally as well, through gestures, movement, and space. But speech is the primary mode of communication in every small group. Furthermore, for our purposes, the communicating members of a small group are in a face-to-face situation. While it is theoretically possible for a group to exist by communicating only through letters or telephone, the face-to-face situation is far more typical in this society.

But our primary concern involves a more specific purpose—the purpose of making decisions. While many aspects of a small group are common to numerous types of groups with a greater variety of purposes, group decision making is not only more common but allows for greater sophistication in developing the group process. We shall, of course, be interested in other group purposes from time to time as they contribute to our understanding of group decision making, but the emphasis of the book remains on decision making.

This first chapter considers the group context from several perspectives and introduces the scope and purpose of the remaining chapters. In many ways our treatment of small group decision making is somewhat unusual. While some books consider group decision making in the context of a public discussion, other books focus on groups whose purposes are other than that of making decisions. This initial chapter surveys some of those other approaches and, by way of contrast, introduces the group context to be employed in the present treatment of group decision making. The chapter also considers some of the mystique of conventional wisdom surrounding group decision making and outlines the chapters to follow.

PUBLIC DISCUSSION AND THE GROUP CONTEXT

Training in public discussion as a form of group decision making was a natural outgrowth of interest in public speaking. The term "discussion" implies much more than mere conversation or public speaking. People "converse" randomly about many subjects, and they may or may not converse with serious intent. But people "discuss" issues by focusing on a particular topic of serious concern to discussants. Group discussion, then, implies task-oriented conversation. Public discussion implies the presence of an audience so that the discussants share their views not only with each other but with nonparticipating onlookers as well.

A public discussion is a tool or device generally used for the purpose of disseminating information to an audience or persuading an audience toward a particular belief or attitude. The public discussion may be viewed as a public speech involving more than a single speaker, although the discussion context is typically much more informal and impromptu. While public discussions were often heard on radio, with the advent of television they lost much of their popularity and underwent significant changes. Nevertheless, the public discussion remains a potentially powerful force in public communication.

Forms of Public Discussion

Perhaps the most familiar form of public discussion is the "panel." Members of a panel discussion are generally experts in a given area who informally engage in conversation oriented toward solving some problem or making some policy decision in that area. Depending on the purpose of the specific panel discussion, members may or may not come to a definite conclusion or decision. The typical purpose of a panel discussion does not include striving for consensus. Rather, members wish to air their views before an audience. Often panel members are selected because they represent a diversity of opinions on the topic.

A panel typically includes a nonmember whose duty is to moderate the public discussion by asking leading questions, assuring that all panel members have equal opportunity to speak, and generally keeping the discussion orderly. Normally the moderator is not an expert on the topic and not actually a contributing member of the discussion. When many people think of a group discussion, they generally think of the panel discussion with a moderator.

Unlike the panel discussion, the "symposium" is much more formal and quite similar to public speaking. In fact, the symposium is not a discussion at all in the sense of an informal conversation. Rather, the symposium includes a series of public speeches oriented around a common theme. Symposium members may partition the topic and present an organized, coherent, and progressive program of speeches concerning that topic. But in the sense of task-oriented conversation and the give-and-take of spontaneous communication, the symposium is not a discussion. In terms of a group context, the symposium is only generally relevant to group discussion.

The audience may also participate in a public discussion. When they do, the discussion assumes the form of a "forum." The old town meeting was based on the principle of a forum with all members of the audience, the citizens of the town, allowed to share their views with everyone else. A moderator also controlled the proceedings of a town meeting, but the group who engaged in the discussion was the audience acting as a committee of the whole. Members of an audience attending a public lecture are often invited to respond to the lecture with questions or refutations of the issues contained in the lecturer's formal presentation. A forum often follows a panel or symposium, too. The forum, then, often occurs in combination with other forms of public communication.

Although many radio programs included panel discussions, television producers apparently considered them unsuited to the electronic medium of video. But current television programming does include some forms of public discussion. Only the format of the discussion has changed. Rather than an informal and unfocused conversation of a panel discussion, the televised public discussion typically involves question-and-answer sessions with a guest expert or group of experts. In fact, such programs seem to be quite popular today with all three major networks including their own versions of the public discussion—NBC's "Meet the Press," CBS's "Face the Nation," and ABC's "Issues and Answers." The televised debates between the Presidential contenders in 1960, John F. Kennedy and Richard M. Nixon, also assumed this format. For apparent reasons, the currently popular late-night "talk shows" are not considered true public discussions.

The question-and-answer form of public discussions generally includes a group of inquisitors who alternately ask questions of the guest expert or experts. A moderator who does not participate directly in the question-and-answer session keeps track of time, keeps the discussion moving, assures the inquisitors of equal question-asking time, and generally serves as a buffer between the questioners and the guest. Often the guest expert is allowed to deliver a statement at the beginning and close of this form of public discussion, but he generally answers questions spontaneously or at least gives the impression of spontaneity in his participation.

Public Discussion and Group Decision Making

The public discussion is not the focus of this book primarily because the public form of group discussion does not include many ingredients essential to group decision making. Most importantly, the public discussion does not typically involve the formation of a real "group." Participants in a public discussion act as individual personalities who perform before an audience. Conversation among participants creates only the illusion of members talking with each other, but the primary purpose of the public discussion remains focused on the audience. Discussants may converse with each other spontaneously, but they are actually talking to the audience in attempting to inform or persuade them.

The primary purpose of a public discussion is simply not group decision making, at least in the sense that group members commit themselves to a goal of achieving group consensus on decisions. The purpose of individual participants is not to make decisions they would not be able to make or make just as well individually. In fact, the final decision regarding the topic of a public discussion is generally within the province of their audience and not of the group participants themselves. Even in the instance of a public discussion which does yield consensus decisions among discussants, the group participant rarely attempts or has the capacity to implement those decisions.

Public discussions occasionally attempt to create an illusion of group decision making. Participants initiate discussion with an apparent spirit of inquiry or with varied opinions and proceed to come to agreement on a common decision. But the discussion is a fake. This pseudo-discussion may be preplanned so that the initial variance of opinions was a hoax designed to impress the audience that the discussants impartially and thoughtfully arrived at their predetermined decisions through reflective analysis of all the issues involved. Actually the members merely use the discussion context as a strategic ploy to persuade an audience to their way of thinking. The pseudo-discussion was formerly not uncommon in radio political campaigning. Members of an "impartial" group appeared to discuss issues for the benefit of an allegedly naïve audience and miraculously came to agreement that one political candidate was head and shoulders above all the rest. Contemporary political campaigns rarely employ this strategy probably because political campaigners realize that voters are not nearly so naïve as once believed.

Thus, public discussion does not seem highly pertinent to group decision making. The primary purpose of the participants in public discussion is not necessarily to make decisions but to disseminate information to a public audience. The purpose is then defined in terms of persons outside the group. Because of the outgroup purpose of public discussion, participants are more public performers than actual group discussants. As ensuing chapters reveal, group decision making inherently involves each group member's commitment to the other members of the group and to the decision-making purpose of the group. Without that commitment intrinsic to the group members themselves, public discussions are only partially relevant to the study of group decision making.

TYPES OF SMALL GROUPS

Sociologists often consider several "levels" of social systems, which differ not only in size but in complexity. A common classification of social systems ranges from minimum to maximum complexity and includes the "individual," the "dyad," the "small group," the "organization," and the "society." Note that the dyad—a dialogue between only two interacting individuals—is a level of complexity between the individual and the small group. Hence, for reasons which shall be apparent in later chapters, the small group requires a minimum of three members.

Our concern is with the small group and its members. Factors outside the boundaries of that social system shall be deemed less important. But many different types of small groups exist within organizations and societies. And not all of these small groups can be characterized by possessing decision-making purposes. While all small groups reflect many characteristics in common, the purpose peculiar to one type of small group renders it quite different from other small groups with different purposes.

Viewing group decision making in perspective necessitates a survey of the common types of groups. And since groups are generally classified according to the purpose they intend to accomplish, awareness of the common types of small groups implies an awareness of some of the purposes performed by small groups and for which small groups are formed and maintained.

During the past ten or fifteen years the "training group," or T-group as it is commonly known, has become extremely popular throughout our society. Despite the numerous variations among training groups, we shall consider all groups which exist for the general purpose of interpersonal growth within the generic definition of training groups. Common varieties of training groups include sensitivity training groups, encounter groups, confrontation groups, awareness groups, Synanon-type groups, discovery groups, sensory awareness groups, creativity workshops, and a host of other variations too numerous to mention.

"Therapy for normal people" is one oversimplified explanation of the purpose served by training groups. Generally a training group attempts to modify the normal behaviors of its members through developing interpersonal sensitivity, human relations skills, mutual trust, and a freer expression of personal feelings. In short, the purpose of a training group is the interpersonal development and growth of its participating members. While specific devices and techniques may vary from one kind of training group to another, the basic purpose of all training groups remains similar—behavioral change through interpersonal growth.

The popularity of training groups has recently reached the proportions of a full-fledged "fad." Perhaps because of this faddish popularity, many extreme and nearly incomprehensible techniques have been associated with every type of training group. For instance, to many people a training group means a group of people sitting in a tepid swimming pool often in the nude, a group of people rubbing soap suds on each other's nude bodies, or a group of people rolling on the floor in leotards or again in the nude. Numerous television dramas and paperback books have encouraged the public to associate training groups with violent interpersonal confrontations, strong language, and people shouting insults at each other. While the Synanon-type group contains violent interpersonal confrontations as a device to stimulate behavioral change, particularly for drug addicts, most training groups do not employ such extreme techniques. Unfortunately, however, the techniques and particularly the extreme techniques of some types of training groups have become synonymous with all training groups in the minds of many members of our society.

One absolutely essential ingredient of the training group is the presence of an expert trainer. The group trainer is more of a nonparticipating observer-consultant than a contributing member of the group. The trainer is a behavioral expert, usually a clinical psychologist or a psychiatrist, who screens participants before group sessions in order to avoid the dangers of potential psychic damage. The trainer possesses sufficient expertise so that he is able to recognize behavioral symptoms of potential mental damage during group interaction and halts the group proceedings before permanent damage is incurred.

The unfortunate reputation of training groups as dangerous to one's mental health is to some extent a result of its faddish popularity. Many former members of training groups, who relished their group experiences, later organize other groups with themselves as the "expert" trainer. Occasionally persons read a book or two on the subject of training groups and consider themselves "expert" enough to be trainers. There have been numerous examples of participants in training groups who have later developed psychoses as a result of their experiences and occasionally have either committed or attempted suicide. The blame for these incidents can probably be placed on unqualified or inexperienced trainers who did not screen members before group sessions and who were not sensitive to dangerous symptoms of abnormal behavior during group interaction. Serving as a group trainer is a highly responsible position and absolutely demands expertise.

Even more dangerous than the well-meaning but overly zealous convert who serves as an unqualified trainer is the equally unqualified charlatan who "sells" his services as a trainer and offers the training group as a patent-medicine cure for all social ills. Any benefits which may occasionally result from unqualified trainers conducting training groups do not offset even one instance of psychological harm. Fortunately, unqualified trainers do not always cause harm. But, of course, they don't typically generate any benefits either. This general problem has become severe enough in recent years that representatives of the National Training Laboratory and the Speech Communication Association have advocated instituting procedures for the professional licensing of group trainers. It is hoped that their efforts will be successful.

The value of training groups led by unqualified trainers is obviously minimal. But some authorities have also questioned the value of genuine training groups—not on the basis of harmful results but that the results are generally superficial and temporary. Behavioral changes in members during training-group sessions have typically proved unique to that specific group context. When members return to their normal social environment, they typically revert to their pattern of pretraining-group behaviors. Repeating group sessions at periodic intervals as "refresher" courses has not significantly affected the nonpermanence of behavioral changes. One familiar explanation for the apparent lack of lasting results is that the training group's social environment is too contrived and artificial or unreal. A number of psychologists and psychiatrists are continuing their attempts to improve the quality of training groups. It is hoped that their efforts will also be successful.

Often confused with the T-group is the use of the group context in the therapeutic treatment of mental illness. Members of a "therapy group" suffer from overtly pathological behavior or abnormal mental configurations previously diagnosed as some form of mental illness. Like the training groups, the purpose of group therapy also involves change of its members, but change in the sense of responding to psychiatric treatment. A psychiatrist is in charge of a therapy group—not as a trainer avoiding the development of psychoses but as a psychiatrist treating patients diagnosed as suffering from mental illness. In an oversimplified sense, the therapy group is a multiple physician-patient relationship. That is, the group exists only as a context for physician-patient treatment just as the one-on-one context of the dyad is a context for individual physician-patient treatment. Obviously the therapy group is a unique use of the group context far removed from our present interest in the use of the group context for decision making.

The "task-oriented group" is a generic term referring to an enormous variety of groups whose very existence depends on performing some task function. An outgroup authority often assigns the task to the group although individuals may, of their own volition, form a group in an effort to perform some task which either cannot be accomplished by a single individual or cannot be accomplished as effectively by individuals acting alone. The nature of the group task varies widely from a group on a factory assembly line whose task is to put bolts A, B, and C through holes

1, 2, and 3, to a group of jury members who ponder trial evidence and decide on the guilt or innocence of a defendant. Some tasks obviously require verbal and oral interaction, such as the jury group, while others require no oral interaction at all in accomplishing their task, such as the assembly line group.

The task-oriented group is by far the most prevalent group in our society. Every human organization—business, educational, service, and political—includes numerous task-oriented groups to carry out the various functions of that organization and other task-oriented groups to coordinate the efforts of all other groups. Perhaps the most interesting of these organizational subgroups are the management groups—those groups charged with the task of organizing the various organizational groups and subgroups into a unitary efficiently functioning organization. Management groups may be the most interesting because they deal directly with issues confronting every social system. And much of being a group member is knowing how to work productively with others in a social situation.

Our present focus is narrower than the broad variety of purposes implied by the term "task-oriented group." Specifically our concern is with one of those purposes, probably the most common group purpose of all—decision making. Decision-making groups comprise the bulk of all groups in most human organizations. Groups decide what new products will be manufactured, how they are to be designed, advertised, and sold. Groups decide which laws will serve to govern a society, how those laws will be enforced, how they are to be interpreted, and even the verdict for those found to violate the laws. Our entire society functions through the organizations which comprise it. And each organization functions through decisions made by groups within that organization. This type of group—the decision-making group—is the primary concern of this book.

DECISION MAKING IN THE GROUP CONTEXT

The decision-making group is undoubtedly the most familiar of all task-oriented groups in our society. Some authorities (Tallman, 1970, and Pollay, 1969) view even the family as a decision-making group. While a T-group and a therapy group are relatively rare because they serve highly specialized functions, literally hundreds of thousands of groups throughout every segment and on every level of our society are making decisions daily. Group decision making is indeed an extremely common occurrence in the day-to-day life of every member of our society.

Moreover, group decision making is vitally important to the functioning of every human organization. Whether the organization functions effectively or ineffectively, group decision making governs every facet of its existence. Our concern, naturally enough, is effective group decision making. And prerequisite to effective group decision making is a thorough understanding of the basic process of group decision making. The need for a comprehensive knowledge of group decision making is obvious in order to analyze and find effective solutions for the ills plaguing our society. The solution to every social problem—crime, poverty, inflation, unemployment, denial of human rights—is ultimately dependent on effective decisions made by groups concerned with and able to cope with those social ills. And effective decisions demand an understanding of effective decision making.

Decision making at every level of society cries out for substantial improvement. We still endure the tragic results from past decisions. Large-scale political decisions in foreign affairs have left our nation in untenable situations in Southeast Asia, Cuba, and Berlin. The effects of decisions made before, during, and since the crises on university campuses in the past decade remain with us today. Decisions made in large cities did not avert or effectively cope with destructive riots—Watts, Detroit, and Chicago. Something is tragically wrong with those management decisions made or not made, implemented or implemented badly. While an understanding of group decision making will not miraculously cure all social problems, it is at least a step, however small, in the appropriate direction.

CONVENTIONAL WISDOM—BARRIER TO UNDERSTANDING

As a high school instructor some years ago, I engaged in an unresolved difference of opinion with an instructor of instrumental music in that same high school. He contended that I "had it easy" teaching students the principles of communication, because high school students were able to benefit from experience. After all, they had spent ten to fifteen years actually communicating every day. But teaching a beginning student how to play the trombone, he maintained, was much more difficult since there was no basis of past experience in trombone playing from which to draw. I maintained that it was precisely for that reason that trombone playing was probably less difficult. Because humans had vast communicative experience, they possessed a large repertoire of alleged "knowledge" gained from that experience—knowledge widely believed and tenaciously maintained whether or not it reflected reality. And that knowledge served to inhibit rather than assist the students' understanding of communication principles.

Layman's knowledge which is widely if carelessly believed falls under the genre of "conventional wisdom." Principles from conventional wisdom are considered credible and true, not because they are actually true, but because they are conventional—because many people believe them to be true. The advertising slogan, "Fifty million Frenchmen can't be wrong," reflects the simplistic wisdom based on conventionality. If so many people believe it to be true, then it must be true. But if fifty million Frenchmen believed the earth were flat, they would be wrong nonetheless. Conventionality may lead to increased credibility, but it has no direct bearing on reality.

Belief based on conventionality often takes the form of a cliché or adage believed to possess truth because it is so familiar. We sometimes call them "old wives' tales" but nevertheless fall prey to the influence of such adages. How and why conventional wisdom gains credibility through familiarity is a matter of some conjecture. The "early to bed, early to rise" axiom may even be traced to Benjamin Franklin's mother trying to urge her recalcitrant son into bed at the appointed hour. Conventional wisdom is also not necessarily easily identified as conventional wisdom. It is difficult to resist the influence of that familiar antecedent which often precedes a principle from conventional wisdom—"Everyone knows that. . . ." Who wants to be "out of step" with the rest of the world!

Dangers of Conventional Wisdom

Because conventional wisdom is conventional does not necessarily make it false. To the contrary, many clichés have some basis in fact. But accepting such "wisdom" at face value is nonetheless dangerous. At its worst, conventional wisdom is blatantly false and leads to greater problems than originally. At its best, conventional wisdom oversimplifies the situation and desensitizes individuals to reality. In the case of group decision making, members either create more social problems for themselves because of false "wisdom," or they are led to inefficient and unproductive effort by the demands of irrelevant "wisdom."

Most importantly, axioms based purely on conventionality masquerade as real knowledge and thwart genuine understanding. In the case of group communication, which abounds with old wives' tales, conventional wisdom severely inhibits improvement of decisional quality and improvement of group communication. In almost no other area of human endeavor do we rely so heavily and so trustingly on conventional wisdom. Although some persons suffering from arthritis continue to wear copper bracelets on their wrists, we generally seek the expert assistance of a physician when illness strikes. We may even "starve a cold and stuff a fever" (Or is it the other way around?), but we don't seriously believe that eating an apple every day will protect us from illness. We generally don't rely on a pain in the foot to predict bad weather or take delight from a red sky in the evening. When we seriously want to know what weather is in store, we seek out the forecasts made by expert meteorologists. But when it comes to communication and the group process, everyone seems to be his own expert, and he reverts to the oversimplifications of conventional wisdom.

Conventional Wisdom about Group Decision Making

A representative list of examples of conventional wisdom pertaining to group decision making follows below. Many of these examples probably appear sensible and eminently reasonable. You will probably discover that you may believe more than a few of them. The list is by no means complete. It samples but a minute portion of the clichés surrounding group decision making. The ten examples chosen from various areas of communication and the group process possess only one trait in common. They are all false!

Relying on conventional wisdom is a formidable barrier to the understanding and knowledge of group decision making. By the time you have read the remaining chapters, you should understand why and how these examples of conventional wisdom are simply not true. At that time you should also be able to add many other examples to the list. When you are able to do that, you have taken one giant step forward toward a robust understanding of group decision making.

The following are examples of conventional wisdom surrounding group decision making. Without exception each item in the list is untrue:

1 Discussion differs from debate in that members of a group discussion do not advocate argumentative positions but maintain an open mind and a spirit of free inquiry. (Corollary) The effective decision-making group exhibits a minimum of argument and interpersonal conflict.

2 Too much interpersonal criticism leads to communication breakdowns or develops communication barriers.

3 To be effective the group should strive for nearly equal participation among group members.

4 Each member of the group should perform certain duties required of group membership. (Corollary) The duties of the leader differ from the duties of the other group members.

5 In the group context getting the job done, that is, making the decisions, is more important than getting along with each other. (Correlative opposite) In the group context developing close interpersonal relationships is more important than the actual performance of the decision-making task.

6 The effective decision-making group normally follows an orderly agenda which directs their progress toward their group goal.

7 Some people are naturally born leaders. (Corollary) Some people possess the characteristics or quality of leadership.

8 The personalities of the members exert the most significant effect on the process of group decision making.

9 In the long run, a group will achieve better results through using democratic methods than achieving specific results by other means.

10 Almost any job than can be done by a committee can be done better by having one individual responsible for it.

AN OVERVIEW OF THE BOOK

The preceding pages have established the primary focus of this book—group decision making. But there are dozens of methods one can use to approach the study of group decision making. The subtitle of this book provides an insight into the perspective employed in the chapters which follow. Although "communication and group process" may imply two perspectives, the remaining chapters shall attempt to illustrate that communication and group process comprise a single unified perspective.

Chapter 2

The Group Process

"Group" and "process" are two words common to nearly everyone's daily vocabulary. We use these words flippantly as though we understood them thoroughly. And, for the most part, our understanding of these words is sufficient for everyday conversation. But writers of textbooks use these words and others as though they and their readers understood the words in the same way. This textbook writer wants to take no chances.

This chapter is devoted to providing a working definition of "group process." Essential to this definition is an understanding of each of the two words individually. To provide these working definitions requires a certain amount of courageous self-assurance. Although the words are common, definitions for them abound. The reader will discover in this chapter (and in others to follow) that the viewpoint expressed in this book is in substantial agreement with other authors and in substantial disagreement with perhaps even more.

PROCESS DEFINED

A single sentence is not sufficient for an adequate definition of "process." As with most terms, process cannot be *defined* nearly so easily as it can be *understood.* A dictionary provides several elements of "process" which offer a starting point for such an understanding. According to any good dictionary, four elements are inherent in a process—*action* or acts, a continuous *change in time,* advancement or *progress* over time, and a *goal* or result. Thus, process clearly implies a time dimension as well as a space dimension in which action occurs in a continuously changing progression toward some goal.

David Berlo (1960, p. 24), discussing the process of communication, offers an excellent and often quoted definition of process:

> If we accept the concept of process, we view events and relationships as dynamic, on-going, ever-changing, continuous. When we label something as a process, we also mean that it does not have *a* beginning, *an* end, a fixed sequence of events. It is not static, at rest. It is moving. The ingredients within a process interact; each affects all of the others.

Berlo's definition is richer than the dictionary's and emphasizes the time dimension as a fluid, ever-changing evolution of ingredients. Because it is so deeply imbedded in the time dimension, any beginning or end of a process is an arbitrary point in time since the "something" is different from one instant to the next. Berlo also provides a clue to why the process is continually changing—interaction among the ingredients. Each ingredient affects and is affected by every other ingredient. The ingredients, then, are interdependent, that is, any change in one of the ingredients affects all the other ingredients.

Clearly implied in the nature of process is a marriage of the space and time dimensions—structure and action. For example, "table" is a statement about the *structure* of various pieces of wood. But the *process* of "table" requires an explanation of how wood was sawed from a felled tree (an arbitrary starting point in time), the sequence of steps involved in cutting and assembling those pieces of wood, applying the finish, etc., until the finished table appears (an arbitrary stopping point in time). Thus, process involves not only structure but how and why structural changes come about during the passage of time.

GROUP DEFINED

A Smorgasbord of Definitions

Marvin E. Shaw (1971, pp. 5–10), in his integration of the research knowledge of small group phenomena, summarizes the various approaches to defining "group." Most of the definitions cited by Shaw indicate that members of a group *share* something in common. And it is that common something which serves to define the existence of a group. One definition considers a group any collection of individuals with shared perceptions. That is, a group is composed of individuals who perceive the existence of a group and their membership in it.

Perhaps more familiar is the definition which stipulates the sharing of a common motivation or goal. Thus, workers unite to form a labor union since they have a common need to satisfy—for example, higher wages and better working conditions. The collective strength of the union, then, possesses the common purpose of securing those goals.

Still another definition based on commonality specifies the sharing of a common fate. That is, a basketball team or a debate team wins or loses as a group and not as individuals. The outcome affects all members of the group as a whole and not each member individually.

Other definitions imply that commonality is insufficient for an adequate understanding of "group." This class of definitions looks to the structure of the group—the relationships and ties among group members which bond them together into a group. Such an organizational definition perceives the social organization as the "glue" of group structure. Thus, roles, norms, values, status hierarchies, power relations, etc., are laws which govern the behavior of group members and tie them to the group. The presence of these ties defines the nature of the group.

A final category of definitions perceives the central element of a group to be interaction among its members so that the members are interdependent among themselves. It is this type of definition that Shaw (1971, p. 10) finds most acceptable—". . . a group is defined as two or more persons who are interacting with one another in such a manner that each person influences and is influenced by each other person." (Although everyone does not agree, this book shall use "interaction" and "communication" interchangeably. The two terms are considered synonymous.) The notion of mutually reciprocal influence among members embodies the concept of interdependence among members of a group. Although for the purpose of this book Shaw's definition is incomplete, it forms the basis for our definition of "group."

The Principle of "Groupness"

Common sense should tell us that every collection of individuals who talk with each other and who even exert minimal influence on each other is not a "group," in the strictest sense of the term. Consider several individuals who congregate in an elevator or at a bus stop. They may carry on a conversation, but they would not constitute a real group.

Arguing whether a particular collection of individuals comprises a group is about as worthwhile as arguing the number of angels who can dance on the head of the proverbial pin. But identifying those characteristics which differentiate a group from a collection of individuals does provide insight into a more complete understanding of the nature of a group. John K. Brilhart (1967, p. 12), for example, specifies five characteristics of a group:

> 1 A number of people sufficiently small for each to be aware of and have some reaction to each other. . . .
> 2 A mutually interdependent purpose in which the success of each is contingent upon the success of the others in achieving this goal.
> 3 Each person has a sense of belonging or membership, indentifying himself with the other members of the group.
> 4 Oral interaction (not all of the interaction will be oral, but a significant characteristic of a discussion group is reciprocal influence exercised by talking).
> 5 Behavior based on norms and procedures accepted by all members.

You will note that Brilhart employs the smorgasbord of definitions within his five characteristics—common perceptions (1 and 3), common fate and common goal (2), interdependence and interaction (4), and organizational structure (5). Brilhart adds to the interaction characteristic the stipulation that a significant proportion of communication will be through speech, thereby virtually requiring that the group be in face-to-face confrontation. He also places a general limitation on size, which is assumed within the framework of a *small* group.

But Brilhart is more concerned with illustrating the principle of "groupness" which he considers a property that groups possess and collections of individuals do not. According to Brilhart (1967, p. 12):

> "Groupness" emerges from the relationships among the people involved, just as "cubeness" emerges from the image of a set of planes, intersects and angles in specific relationships to each other. One can draw a cube with twelve lines (try it), but only if they are assembled in a definite way. Any other arrangement of the lines gives something other than a cube. Likewise, one can have a collection or set of people without having a group. . . .

Brilhart emphasizes that a group exists as something apart from the individuals who comprise the membership. Just as the twelve lines form "cubeness" when placed in the proper relationships to each other, "groupness" forms from the relationships among the members. As the individual lines lose their individual identity when "cubeness" is perceived, so do members lose their identity as individuals when "groupness" is perceived. Shaw (1971, p. 14) appears to be making a similar observation when he states, ". . . a group is real to the extent that it is perceived as an entity."

For several scores of years a controversy existed among sociologists regarding the existence of a "group mind." In oversimplified terms, a group was thought to have a "mind" of its own—a way of thinking and a pattern of emotions quite separate from those of the member individuals. The "group mind" idea was rejected several decades ago on the basis that the group could not be substantially different from the individuals who comprised the membership. A group simply cannot have a mental life external to the mental lives of its members. In analogical terms, a finished product is limited by the raw materials of its composition. Without sulfur, oxygen, and hydrogen, for instance, sulfuric acid simply cannot exist.

Although a "group mind" is not implied, a group does possess an identity of its own apart from the identities of its individual members. In fact, individual members often take on the identity of the groups to which they belong as part of their identity as individuals. For instance, John Doe is identified as a Democrat, a student, a communication major, a suburbanite, a Kiwanian—all groups with corresponding identities and with alleged characteristics of their own. We shall return to this point in Chapter 7 when we discuss the law of partial inclusion.

The Group as a System

The identity of a group apart from the identities of its individual members—"groupness"—has been established. A more common method of expressing this same principle is literally a cliché—that is, a group is "more than the sum of its parts." This principle of nonsummativity assumes that individual components comprise a single entity and, further, is characteristic of a *system.*

An entire body of theoretical knowledge, commonly known as general system theory, may be beneficial to furthering our understanding of the group process. A "system" may be defined simply as an entity which behaves as an entity because of the interdependence of its component parts. A group-system, then, is a group which behaves collectively as a group because of the interdependence of its members. Every system possesses three elements which describe its existence— *structure, function,* and *evolution.*

The *structure* of a system may be regarded as the physical arrangement of components in space at any given point in time. If a cake were considered as a system, the components of the cake are the ingredients—flour, shortening, baking powder, eggs, milk, etc. After they are mixed in the bowl, these ingredients are relatively homogeneously arranged in the structure of batter in which the dry ingredients (e.g., the flour and baking powder) are suspended in the homogeneous liquid mixture (eggs, milk, shortening). The important thing to remember about systemic structure is the limitation imposed by space. Time is static in the determination of structure. Thus, the above structure of the cake is a description of the arrangement of ingredients at a specific point in time—the batter stage, after ingredients are mixed and before baking. Naturally, the structure of the cake is different from one point in time to another. Thus, a system undergoes continuous structural changes as time passes.

The *function* of a system may be defined as the relationships among components in time. The function of a system provides order and regulation of the system. The complex of structure and function combined is necessary to describe the process of a system's operation. To return to the cake analogy, the process of making a cake cannot be explained by merely listing the ingredients in proportion but must include the steps of mixing in the proper sequence, preheating the oven to a certain temperature, baking in the oven a specified length of time, and so forth. The system functions according to laws or rules which must be followed if cake making is to proceed normally. Not abiding by these rules, e.g., setting the oven temperature too high, will result in an abnormal process in which the cake bakes too fast, burning the outside to a crust and leaving the batter inside underdone.

The function of a system is the day-to-day operation of the system. Our society provides laws which allow the system to function in a desired (that is, normal) manner. As structure refers to relationships among a system's components in space, function refers to the relationships among those components in time.

The *evolution* of a system embodies the history of the system—its progressive and possibly regressive changes through time. Every system needs a history—time to develop into an orderly structured and functioning system. The behavior of the system contains that history. Open systems, of which a group is one, possess the capacity of self-determination. Hence, the system itself may artificially accelerate the process of systemic development. For example, when this country was founded in the late eighteenth century, it possessed little history of an independent, democratic American society. To the contrary, its history was that of English colonists and distant subjects of a monarchy. Thus, a history was virtually created by emphasizing relatively minor events of the recent past and incorporating them as important elements in the culture. Perhaps the best example is Patrick Henry's speech before the Virginia House of Burgesses—a very minor event at the time in parliamentary debate over a trivial issue. The speech attributed to Patrick Henry which we know today was actually written by someone else decades after Henry had delivered it. In fact, Patrick Henry probably never did utter exactly the now famous words, "Give me liberty, or give me death!" But the speech epitomized the ideal of the new nation and became an enduring part of its history, undoubtedly accelerating the development of our nation-system.

We must not confuse, however, the history of a system (its evolution) with the normal day-to-day regulation of the system (its function). To be sure, the time dimension is inherent in both function and evolution. But systemic function is essentially repetitive and cyclical while systemic evolution chronicles regular, enduring change along the broader time dimension. For example, the punishment for breaking society's laws is a portion of systemic functioning, repeating itself in the everyday regulation of the system. Several centuries ago, our society punished lawbreakers with flogging, burning at the stake, beheading, and other inhumane treatments. These elements now belong in our history but do not characterize the contemporary functioning of our society. Although capital punishment was recently a portion of our nation's systemic functioning, the Supreme Court made it a part of our history. We are now experiencing a transition period in which our system is making a functional change. Evolution of the system chronicles the evolving of these structural and functional changes as the system develops and changes its character over time.

The principles of "groupness" and "process" are consistent with the evolution of a system. It takes time for a collection of individuals to form "groupness." And the process of forming a group from a collection of individuals is embodied in the evolution of the group-system. Those evolutionary changes as the group changes its character are also included in the system's evolution.

In discussing these elementary principles of a system, we must not forget that an entity with structure, function, and evolution is a system specifically because of the interdependence of its component parts. Any change in the components' structural or functional relationships leads to a different system. The functional change in the cake which results from baking too hot and too fast results in a system which is not a cake. It may resemble a cake, but it is not a cake. Consider a structural change such as omitting the baking powder. That thing in the pan which has the taste and texture of a cellulose sponge is not a cake. It is a system which is different from a cake. The same is true of a group. Any structural or functional change will result in a different group. It may resemble the former group and may even contain many of the same people, but it is a different group.

The Group as a System of Behaviors

If the point is not yet clear after the discussion of the many definitions of a group, we shall be explicit now. None of the definitions of a group is false or incorrect. That is, each definition is true and correct. As Shaw (1971, p. 5) says, ". . . it is evident that different authors are simply looking at different aspects of the same phenomenon." It is a matter of fact that the observation of reality must always proceed from the perspective of the observer. And perception is always fragmentary. Remember the fairy tale about the blind men who encountered their first elephant. One blind man felt the legs and perceived the animal to be like a tree trunk. Another perceived only the body of the elephant and assumed it to be like a brick wall. The man who felt the ears thought it was like a fan. Observation of the tail and trunk resulted in conclusions of a rope and snake. The point is that none of the blind men was incorrect. Each perceived the same phenomenon from a different perspective and generalized about the whole phenomenon on the basis of his perceived information.

The truth of the matter is that reality is quite elusive. It is not so much *discovered* by man as it is *constructed* and manipulated. When considering human behavior from a process perspective, we confound even further the problems involved in constructing reality. Berlo (1960, p. 25) explains:

> The basis for the concept of process is the belief that the structure of physical reality can not be *discovered* by man; it must be *created* by man. In "constructing" reality, the theorist chooses to organize his perceptions in one way or another. He may choose to say that we can call certain things "elements" or "ingredients." In doing this, he realizes that he has not discovered anything, he has created a set of tools which may or may not be useful in analyzing or describing the world. . . . The dynamic of process has limitations; nevertheless, there is more than one dynamic that can be developed for nearly any combination of events.

In "constructing" his definition or his "reality" of a group, each author attempts to organize his perceptions by emphasizing those "elements" which he considers most significant. By creating his "set of tools" he has used only one "dynamic" for describing a group and has based his definition of group on that perspective.

The perspective of this book is communication. It should not be puzzling, then, that our definition of a group will utilize that perspective.

The common method of defining a group has viewed individual human beings as the components of the group-system. The definition which follows does not deny that human beings comprise the group, but the individual person is not the primary unit of analysis. Rather, what the individual does—how he behaves—constitutes the set of tools used to describe, analyze, and define the group.

If components of a system are interdependent, they influence and are influenced by each other. Unless we consider some form of supernatural power, the only means by which one person can influence another is by the behaviors he performs—that is, the communicative exchanges between people provide the sole method by which influence or effects can be achieved. Our emphasis, then, is on what the group member does and less on what he thinks and feels. Thus, the components of our group-system are the communicative behaviors produced by individual members.

Karl Weick (1969, p. 46), in discussing "collective structure," stresses the point that as people organize into a group-system, they organize their behaviors:

> . . . the elements potentially available for a collective structure consist of the behaviors that can be produced by A and the behaviors that can be produced by B. . . . The collective structure can involve only those behaviors that A and B are capable of producing. A collective structure exists when behaviors of two or more persons become interstructured and repetitive. The unit of analysis now becomes the interact or double interact and *not* the act. To identify instances of collective structure, we look for instances in which, with regularity, A emits an act which is followed predictably by an act from B, and B's act then determines A's subsequent act.

A collection of individuals, then, develops into a group as each member interlocks his behaviors with each other's. Consider an analogy of a basketball team. All the previous definitions of "group" are applicable to the team. But for our purposes, the team possesses "groupness" to the extent that the behaviors of the players are interdependent, interstructured, and predictable. Sportscasters are fond of saying that a team has played together so long that they "know each other's moves." To rephrase this cliché, one player can, on the basis of his own act, predict what another player will do next and what he himself will do subsequently. A "fast break" or "out-of-bounds play" is based on structuring the players' behaviors interdependently so that the result of the cluster of interdependent behaviors is a man "free" to take a shot. On the other hand, some basketball teams are characterized by "free-lancing," which may be another way of saying that the players' behaviors are not interdependent but are based on individuals behaving as individuals. Hence, a free-lance team is more a collection of individuals than a group.

Weick expresses more concern, however, with the "interact" or "double interact" and less with the single act. Actually, interacts and double interacts are simply groupings of acts. An interact is composed of two contiguous acts, while a double interact is a combination of three contiguous acts. A emits an act (a single act) which is followed by an act from B (an interact) which is followed by a third act from A (a double interact). If the emphasis is on interdependent acts, the more important unit of analysis is the interact or double interact. In this way, acts are seen within the context of preceding and succeeding acts. The structure of the group, then, is those sequences of acts which recur so often that one can predict what kinds of acts tend to follow or precede other kinds of acts. Because interdependence of individuals is achieved by mutual influence through communication, the organizing element of the group system is communication. And communication and communicative exchanges— acts, interacts, and double interacts—are the ingredients for analyzing the system—not the individual members.

Viewing a group as a system of behaviors may be disconcerting to some. A system of behaviors is not tangible. You can't touch or hold a behavior. It doesn't exist in space. Hence, a group seems somewhat mystical as a result. In a way, this is very true. Groups are less tangible than we often believe. But communicative behaviors can be observed— unlike such internal phenomena as interpersonal liking, beliefs, and feelings. And communicative behaviors are apparently the only method by which interdependence or mutual influence can be achieved or observed.

Therefore, a group shall be defined as a collection of individuals whose communicative behaviors—specifically, acts, interacts, and double interacts—become interstructured and repetitive in the form of predictable patterns. To the extent that the communicative behaviors of group members are interstructured, the attributes used to characterize a group may be assumed to exist.

THE LEADERLESS GROUP DISCUSSION (LGD)

For the purpose of explaining the "natural" process of a group, this book shall consider the leaderless group discussion (LGD) the prototype of a group. Contrary to the implication of its name, the LGD is not a group of talkative people without a leader. The characteristic which distinguishes an LGD from other groups is self-determination. That is, an LGD is affected or influenced by a minimum of authority or forces external to the group. For example, a committee formed within a larger organization is subject to the demands and pressures of the larger organization. The organization imposes on the committee certain assigned duties, deadlines for task completion, etc., and the activities of the committee are restricted by the need to meet the needs and goals of the organization. The LGD, to the contrary, has a broader capacity to decide for itself its own goals, its own norms, its own roles, and its own status hierarchy. Rather than the leadership assigned by some external authority, the LGD determines its own leader. Hence, "leaderless group discussion" implies not the absence of leadership altogether but the absence of externally assigned leadership.

The analogy of making a cake breaks down at this point. In terms of a system, the cake is more of a "closed" system, and a group is more "open." While the components of the cake were at the mercy of their environment—for example, the heat of the oven—components of the LGD interact with their environment and, to a large extent, create their own environment. While the cake's ingredients are not capable of self-determination, members of an LGD must exercise self-determination.

A second characteristic of an LGD concerns the external pressure on all status levels. We shall assume the membership of the LGD to be peers at the time the group is formed. A large organization endows its members with status and structures those status levels into a hierarchy. A corporation, for example, has directors, managers, assistant managers, foremen, and assembly line workers. A committee formed within this corporation would reflect the status hierarchy of the larger corporation. Consider the military—perhaps the most status conscious of all human organizations. Members of the military visibly display their status on their sleeves or shoulders. Understandably, a group composed of military personnel would be highly susceptible to the status demands of the larger organization. But to avoid the external pressures of a larger organization's status hierarchy, the LGD is generally thought to be composed of members with the same initial status.

For our purposes, we shall also consider an LGD to be a zero-history group. That is, our LGD is observed from its first formation—the point of zero history. We have already established that the process of developing groupness takes time. So that the complete process of group formation can be observed, observation of the group must begin at the point of its inception as a collection of individuals. The zero-history group, then, embodies the total history of the group.

To the extent that external forces impinge upon the self-determination of the group members, the "natural" group process is incomplete. This is not to say that a group which is subject to external pressures is not natural. Indeed, most groups in the "real world" are probably not LGDs. But an LGD embodies the entire group process—the development of its entire group culture. Our purpose is to look at the entire group process. The LGD allows us to do that. A non-LGD reflects something less than the whole process with a portion of the group process predetermined by external authorities. Thus, the LGD reflects the group process in its "pure" or "natural" state.

Realistically, of course, no group is totally free from external authority nor is a group totally controlled by external forces. In fact, forming a true LGD in a classroom is practically impossible. Every classroom group is subject to external restrictions—the presence of the instructor, the "captivity" of the classroom, the status distinctions from the student culture, the environmental pressure of classroom assignments and the end of the quarter or semester, or the due date for a group project. Even if the instructor does not assign a specific task but allows the classroom group to select its own, the group is "forced" to choose its own task rather than voluntarily forming around a common need which is "felt" by the group members. But even though a classroom group is not truly an LGD, external restrictions are or can be quite minimal. While the LGD is defined in its "pure" form, realistically we expect that the LGD in real life is to some extent "impure."

SUMMARY

Understanding the nature of group process requires an understanding of the nature of "group" and "process" separately. Process involves the dynamic relationships of events in an ongoing, continuous sequence of time. Each ingredient of the process affects and is affected by every other ingredient as changes in the process evolve through time. While many perspectives have been used to define "group," this book utilizes the perspective of interdependence and interaction. A collection of individuals develops "groupness" over time so that the identity of a group exists apart from the identities of its individual members.

A group is conceived to be a system characterized by its structure (the pattern of relationships among components at any given point in time), its function (the regulatory recurring day-to-day relationships among components through time), and its evolution (the continuous evolutionary changes of structure and function through enduring time). Rather than perceiving individual members as components of the group-system, this book considers communicative behaviors as the units for defining, observing, and analyzing the group-system. Thus, a group is a collection of individuals whose communicative behaviors—specifically, acts, interacts, and double interacts—become interstructured and repetitive in the form of predictable patterns. The prototype group which embodies all the elements of group process and is minimally inhibited by external or environmental constraints is the leaderless group discussion (LGD).

Chapter 3

Dimensions of the Group Process

Our society has long tended to draw rather clear distinctions between allegedly opposing phenomena. For example, we classify a person as a liberal or a conservative, a Democrat or a Republican, a blue-collar worker or a white-collar worker. It is no wonder, then, that we differentiate between two dimensions of group decision making—task and social. Because people are involved in a group, the social dimension is evident. And because the group is expected to come to agreement on a decision, the task dimension is also important.

It is unfortunate but true that the task and social dimensions of group decision making are often viewed in conflict with each other. This view seems to reflect the hackneyed conflict between reason and faith, science and humanities, classicism and romanticism, logic and emotions. There have been numerous attempts to provide detailed plans and instructions for making a group decision which avoids social or emotional influence. The assumption underlying these proposals is apparently that a decision is better when based on an impersonal and critical evaluation of the facts. We are cautioned against emotional reactions in the apparent belief that such reactions lower the quality of the final decision.

The purpose of this chapter is to provide an insight into the task and social dimensions of group process. Consistent with the perspective of interdependence involved in the group process, the two dimensions will be viewed as inseparable and interdependent. This chapter will further illustrate how the social dimension affects group decision making and consequently, how group decision-making tasks are or should be fundamentally different from decision-making tasks performed by individuals.

THE TASK AND SOCIAL DIMENSIONS

Both the task and social dimensions are inherent in the process of group decision making. No decision-making group exists without both dimensions, each of which is vitally important in order to understand effective group decision making and to participate effectively in a decision-making group. The task dimension refers to the relationship between group members and the work they are to perform—the job they have to do and how they go about doing it. The social dimension includes the relationships of group members with each other—how they feel toward each other and about their membership in the group.

For some reason the task and social areas of the group process have typically been viewed separately. Tuckman (1965), for example, indicates that two problems continuously confront a group during its period of development—group structure (social) and task activity. Thus, group members deal with each type of problem separately throughout their existence as a group. According to Tuckman, certain comments aid in developing the group structure, and other comments are directed toward accomplishing the group's task. Robert F. Bales's (1950) system of classifying behaviors or acts of group members (Interaction Process Analysis), also, specifically labels every comment as either oriented toward the social area or oriented toward the task area. Such a total separation is probably unwise. Common sense should tell us that a comment such as "Aw, you don't know what you're talking about!" implies not only an outright rejection of a contributed idea (a task comment) but an impact as well on the social relationship of at least two members. Bales's (1970, pp. 471–491) recent revision of his Interaction Process Analysis (IPA) categories of acts seems to reveal second thoughts about drawing such a clear distinction between social and task comments. (Bales's IPA system will be discussed in more detail in Chapters 7 and 8.)

Our viewpoint agrees with the position of Kelley and Thibaut (1954,

p. 736) who feel that the task and social dimensions of group process are highly interdependent—in fact "virtually indistinguishable" from each other. That is, one may separate the two from a theoretical perspective, but the interaction between the two makes them virtually inseparable in practice. Cattell (1955) and Bales (1953), on other occasions, have also emphasized the interdependence of the two dimensions.

There is a reason for using the term "dimension" to refer to the task and social areas of group process. Figure 1 illustrates the two-dimensional existence of a plane geometrical figure. A rectangle exists in two dimensions—height and width. Height cannot be separated from width without destroying the rectangle itself. Although the height or width may be observed and measured separately, the two dimensions are inseparable within the definition of the rectangle. The same inherent and inseparable relationship is true of the task and social dimensions of a group process. Without either dimension, the group process does not exist.

Several people have attempted to separate the task from the social dimension in order to observe more closely the behavior or acts of group members related to the task dimensions. Scheidel and Crowell (1964) attempted to observe those acts specifically related to the development of ideas. Fisher (1970a) sought to isolate those acts which were directly related to the making of group decisions. In terms of an actual separation of the task from the social dimension, both attempts were probably abortive. It would probably be more accurate to say that Scheidel and Crowell and Fisher viewed a single interdependent group process from the perspective of the task dimension. In other words, group members make a decision and develop ideas at the same time and in the same manner that they develop a group structure and get along together.

PRODUCTIVITY AND COHESIVENESS

You can probably remember being a member of a group which you thoroughly enjoyed. There was an esprit de corps among the members, a

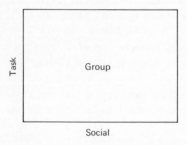

Figure 1 "Dimensions" of the group process.

spirit of camaraderie, a feeling of close personal ties. You undoubtedly felt the group was worthwhile and rewarding to you, and you felt a sense of loyalty to the group—a personal commitment. In a group such as this, members are proud to be members. Occasionally such groups evolve from classroom groups. The following comments, for example, are selected from each member's final diary. They were members of a group formed within a class studying group communication. Their feelings were unanimous:

> "I feel a close bond with the other members of our group and would like to continue working with each one."
> "I am very grateful for this group experience and feel a very close bond of friendship and understanding with each member."
> "What I really want to emphasize is the way that we learned to function as free-thinking people unacquainted, really, with the others (at the beginning of the term) and evolve into an extremely cohesive group."
> "I developed a great amount of respect for and a relationship of oneness or unity with each member individually and the group as a whole."
> "It may sound a little corny, but I feel [list of the other members' names] are good friends and, when this class is over, I will feel like, if nothing else, I have made some friends for life."

On the other side of the coin, you have probably been involved with groups which were less than appealing. There may have been bickering among some members, but probably you were more bored than hurt by the group experience. Rather than feeling a sense of commitment or pride in the group, you probably searched for excuses to avoid group meetings. If you had any choice in the matter, you probably dropped out of the group. Otherwise, you endured it only as long as you had to. One comment from a final diary of another classroom group illustrates this type of group: "One thing that really affected the development and behavior of our group was being able to get together for a meeting. It seemed that the five of us could never find one time that was good for everyone. But as they say, you can always find time for the things that are important."

The two types of groups depicted above illustrate a difference in "cohesiveness"—the ability of group members to get along, the feeling of loyalty, pride, and commitment of members toward the group. It would not be inaccurate to say that cohesiveness is, more than anything else, the degree of liking that members have for each other. To the extent that members like each other, they are committed to the group and feel loyal and proud of their membership status. Cohesiveness may also be viewed as the output of a group's social dimension. That is, cohesiveness is not a process so much as a state of being. As "groupness" emerges from group interaction, the group may be characterized at some level of cohesiveness. Such a characteristic describes the outcome of the process in the group's social dimension.

In a similar fashion, the output from a group's task dimension may be described as "productivity." To the extent that a group accomplishes their task, they are productive. Like cohesiveness, the amount of productivity is not always easily determined. Of course, the productivity of a group on a manufacturing assembly line may be measured by counting the number of products they complete in a given time period. Or the productivity of a basketball team may be determined by the number of games they win. But what of a decision-making group? The number of decisions is seldom a good indication of productivity. A jury, for example, may have only one decision to make—the guilt or innocence of the defendant. As in most decisions, quality rather than quantity is the best determinant of a decision-making group's productivity. And decisional quality is exceedingly difficult to measure.

Despite the difficulties of observing and measuring productivity and cohesiveness, they serve as useful concepts to describe the general success of a group along its task and social dimensions. Caution must be exercised, however, in utilizing these descriptive terms. Cohesiveness and productivity are not qualities which a group does or does not possess. Each is a characteristic which describes to some degree the success of the group process in every group.

In every group cohesiveness and productivity exist, and each exists in some amount. That is, a group's productivity or cohesiveness should each be visualized as some point along a continuum. For example, a group may be a low cohesive group, moderately low, moderately high, high, and so forth. Another analogy may illustrate this point. Height is a characteristic which describes every person. We measure height conveniently in feet and inches, and everyone has height to some degree. We may describe someone as tall or short, but we would never say that he has no height. In the same way, we may describe a group as low cohesive or low productive, but it is foolish to say the group is not productive or not cohesive. Even though we commonly use such expressions to characterize a group, we must keep in mind that we actually mean that the group is rated at the lower end of the continuum of either productivity or cohesiveness.

Since the interdependence of the task and social dimensions has been established, it seems reasonable that the outputs of these dimensions—cohesiveness and productivity—should also have an interdependent relationship. Although we can visualize a group whose members hate each other but are able to be quite productive, this type of group is unusually rare. Common sense would dictate a direct relationship between productivity and cohesiveness—that is, the more cohesive a group, the more productive it is likely to be. And this dictum is true—up to a point. As groups raise their level of cohesiveness, the more likely they will raise their level of productivity. Conversely, the more productive the group, the greater the likelihood that they will be more cohesive. However, the relationship breaks down toward the upper end of the two continuums. Figure 2 illustrates this curvilinear relationship between cohesiveness and productivity. According to this illustrative diagram, extremely cohesive groups are more likely to have moderate to low productivity. Although the productivity of highly cohesive groups probably doesn't sink to the level of extremely low cohesive groups, they are not nearly as likely to be as productive as groups with moderately high cohesiveness.

Several explanations account for this phenomenon. First, the group may have been together so long that their original purpose—their

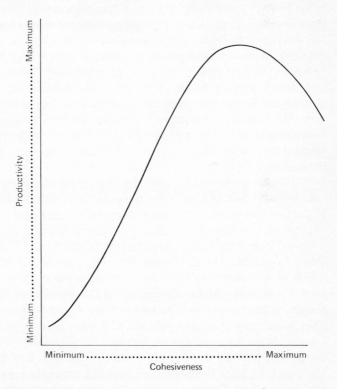

Figure 2   The curvilinear relationship between cohesiveness and productivity.

task—has suffered due simply to the fact that the members enjoy each other's company too much. Many local community service organizations find that over the years the primary purpose of their organization has changed from assisting their community to having a good time. The greater proportion of their activity, then, is socializing rather than working on community service. I am familiar with one group whose purpose, at the time the group was formed, was to raise money for an annual charity drive. As far as I know, that group still raises money annually; but the group continues to meet regularly during the year to play cards, eat dinner, and generally have a good time. The greater proportion of their effort is social enjoyment and not raising funds.

Another explanation is advanced by Clovis R. Shepherd (1964, pp. 94–95). He indicates that a highly cohesive but low productive group has a great deal of "reserve productivity." That is, the group is capable of much more productivity but simply does not expend the effort to be productive. Hence, their productivity lies dormant or in reserve. The classic example is the bright student who does just enough work to earn a passing grade but doesn't earn the A that his high intelligence would lead one to predict. His teachers, parents, and friends would say that he isn't working to capacity. Another example is the athletic coach of a losing team who bemoans the fact that his players are capable of winning every game but just aren't playing to the level of their abilities. In either case, the assumption is that the group or individual is capable of superior productivity but actually achieves only average or below average productivity—hence, the term "reserve productivity." If actual productivity and reserve productivity were added together, the total would be a superior level of productivity.

Whatever the explanation for the curvilinear relationship between cohesiveness and productivity, the point to remember is that the outputs of the two dimensions of group process affect each other reciprocally. For example, an increase in productivity tends to increase the cohesiveness of a group. Recall the Green Bay Packers football team coached by the late Vince Lombardi. The coach and the team possessed all the characteristics which would normally lead to low cohesiveness. The coach was aloof from his players—highly dictatorial and a slave-driver. The players were literally forced to perform behaviors they would normally find abhorrent. They were subject to stringent training rules more appropriate for Little League juveniles than mature adults. They endured tortuous practices above and beyond the normal practice routines. But they won games! They literally ruled the National Football League during the decade of the 60s and became famous for their "Packer pride." Apparently the team was a tightly knit, highly cohesive group. We can only wonder how cohesive they would have been had they been a losing football team.

Conversely, an increase in cohesiveness generally precipitates a corresponding increase in productivity. The classic example of this phenomenon is commonly known as the "Hawthorne effect." Deriving its name from a series of investigations performed in the Hawthorne plant of the Western Electric Company, the Hawthorne effect generally refers to the increase in productivity which results from an environmental change in the social dimension. Organizational managers may single out a work group within the organization and give that group special attention or special favors, such as enlisting their aid in a research situation. That group is likely to increase its productivity as a result. Athletic coaches talk about getting their players "psyched up" for the big game with a great deal of group activity, shaking hands, yelling together, and so forth. They believe their teams play better in the proper socioemotional atmosphere. Examples, based however vaguely on the Hawthorne effect, are common to all of us. The background music in an office is intended to make the social environment more pleasant so that the office workers are more productive. I have an uneasy feeling that as customers in a store with soothing background music piped in, we are expected to purchase more products in the pleasant environment of that store.

Occasionally, however, the increase in productivity precipitated by an increase in cohesiveness may be more a rationalization by the group members to account for their otherwise low level of productivity. That is, the group members probably realize their group has accomplished little in their task dimension, so they rationalize that their group actually accomplished more than they did. One method of rationalization is to change the nature of the task. A classroom group often feels their decision-making task was not very worthwhile, anyway, so they arbitrarily change their perceptions of what the task really was. The following excerpt from a classroom group's final self-analysis illustrates this rationalization:

> Because our information would not be used for anything of real importance, we felt we were wasting our time to meet. . . . The only real purpose in our group was to get in the assignments. . . . As it turned out, our group was more a social group than anything else. We never really got into any real conflicts. But we felt some very important things came out of the experience of being in a group. We learned better how a group functions and why. . . . All the different topics that we had discussed in class about what happens in a group became clearer to us as we related to each other about what had happened in our group. This gave all of us a better understanding of group methods.

In reality, little "groupness" ever emerged for these individuals. They experienced a spurt of social success toward the end of the term and began the problem of rationalizing their previously low productivity.

Although they did perceive the "real task" of the classroom group, they were probably writing more to "apple-polish" the instructor than they were actually describing their group's productivity level. It is unfortunate but probably true that the latter comments are more typical of the classroom group than the comments of the extremely cohesive group cited earlier.

INDIVIDUAL DECISION MAKING
VS. GROUP DECISION MAKING

Surely the process of making decisions in a group differs from that of an individual working alone. This statement should not be too startling. After all, a group is different from a single individual. For one thing, there are more people in a group. This bit of wisdom contains several important implications. A group possesses a greater variety of resources. There are more minds to contribute to the decision-making effort, more sources of information. Unlike the lone individual, a group is able to divide labor among its members, having one individual work on his specialty, another working on another specialty, and so on.

On the other hand, a group possesses potential problems not inherent in individual decision making. The problem of achieving consensus is present in a group. The many examples of "hung juries" are ample evidence of the existence of this problem. And with the addition of more people there is greater opportunity for conflict. At the same time, there are many more sources to generate new ideas. And there are more viewpoints from which to evaluate critically those ideas. In other words, a critical exchange of ideas is much more easily accomplished by a group.

The Risky Shift

Among the differences discovered when individual and group decision making have been compared is the phenomenon commonly known as the "risky shift." Simply stated, the risky shift refers to the fact that groups tend to gamble more than their individual members do if each was making the decision alone. That is, a group tends to select an alternative that has a bigger payoff but a lower probability of attainment. If groups and their individual members were to place bets on a horse race, for example, the risky shift would predict that the group decision would be more likely to place the bet on the 100-to-1 shot than would any of the decisions made by the members deciding alone. Although there are exceptions to this rule as there are to every rule, the proof is quite conclusive that a given individual is likelier to make a decision involving greater risk when he is in a group rather than when he is making the decision by himself. Thus, group interaction apparently stimulates individual members to take greater risks and to be less conservative than they would as individuals.

Much time and effort have been expended in order to explain the "risky shift." Shaw (1971, pp. 73–79) documents the major results of those efforts. While it is not our purpose to provide a detailed account of the various explanations, we will summarize them briefly and critically. One explanation asserts that risk-taking is a personality trait of individuals. Thus, groups composed of high risk-takers will tend to make riskier decisions. This explanation may be true, but the findings indicate that generally all groups make riskier decisions than their members do individually.

A second explanation stipulates that risk-taking is a value shared by members of a certain culture. This may also be true—particularly if the culture is composed of mountain climbers. But this explanation does not account for why groups generally tend to make riskier decisions even compared with individual members of the same culture.

Another hypothesis explains that the group's risky shift can be attributed to the influence of a risk-taking leader. Such an explanation is simple to understand and too easy to believe. But not only does some research indicate that this explanation is probably not true, the nature of group leadership described in Chapter 5 would cast serious doubt on the credibility of this hypothesis.

A final explanation, and one which probably has the greatest evidence to support its acceptance, attributes greater risk-taking in a group to a diffusion among group members of the responsibility for the group decision. Such an explanation corroborates the conventional wisdom gained from the experience of viewing a lynch mob on a TV western. Each of the good citizens of the frontier town wouldn't think of lynching the man in the jail. But in the anonymity of the mob and the overwhelming feeling of group support, "mob fever" results. Examples of "mob fever" and "leaping on the bandwagon" should readily come to mind with a minimum of thought.

The fact is fairly well established that groups do make riskier decisions than individuals. We should probably accept that fact and expect a group decision to involve greater risk. But *why* groups make riskier decisions may be a moot question. It is certainly less important than *how* groups make riskier decisions, that is, discovering what *behaviors* in the group lead to greater risk-taking and how these behaviors are interlocked with each other in a pattern of interaction unique to group decision making. Unfortunately, this knowledge is not totally available to us at the present time. One plausible explanation of the risky shift based on interaction patterns may be that the communicative patterns of social conflict alleviate the fears and initial conservatism of individual members. Those conflict patterns will be discussed in Chapter 6.

Efficiency and Speed

Few people have accused a group of being efficient. Referring a proposal to a committee in order to kill it is a well-known parliamentary tactic. Simple arithmetic should illustrate that, in terms of man-hours expended, groups are destined to be more inefficient than individuals. Assume that one person can perform a task in one hour. A three-man group would be required to perform that task in twenty minutes in order to equal the one man-hour expended by the individual. If the task is decision making, a group would probably spend more than one hour—hence, an excess of three man-hours.

Compared to individuals, groups are abominably slow. You will recall that it takes time for "groupness" to evolve. The group must establish a history before it can function effectively as a decision-making system. For a group member, patience is an important virtue. Inevitably group members become highly frustrated, particularly in the early stages of group development, over the group's apparent lack of progress. Members are anxious to "get the show on the road," to quit wasting so much time and attend to the task at hand. Although these feelings of frustration and discouragement are typical, they should not be considered seriously. Progress is not very visible in the early stages of group development, but the seemingly rapid progress later is a direct and cumulative result of the activities which have come before. (Chapter 7 discusses the process of group development during decision making.)

David Berg (1967) provides one possible explanation for the apparent inefficiency and slowness of group decision making. In his analysis of the duration of themes discussed during group interaction, he discovered a group's effective attention span is quite small. In fact, the average length of time a group discusses a single theme is only fifty-eight seconds! In other words, groups tend to jump from topic to topic very quickly without dwelling on any single topic for very long. As described in Chapter 7, groups tend to make decisions in spurts of activity while an individual may be more capable of lengthy periods of sustained effort.

At this point one might be tempted to ask, "If groups are so slow and inefficient as a decision-making system, why bother with them at all? Let individuals make all the decisions." If efficiency and speed were the sole criteria by which decision making is judged, no one should bother with groups. But the quality of the decision is infinitely more important than the time expended to make it.

Although it is difficult and often impossible to measure accurately decisional quality, there is a deep-seated feeling that in many cases groups will make better decisions than individuals. Our jury system, for example, is based on this premise—that a group of peers is more likely to arrive at a better or more accurate verdict than a single individual, even a judge. The principle of a democracy also operates on this assumption. If it didn't, we would disband the Congress and the Supreme Court and make the President a dictator.

Common sense tells us, then, that in some cases a group, even an occasional group of nonexperts, will make higher quality decisions than a single individual—even an expert individual. It is this feeling, perhaps, that sustains our interest in group decision making. But it is more than a mere feeling. There is incontrovertible evidence that some situations virtually demand decisions made by groups and not by individuals. Our next problem is to identify those decision-situations.

The Group Task

For years small group researchers compared individual decision making with group decision making attempting to determine whether, in fact, two heads were better than one. After numerous studies and conflicting results, researchers revised their perspective. As Collins and Guetzkow (1964, p. 57) point out, "It seems more profitable to ask, 'On what kinds of tasks and in what environments will the group perform better than its individual members working separately?'" It seems reasonable that the impact of the social dimension of a group (for example, more information resources, capacity to divide labor, social conflict, critical analysis, demands of consensus) would give the group a distinct advantage for some decision-making tasks.

James H. Davis (1969, p. 33) distinguishes some characteristics of the group task which are different from a task for individuals.

> Some tasks could reasonably be presented either to individuals or to a group. A word puzzle, for example, presents a challenge to an individual person as well as to a set of persons who cooperate in its solution. This type of task is defined in terms of individuals but the definition remains applicable to groups as well. On the other hand, a number of tasks are impossible, or undefined, for individual persons apart from a group. For example, the major chore facing a group may be reaching agreement on some political issue. An individual subject may have no doubts as to his own position, but be distressed to find others in disagreement. The resolution of this disagreement in order to achieve consensus may represent a formidable task for the group, but there is no counterpart to this task for the isolated individual.

It is clear that some tasks, such as an algebra problem or a crossword puzzle, may be performed by either an individual or a group. But the social dimension of the group process could add nothing to the solution of such a problem. Nevertheless, as Davis points out, some tasks require the critical exchange of conflicting viewpoints, such as a political issue. In this task a group has a distinctly superior advantage.

Zaleznik and Moment (1964, p. 143) provide further direction in our search for the group decision-situation. They point out that a group functions under a condition of "psychological interdependence" so that the productivity of the group is more than the sum of the outputs of the individual members. If a group were to perform a task just as easily performed by an individual, the output would be simply the total of the outputs from all the individual members. If one of the members were absent one day and the other members continued working at their same rate, the productivity of the "group" would decrease. In other words, the activity of any of the members has no influence on the group activity. There is simply no interdependence among members. The authors go on to say:

> The output of the problem-solving group is of an entirely different nature. The contributions of the individual members do not accumulate by simple addition to determine the group's output. The output is *more than* the aggregate of individual contributions, or in some instances less. *Such a group deals with the kind of problem that actually requires group activity for its resolution.* (Emphasis added.)

The principle of nonsummativity (that is, the whole is greater than the sum of its parts) which Zaleznik and Moment call "psychological interdependence" is described by Collins and Guetzkow (1964, p. 58) as the "assembly effect." According to Collins and Guetzkow:

> *An assembly effect occurs when the group is able to achieve collectively something which could not have been achieved by any member working alone or by a combination of individual efforts.* The assembly effect bonus is productivity which exceeds the potential of the most capable member and also exceeds the sum of the efforts of the group members working separately.

The importance of the principle of nonsummativity cannot be overestimated. If a group performs a task which an individual could just as easily perform, the group cannot surpass the efforts produced by its most competent individual member. But if group activity is *required* to make the decision, the group can easily exceed its most competent member. The most capable individual in the group is still incapable of producing the critical exchange of ideas developed by the demands on the group to achieve consensus.

We should now be able to define the type of decision-situation which is unique to the group process. For our final assistance we turn to Norman R. F. Maier's (1963) distinction between the type of decision which requires high-quality technical expertise and the type of decision which requires group acceptance and commitment. To illustrate this distinction, the solution of a sophisticated mathematics equation requires a person who has considerable expertise in mathematics. You or I would be at a loss to solve the problem since we simply do not possess that extent of mathematical expertise. For such an individual task there exists only one "correct" answer or one "best" answer. On the other hand, if our problem involved deciding who should be the next President of the United States, we are dealing with a totally different kind of problem. The expert in political science or economics has no greater voice in this decision than you or I. His vote is equal to yours or mine. For such a problem no single "correct" or "best" answer exists (although each of us is probably convinced than one person would be better than any other).

The solution to the group task, moreover, has no external means by which the correctness of the decision can be validated—unlike the mathematics problem, which is wholly determined by the technical laws of mathematics. The sole criterion for validating the group decision is group acceptance or group commitment to the decision once it is made. Thus, the only means to validate the decision is whether it achieves consensus. Of course, the passage of time would allow a better judging of the quality of the decision. But remember that the decision-situation changes from one point in time to another. What was a "good" decision during the campaign might prove to be less "good" after the elected candidate has been in office for a few years. Because decision-situations change, incumbents are sometimes defeated in bids for reelection.

Of course, it is not always simple to distinguish among group decision-situations and individual decision-situations. For example, a person suffering from a heart ailment would be well advised to follow the diagnosis of the most expert heart specialist. This decision-situation obviously requires high-quality technical expertise. But if several equally expert heart experts disagreed on the diagnosis, should the patient determine which physician is the most expert, or should he ask the specialists to come to some form of group consensus? Such questions, however, are rather academic. But they do serve to illustrate that distinguishing between an individual or a group task is not always a black-and-white distinction.

An important point to remember is that neither groups nor individuals are superior to the other as a decision-making system. An individual with expert qualifications should be expected to outperform a group on an individual task, and a group should be expected to outperform an individual on a group task. If the task requires high-quality technical expertise, the available individual most expert in that technical specialty should perform that task. If the task requires group commitment or consensual validation, a group should be expected to perform that task. And unlike individual tasks, group tasks do not have a single "correct" or "best" answer. Many problems arise when groups are expected to perform a task just as easily performed by an individual. Few will deny that there are too many "committees" in the world. But when the situation warrants it, a committee decision is essential if the decision is to be of highest quality.

SUMMARY

The "group process" embodies two dimensions—the task dimension and the social dimension. Despite numerous attempts to separate them and a pervasive tendency to consider them in conflict with each other, the task and social dimensions of a group process are inseparable and interdependent. Although they may be separated theoretically, the task and social dimensions exert mutual and reciprocal influences on each other so that they are virtually inseparable in practice.

Productivity and cohesiveness may be considered the outputs of the task dimension and social dimension respectively. A curvilinear relationship exists between task and productivity so that as the cohesiveness of a group increases, its productivity also increases up to a point of diminishing returns. As a group approaches extremely high cohesiveness, it tends to decrease in productivity. Thus, the group with the highest productivity is generally a group with only moderately high cohesiveness. Consistent with the interdependence of the task and social dimensions, productivity and cohesiveness are also interdependent, each exerting influence simultaneously upon the other.

A vast quantity of investigations have compared individual decision making with group decision making. While the group process embodies two dimensions (task and social), the individual process has only the task dimension. The two-dimensional nature of groups results in several points of comparison with individuals. Groups tend to make riskier decisions than do their individual members making decisions alone. And, compared to individuals, groups are inefficient and slow. But for many situations group decisions are virtually necessary because of the superior quality of the decisions.

There are some tasks which can just as easily be performed by individuals or groups. For those tasks group activity adds nothing to the efforts of the most capable member. These tasks are those whose accomplishment requires high-quality technical expertise and for which there is one "correct" or "best" answer validated by the subject matter of the technical specialty.

Other tasks, however, require group acceptance or group commitment for successful performance. For such tasks no single answer may be externally validated as "best." The sole means of validating this type of decision is whether it achieves consensus. These situations comprise the type of task which may be uniquely labeled, the group task. A group decision, because of the "assembly effect," will undoubtedly be superior to the decision made by even the most competent group member working individually.

Chapter 4

The Socioemotional
Climate

Our society has long recognized the worth and dignity of the individual. The individual's right to life, liberty, and the pursuit of happiness is inviolate. Advertisements sell products with the appeal to get away from the crowd and assert your own individuality. Laws protect the individual's right to privacy, to earn a living, to gain an education—in short, the right to be an individual. But we also recognize that the human individual is a social being. Although a few isolated hermits do exist, the human animal seeks the company of other humans and apparently needs membership in a variety of social systems.

To understand a group is to understand the relationship of the individual and the group. Moreover, to understand the relationship of an individual and the group is to understand the individual. This chapter deals with the reciprocal relationship between the individual and the group. Specifically, the development of the miniculture which constitutes a group entails the development of a climate which socializes the uniqueness of the individual and his emotional makeup into the social system of the group. The term "socioemotional climate" refers to this merger of individual and social system.

PERSPECTIVES ON THE SOCIOEMOTIONAL CLIMATE

The most common perspective used to discuss the socioemotional climate of a group is cohesiveness. But cohesiveness is a very general and abstract concept which is virtually synonymous with socioemotional climate. Understanding how cohesiveness develops is indeed equivalent to understanding the development of a group's socioemotional climate.

Interpersonal Attraction

One common approach to discussing cohesiveness is to discuss how and why people are attracted to each other, that is, how and why people like each other. The assumption is that people who like each other develop a cohesive group. So a cohesive group is cohesive because members develop interpersonal liking.

Numerous factors have been associated with interpersonal attraction. One rather consistent factor is similarity, particularly similarity of attitudes. In typical "birds-of-a-feather-flock-together" fashion, people with similar attitudes toward objects tend to congregate together and reinforce each other's attitudes. Such reinforcement is evidently a pleasing experience, so that the people with similar attitudes tend to like each other.

Theodore M. Newcomb's (1953) AtoBreX system provides one explanation of this phenomenon. Figure 3 illustrates the minimal AtoBreX system in which A and B are persons with positive or negative attractions toward each other and with positive or negative attitudes toward some object X. If A and B have similar attitudes (either both positive or both negative) toward object X, Newcomb postulates that they will experience a "strain toward symmetry" so that their attractions toward each other will be positive. A symmetrical AtoBreX relationship involves positive attractions between A and B along with similar (both positive or both negative) attitudes toward X. Newcomb's approach also emphasizes the importance and even the necessity of communication in order for A and B to inform and to influence each other about their attitudes.

A second factor associated with interpersonal attraction is frequency of interaction. As people communicate with each other more

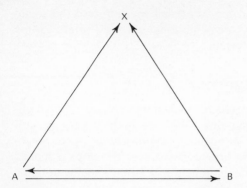

Figure 3 The minimal AtoBreX system. [*From Theodore M. New-comb, "An Approach to the Study of Communicative Acts,"* Psychological Review, *60, 1953, 393–404. Copyright (1953) by the American Psychological Association, and reproduced by permission.*]

frequently, they increase their attraction toward each other. There is little way of knowing, however, whether greater frequency of interaction is a cause of interpersonal attraction or its effect. That is, is a person attracted to another because he communicates more frequently with him? Or does he communicate more frequently with another because he likes him? One certainly tends to communicate most often with his friends and is more apt to be friends with those with whom he communicates most often. At the very least, we can say that interpersonal liking cannot be achieved without some interaction. And in addition we would probably decrease the frequency of our interaction with people we don't particularly like.

A third factor associated with interpersonal attraction is the perception of reciprocated attraction. Interpersonal liking is a two-way street. A will tend to be attracted to B if he perceives that B likes him. (This phenomenon of reciprocal attraction is consistent with the norm of reciprocity to be discussed later in this chapter.) Perception of the other person's attitudes and feelings is certainly important to interpersonal attraction. And our perceptions can be based only on what we see and hear the other person do or say. In other words, communication provides the data—the raw materials—on which we build our perceptions of others.

One additional variable often associated with interpersonal attraction is also directly linked to communication—self-disclosure. Self-disclosure may be defined simply as statements made to another about one's self—what one thinks, feels, believes, wants, needs. Erving Goffman (1959, 1963, 1967) discusses the presentation of one's self to another as a normal phenomenon of human interaction. Although Goffman does not explicitly discuss self-disclosure, he assumes that presenting or disclosing one's self to another is an inevitable and unavoidable experience. When man communicates with someone else, he is engaged in an act of self-disclosure to another. Goffman assumes further that the self may be "presented." That is, the communicator attempts to manipulate the perceptions or impressions of others by presenting data through his communicative behavior that is designed to present his self in the way in which he wants it to be perceived.

Brenda Robinson Hancock (1972), in a pilot research project, has discovered some important implications concerning self-disclosure via communicative behavior. Hancock's preliminary results indicate that while groups of friends and groups of acquaintances tend to discuss many of the same topics, friends tend to discuss intimate topics for longer periods of time and use much more intimate language. That is, friends tend to be more self-disclosing in their communicative behavior than acquaintances.

Whether self-disclosure, like frequency of interaction, is a cause of interpersonal attraction or its effect is quite unclear at this time. But self-disclosure through communication must be regarded as one of the factors linked to interpersonal attraction.

Member Satisfaction

Cohesiveness may also be viewed as the extent to which members enjoy or are satisfied with their group experiences. Rather than viewing an individual's relationship with another individual, this perspective on cohesiveness attempts to view one element of an individual member's perception of his group as a whole. Although the term "satisfaction" may imply that group membership satisfies some "need" of an individual, the term is used here in a much broader sense to refer to morale, loyalty, or any way in which individual members are pleased with their group membership.

Heslin and Dunphy (1964) summarized 450 studies linked to member satisfaction and discovered three variables which explain most instances of members' satisfaction with their groups. Heslin and Dunphy labeled these three factors *dimensions* of member satisfaction. They include "status consensus," "perception of progress toward group goals," and "perceived freedom to participate." Status consensus implies the degree of agreement among members on the identity of the leader or other high-status members. If all members rank the same individual(s) high, then status consensus is said to be high.

Significantly, the actual progress toward group goals and actual participation are not clearly associated with member satisfaction. Recall from Chapter 3 that group members can manipulate their perceptions of group productivity. Thus, it is the perception of progress that is important to member satisfaction rather than actual progress made.

Common sense should tell us that all members in a group do not participate equally. Furthermore, members probably should not participate equally. Some members have more ability than others and should be greater participators than those of lesser ability. Nor do all members have an equal need to participate. Some people are more extroverted than others. What is important, however, is not equal participation but the perceived freedom to participate. If the member feels he has an equal opportunity to participate, whether he chooses to participate or not, he is satisfied with the group. It is a fact of life that all group members do not participate equally. It should be equally apparent that perceived freedom to participate and not equal participation should be the goal of a group whose members are happy with their group experience.

Group Identification

Another perspective from which to view the individual and his relationship with the group is the extent to which he identifies himself with that group. Many discuss group identification as the member's internalization of group goals—the extent to which the group goals become the goals of the individual members. Group identification here implies a broader meaning. To the extent that each group member feels a part of his group or recognizes his membership in the group, group identification may be said to exist.

There are some observable manifestations of a growing group identification even in the classroom group. Student members will change their classroom seating patterns and begin to sit beside or near their fellow group members. The member will begin to refer to his group in the first person as "my" group or "our" group. When members fill out diaries of their reactions after each group meeting, the diaries themselves reflect a developing group identification. A diary in the early stages of the group meetings will include a reference to another member in the third person, for example, "I am having trouble with one of the people in this group. He seems to criticize everything I say." Later, that same member will use first names exclusively in referring to fellow group members—"Steve is still the critic of our group. But I am beginning to realize that he just wants us to think about what we are saying."

Occasionally group members have difficulty establishing group identification so that an impetus is needed to stir feelings of unity. An instance of one such group provides a possible impetus for increasing group identification. One group member, frustrated over the obvious apathy of his fellow group members, sought help from his instructor. This group, as could be expected, was not very productive and had received a rather low evaluation on a preliminary group project. The members were naturally disappointed over this grade. The instructor and the student arranged a conference at which time the entire group complained as a group to the instructor about their low grade. During the conference the instructor remained firm and justified the low grade—often using rather shaky grounds for his justification. The conference proved to be successful in that the group developed much closer ties of identification. They became united against a common "enemy"—the instructor. At the end of the term when they were informed of the incident, the group members had almost forgotten it. Group identification, in this instance, was spurred by conflict with some outgroup foe but was maintained in the absence of the foe.

BEHAVIORAL STANDARDS

Developing the socioemotional climate is essentially a process of acculturation. Often acculturation implies a new member joining a preestablished culture such as a European immigrant to the United States, a Midwesterner moving to New York, or a Southerner moving to the North. There are certain modes of behavior which are acceptable within a given culture and others which are unacceptable. People in a given culture have established certain expected patterns of doing and thinking which must be learned by the newcomer. One familiar example is the American in a Latin American country who arrives at 2:30 for a 2:30 appointment and can't understand why his host considers him rude to have come so early. Each culture develops its own rules for behavior which may be quite different from another culture's. The alien newcomer adapts his behavior patterns or experiences pangs of "culture shock."

The LGD, however, has no established standards of behavior but develops its own. The development of those standards is cumulative and implicit but nonetheless evident. The LGD soon establishes constraints on the behaviors of its members. That is, the individual member's range of behavioral choices available to him is narrowed during the process of group development. The member soon learns what is expected of him and what he expects of others. And in the LGD he has had a voice in formulating those expectations.

Roles

Comparing the concept of a social role with the dramatic role portrayed by an actor on stage is an all-too-familiar explanation. Even Shakespeare believed that all the world was a stage and life was just acting out one part after another. But we must not conform too closely to this analogy if we are to capture the richer meaning of the social role. While the stage actor does create a role, he is limited by the playwright's lines and the foreknowledge of the play's conclusion. He must also divorce his "self," to a large extent, from the character he portrays. One's social role, on the other hand, is a reflection of self, and the specific behaviors which constitute the social role are much more spontaneous. And of course one cannot rehearse most of these behaviors beforehand.

Role, for our purposes, is a position in an interlocking network of roles which make up the group. But each role must be defined in terms of the behaviors performed by the individual occupying that role rather than by some preordained position which exists apart from the identity of the individual occupying the position. If we were to view role in its broader sense, we might consider "president" of a government or a large organization to be a "role." But this type of role is defined as a position with specific duties and privileges which exist independent of the person who occupies that position. The role definition governs many of the behavioral choices of the person who occupies that position. And the position always exists in the organizational structure despite the identity of the person who occupies it.

The "role" of father in a family group is also determined by factors other than behavior. The father is determined biologically (or legally, in the case of adoption) rather than by actual behaviors performed. But in the LGD no such preestablished network of roles exists to be passed out among the members. Thus, each member, together with his fellow LGD members, works out his own role through his communicative behaviors. His role, along with his role's relationship with the roles of the other members, can be defined *solely* in terms of the behaviors performed by him and his fellow group members.

Although it is impossible to formulate a complete list of all possible roles in a group, Benne and Sheats (1948) have classified some roles which were commonly observed in training groups. Their classification scheme includes three types of roles—group task roles, group building and maintenance roles, and individual roles. Although we will find it difficult to sustain such a clear-cut distinction between roles serving only task functions and roles serving a purely social function, these three role types indicate that some roles are not oriented toward group goals but apparently fulfull some purely individual needs. While these roles cannot be considered a comprehensive list, they do serve to clarify some typical examples of roles often developed through small group interaction:

Group task roles	Group building and maintenance roles	Individual roles
Initiator-contributor	Encourager	Aggressor
Information-seeker	Harmonizer	Blocker
Opinion seeker	Compromiser	Recognition-seeker
Information giver	Gate-keeper and expediter	Self-confessor
Elaborator	Group-observer and commentator	Playboy
Coordinator	Follower	Dominator
Orienter		Help-seeker
Evaluator-critic		Special interest pleader
Energizer		
Procedural technician		
Recorder		

As Benne and Sheats point out, one member may perform several different roles, and several members may perform the same role. But LGD roles are quite idiosyncratic to the particular group. One five-member group may have a network of roles totally different from the role network of another five-member group. No role appears to be universally present in all groups or even in most groups with the exception of the role of leader. But because the leadership role is unique and so important, an entire chapter of this book is devoted to it.

Bormann (1969) provides one possible explanation for the idiosyncrasy of roles. His stimulus-response model of role emergence suggests that roles develop through a pattern of response reinforcement. As a member performs a given behavior, the other members either encourage it or discourage it by their reactions. If they encourage it, the model postulates that the member will repeat that behavior until it becomes his role behavior. If the members discourage his behavior, of course he will cease performing this behavior. Whether the reason for the idiosyncratic nature of roles is due to response performance seems a trivial question. At this point, it is enough to know that roles are generally idiosyncratic to the group.

You will recall from a few pages earlier that the individual member develops that pattern of behaviors which constitutes his role in conjunction with his fellow group members. Thus, the role that an individual develops in one group may be quite different from his role in another group. A role, then, is not wholly determined by those innate personality traits possessed by an individual. He doesn't carry his role with him from one group to another. A role is more like a suit of clothes which he puts on and takes off to fit the occasion. His behavior pattern in one group may be quite different from his behavior pattern in another group as the demands on his behavior change.

One reason for the different roles developed by the same person in different groups is the interdependence of the task and social dimensions. The nature of the task stimulates certain expectations or requirements so that the network of roles is affected along with all elements of the social dimension. An example from a classroom group may serve to illustrate this phenomenon. One girl, whom we shall identify as Margie, felt her contribution to a group was limited to follower and information giver. Although bright, Margie was extremely shy and found it difficult to assert herself in any social setting. In a classroom group discussing problems of educationally disadvantaged children in urban ghettos, she found her behavior pattern quite different from what her personality traits might have predicted. Her fellow members discovered she had had summer experience in social work and consistently turned to her for critical advice, recognizing her expertise based on personal experiences. Margie became a critic-evaluator and by far the most frequent contributor to her group. Rather than being a follower, Margie found herself in a role of dominance due to the nature of the task and her relationship with it. Of course her personality was unchanged. She remained shy and nonassertive. But in the role network of this particular group working on this particular task, Margie's behavior pattern was assertive and her role was quite dominant.

In contrast to Margie, Steve was a BMOC ("Big Man On Campus")—a starting member of the football team, officer in his fraternity, handsome, and loaded with personal charm. It was simply not possible to dislike Steve. Everyone liked him from the first meeting, including his fellow classroom-group members. Steve was used to being a leader and seemed to have the "knack" of exerting the forcefulness of his personality on whomever he came in contact with. But as the pressure of time to complete their task impinged upon the group, the other members became increasingly disenchanted with Steve's role behaviors. Steve discovered that his personality and charm were insufficient to meet the demands of task accomplishment. Bewildered by the social ostracism from his fellow group members and frustrated because his contributions were consistently rejected or ignored, Steve uncharacteristically remained silent and became a habitual absentee. For Steve, the experience of being in that group was obviously socially painful.

Occasionally role strain or role conflict occurs in groups in which the member finds that the demands on his behavior are more than he can perform (role strain) or that his role behavior contradicts his role behaviors in other groups (role conflict). Actually, the LGD is virtually free from the problem of role strain since the member works out his role's behavior pattern in cooperation with the other group members. Rarely does the individual commit himself to an emerging pattern of role behaviors which he can't adequately perform.

Role conflict may occur as it apparently did in Steve's case. Generally, however, a person is able to keep his role in one group quite distinct from his role in another group. At a common-sense level, you behave differently at home with your family group from how you behave with a group of your close friends. And that behavior pattern is different from your behavior pattern in a classroom. And you behave differently at a football game from what you do in a fancy restaurant. If role strain or role conflict does occur, the LGD irons out the problems with a minimum of difficulty. Implicitly and often without being consciously aware of it, we make changes in our role patterns as we move from group to group. And we do it as easily as putting on a different set of clothes. This is the nature of social roles.

Norms

Conformity by members to certain behavioral conventions, specified or unspecified, is a normal and consistent phenomenon of every social system. The punishment for nonconformity is often not clear, but the pressure to conform is strong, nevertheless. We consistently follow the changing fashions of dress and music, for example. What was conformist yesterday may be nonconformist today, but we continue to heed the changing social whims in an overt drive to avoid being abnormal.

The human animal apparently possesses a strong desire to follow the herd. At one time or another, you have probably proved this point with some variation of the "emperor's-new-clothes" prank. I can recall several instances as a teen-ager with a group of friends downtown on a Saturday night. We would stop at a busy corner and stare upward at a purely arbitrary point in the sky. We would engage in totally meaningless but animated conversation about this imaginary phenomenon we were allegedly observing. We would frequently point to it, "oohing" and "aahing" over the magnificence of the sight. Within minutes a crowd would have gathered, all of whom would be staring and pointing to the sky. When we felt the crowd was sufficiently large, we would quietly slip away and congratulate ourselves on our remarkable ability to manipulate human behavior.

Although we can be confident that norms do exist, we are not always certain how and why they function in a social system. Jack P. Gibbs (1965), attempting to provide some order to the confusion about social norms, distinguishes among three definitional attributes of norms which serve to clarify in part their functioning—collective evaluations, collective expectations, and reactions to behavior. The attribute of collective evaluation implies the social system's evaluation of what behavior *ought* to be while collective expectation implies what the social system expects behavior *will* be. Collective evaluations include contemporary social mores or customs with people's evaluations often indifferent to instances of nonconformity. For example, we feel traffic laws ought to be obeyed, but we often roll through stop signs and exceed the speed limit on freeways. We know we ought to fasten our seat belts, but we often ride in automobiles unfettered by the uncomfortable webbing. On the other hand, collective expectation implies no evaluation of the behavior on the part of the members of the social system. For instance, we expect that Americans will drink coffee and the British will drink tea. We would even probably label abnormal those who do otherwise. But in no way does this expectation place an evaluation on the behavior in the sense that they ought to drink coffee or tea.

The third attribute, reactions to behavior, implies the existence of rules or laws which are enforced by some authority. That is, nonconformity to the norm will result in sanctions or punishment to the nonconformist. If we rob a bank, for instance, we will be put in prison. If we wear clothes that are out of style, our friends will laugh at us. In either case, the definitive characteristic of the norm is not the expectation or evaluation of the behavior necessarily, but the sanctioning reactions to nonconforming behavior. Nor does the norm always have the collective support of the members of the social system. Many of the laws of our nation have not had the collective support of the populace. The law in the form of a constitutional amendment prohibiting the sale or use of alcoholic beverages may be the prime example, although there is strong evidence that many of our current laws concerning marijuana possession and usage lack the collective support of the people. But they are norms nonetheless in that sanctions are placed on nonconforming behavior.

An LGD norm, however, should always be a reflection of values shared by the group members. Since the members develop their own norms of behavior, they develop only those which have collective support. On the other hand, many of the rules of non-LGD social systems are formulated without consideration of whether they have collective support. One glittering example would be rules which govern the operation of prisons which are formulated despite nonsupport by the inmates.

Authorities beyond their control formulate and enforce these norms. But as rules for establishing standards of behavior for members of the social system, they must be considered to be norms of that social system. The LGD, of course, is free from such an external authority and, thus, develops only those norms which do gain collective support. In fact, norms develop only because they gain collective support.

The process of developing norms in an LGD is not particularly difficult to understand. Simple repetition of behavior patterns endows those behaviors with normalcy often before we become aware of it. Think about the seating habits in your various classes. After a few weeks in most classes, you can notice the students, including yourself, seated in approximately the same seat day after day. If you come to class late and find someone else sitting in "your" seat, you probably feel slightly irritated.

Realistically, the development of norms is more complex than simple repetition when dealing with norms based on the vast range of communicative acts. Norms develop through the functioning of feedback loops. Although feedback mechanisms will be discussed more fully in Chapter 7, a simple example might clarify the influence of feedback mechanisms on communicative behavior. The members of one classroom group established a norm of argument based on personal assertions and verbally forceful dialogue. Early in the group's history, one or two members presented documented evidence to support their positions and were consistently laughed at. They then questioned the accuracy of some asserted statistics and were again shouted down. Soon they, too, adopted the norm of assertiveness and forcefulness to support their positions. Once begun, they continued to assert positions and to be increasingly forceful in their assertiveness so that the group interaction became a verbal free-for-all. The feedback loops functioned through the predictable sequence of communicative acts in order to establish the norm that lasted through many hours of interaction.

Like roles, norms are also quite idiosyncratic and vary from group to group. Most cooperative groups are shocked when they first observe a Synanon-type training group with its violent and often abrasive confrontations among members. But these confrontations are the norm for such a group developed over the course of their interaction. You probably have friends with whom you exchange insults as a form of greeting but would consider that same behavior abnormal in another group in which politeness is the norm. Many people cannot appreciate the humor of insult-comedians such as Don Rickles and Jack E. Leonard because they are not "normal" comedians who tell funny stories and are "gracious" to their audiences.

As a classroom instructor, I strive to encourage a classroom norm of argument—a free exchange of conflicting opinions and ideas. Students engage in verbal conflict with other students and with the instructor. Many students and instructors are uncomfortable with this norm and consider it inappropriate and disrespectful and disruptive. The point is that no norm is more "correct" than another. Rather, social norms vary from one social system to another and may even conflict with each other. Therefore, a norm developed in one social system is appropriate for that social system but may be quite inappropriate in another.

If any social norm is universal among various social systems, it is the norm of reciprocity. Something of a do-unto-others norm, the reciprocity norm functions by reciprocating similar behaviors in response to the behavior of others. That is, if A helps B, B feels compelled to reciprocate that help. If A likes B and B perceives that liking, B will more than likely begin to like A. If A confides to B some rather intimate self-disclosing information, B will tend to respond with intimate self-disclosing statements of his own. The norm of reciprocity creates something of a snowball effect as each person's behavior reinforces the similar behaviors of the other. For this reason, perhaps, a norm embodying a pattern of communicative behaviors develops rather quickly through continuing group interaction.

SOCIAL TENSION

The feeling of tension is familiar to all of us. When one feels tense, he is nervous, irritable. Television commercials have endowed tension with a certain fame, along with its accompanying headache. But tension does indeed have its physiological signs—contracted muscles, the familiar sweaty palms, averted eye gaze. This is the tension experienced by a single individual. Social tension, however, is not unlike the tension experienced by an individual. Individuals in a group suffering from extreme social tension exhibit many of the signs of individual tension. Extreme social tension is characterized by an electric atmosphere. The very air seems brittle enough to crack at the drop of the proverbial pin. Individuals are uncomfortable. All in all, extreme social tension is not a pleasant experience.

Primary and Secondary Tension

Bormann (1969) distinguishes between two types of social tension—primary and secondary. The difference is one of kind rather than degree. During the initial period of a group's formation, primary tension is inevitable and to be expected as a normal occurrence. One might compare primary social tension to the feeling of stage fright. Social inhibitions create a lack of assurance on how to behave. Comments are quietly spoken and very tentative. Long pauses occur between comments. Members rarely interrupt each other during primary tension; and if two members should speak at once, profuse apologies reveal the extent of primary tension present.

Overall, group interaction during periods of primary tension is of very low intensity. Members are overly polite to each other and overtly strive to avoid anything which might involve social repercussions. But a group needs time and activity to "break the ice." After all, a social *system* does not yet exist, and members do not know what to expect or what is expected of them. Primary tension is normally overcome without great difficulty as interaction is allowed to continue, although it may recur briefly at the beginning of each new group meeting—particularly if a relatively long period of time transpires between meetings. Generally, once the ice is broken, a group need worry no more about social problems stemming from primary tension. Typically, such tension is not a serious problem in a group's socioemotional climate.

Secondary tension is potentially much more serious. Unlike primary tension, secondary social tension is not always predictable or easily overcome merely through the passage of time. The hallmark of secondary tension is typically an abrupt departure from group routine. Sometimes a sharp increase in tension begins with an outburst from one of the members. There may be a heated exchange between two or more members. A flurry of verbal activity will be followed by an unbearably long pause. During the heated exchange members may attempt to shout over each other's comments for extended periods. Usually two or three members will do the bulk of the talking while other members remain rigidly silent, staring at the floor. Extreme secondary tension is definitely an unpleasant sensation and, if uncontrolled, threatens the social health of the group.

The causes of secondary tension are many and varied. Overt interpersonal conflict, occasionally even a personality conflict, may precipitate severe secondary tension. Environmental pressures, such as a shortage of time to accomplish the task, will cause a sharp rise in secondary tension. Quite often, a feeling of frustration of the members foments tension. Such frustration may stem from an acknowledged lack of success in task accomplishment or the feeling that the group performance was far short of expectations. A nonconforming member might cause frustration—particularly one who is habitually tardy or absent from group meetings or who consistently fails to fulfull promises made to the group. Whatever the cause, extreme secondary tension, once experienced, must be brought under control if the group is to survive.

Managing Social Tension

Up to this point we have discussed tension as harmful and destructive to a group's socioemotional climate. Certainly *excessive* tension is harmful to the group, but some tension is both normal and essential. In fact, tension is always present in a functioning group. Tension implies activity. An actor, for instance, is not relaxed when he is performing. He is tense, concentrating on his art. The successful athletic team is "up for the game." After a group overcomes the natural social inertia in the early stages of group development, the members experience tension. Members are alert, on their toes—tense. The functioning group is not at rest but active and, hence, is experiencing some degree of tension.

In point of fact, it is tension which holds the group together. While excessive tension may act as a centrifugal force which threatens to tear the group apart, controlled tension functions as a centripetal force which holds the group together. Place the opposite poles of two magnets together and they will be drawn toward each other. I am sure you have seen the simple experiment of placing a sheet of paper on the magnets and sprinkling iron filings on the paper in order to see the activity of the lines of attraction bonding the two magnets together. Although the magnets seem at rest, they are in fact exerting force which holds them together. Another simple demonstration of the bonding characteristic of tension is to bend your elbows and place your palms together in front of you. Push your palms together exerting as much pressure as you can. You may notice your hands quivering, but they are essentially still, held together through the tension of pressure. In a similar manner tension holds the members of a group together and allows them to function effectively as a social system. Members interact, and interaction inherently implies some level of tension.

The problem of social tension, then, is not that it exists, but that it exceeds an optimal level. Every group has a *tolerance threshold* of social tension above which they cannot function effectively as a group. If the tension level is below that threshold, the group is able to function well. But when the tension level rises above the group's tolerance threshold, it becomes the overpowering priority in the group's socioemotional climate. The group must reduce that tension level before they can do anything else.

Of course, the tolerance threshold varies from group to group. Some groups can tolerate a rather high level of tension. That is, some groups are able to function effectively although a rather high level of tension is present. Another group whose tolerance threshold was lower would find that level of tension intolerable. Just as some individuals can endure more pain than others, some groups can endure more tension than others. The problem for the group, then, is to develop successful mechanisms for reducing tension when it rises above their tolerance threshold.

Figures 4 through 7 illustrate graphically the rise and fall of a group's tension level. Of course, tension cannot be measured very accurately, so these graphs serve only illustrative purposes. The group illustrated in Figure 4 overcame the initial primary tension but were unable to control secondary tension. Thus, the secondary tension level remains above the tolerance threshold, and the group is unable to function effectively throughout. For the members of this group, their socioemotional climate is extremely unpleasant. No group can withstand indefinitely the pressures of secondary tension above the tolerance threshold. One can predict that the life expectancy of this group is quite short. They will probably disband their group rather than suffer this social agony much longer.

Figure 5 illustrates an unusual type of group but one that occasionally occurs. Members of this group were never able to overcome their initial primary tension. Obviously there is very little "groupness." They remain a collection of individuals. Members do not identify with the group, exhibit extraordinary apathy, and have virtually no commitment to either the group or the task at hand. One is reminded of the community meeting

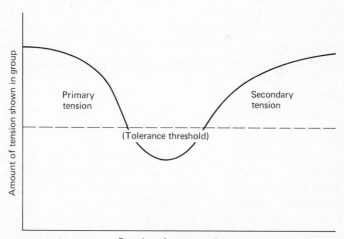

Figure 4 Tension curve of an hypothetical group (uncontrolled secondary tension). [*Figures 4–7 adapted from Fig. 11, "Secondary Tension Curve," from* Discussion and Group Methods: Theory and Practice *by Ernest G. Bormann (Harper and Row, New York, 1969, p. 172).*]

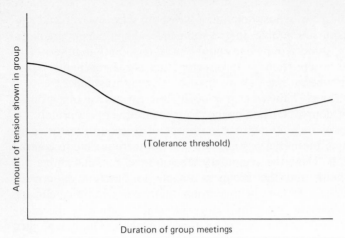

Figure 5 Tension curve of an hypothetical group (uncontrolled primary tension).

called to protest apathy, but no one showed up at the meeting. This group or, more accurately, collection of individuals will not exist too long either. If the members do continue to meet (in the event that they are a "captive" aggregation who are compelled to meet), they will accomplish little.

Such groups are quite atypical. Communication among even "captive" individuals generally produces some degree of interdependence among members. But one classroom group did correspond to this graph quite closely. In approximately twenty hours of meetings, all of which were recorded on audiotape, their interaction patterns in their first hour of meeting time resembled closely the interaction of nearly every other hour of meeting time. They continued to speak with extremely low intensity and never interrupted each other. Pauses between comments were long and painful, some thirty seconds or more in duration. Needless to say, this group also showed little outward sign of group identification, nor were they very productive.

At first glance, the group illustrated in Figure 6 seems ideal. They overcome primary tension and never suffer from secondary tension above their tolerance threshold. They seem to be a happy, healthy group of contented individuals. And that may be true. More likely, however, members of this group are either bored stiff or are suffering from an abnormal fear of social tension. It is simply not healthy, perhaps not normal, for a group never to experience secondary tension above their tolerance threshold. One explanation for never doing so would presume that the members simply don't care enough to get excited about anything.

As a result, members do what they are told but have little commitment to the group's activities. Another plausible explanation would presume the members to be hypochondriacs about social tension. They fear tension so much that they conscientiously avoid any stimulus which would raise the tension level above the tolerance threshold. Hence, members retreat or take flight from any potential source for a social problem. Rather than solving their social problems, they ignore them and hope that they go away.

Of course a "perfect" social system exemplified by Figure 6 might exist. The members might be ultracompatible, and social tension just never rises. Or their tolerance threshold may be so high that the tension. level experienced never exceeds it. Nevertheless, the group develops no history in its behavior pattern as a system which would indicate its success in alleviating social problems when they might arise. If their environment were a Garden of Eden, perhaps problems would never arise. We can only wonder, though, what would happen to such a group if and when "the going gets rough." Without successful past behavior, their ability to cope with excessive social tension remains highly questionable.

The group illustrated in Figure 7 is most likely to resemble the ideal socioemotional climate. This group has frequent moments of secondary tension above their tolerance threshold, and they consistently dispel the excess of tension. This group successfully manages their social tension

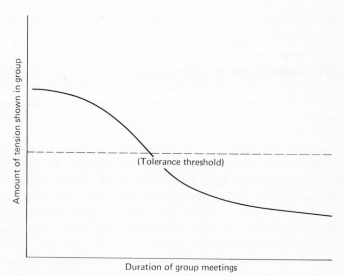

Duration of group meetings

Figure 6 Tension curve of an hypothetical group (absence of secondary tension).

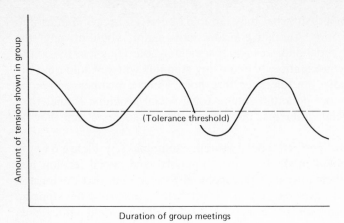

Figure 7 Tension curve of an hypothetical group (frequent periods of secondary tension).

and obviously has no fear of secondary tension. Their past behavior is a series of instances of successful tension management. The members have obviously developed mechanisms for successfully coping with secondary tension and have incorporated them into their system's function patterns. The social fabric of this group is strengthened with each success in managing social tension. Their socioemotional climate is vibrantly healthy, and their members undoubtedly find the group exciting and stimulating.

Lest the point is not yet clear, we must emphasize that the *amount* of social tension above or below the tolerance threshold is relatively insignificant. What does matter is the ability of the group to manage their tension level successfully. Thus, the group in Figure 7 is characterized by the *frequency* and not by the amount of excessive social tension they experience. Each period of tension above the tolerance threshold is quite brief. Members do not suffer extended periods of excessive tension but invoke tried-and-true mechanism-functions for reducing the tension when they need to. Unlike the group illustrated in Figure 6, this group has the devices at its disposal, that is, within the system's function patterns, to cope with problems of social tension—actual and potential.

It should be apparent at this point what a healthy socioemotional group climate looks and sounds like—at least from the viewpoint of tension management. A healthy group is apt to be noisy. Its members are uninhibited and probably not governed by norms of politeness. There are frequent disagreements, arguments, and constant interruptions which reflect the members' eagerness and commitment to their group—high group identification. Members who are not major contributors to the group's verbal interaction are actively a part of the group. They are alert and nonverbally appear interested in the comments of others.

The mechanisms developed by successful groups for reducing excessive tension are also many and varied. Moreover, what works in one group may be totally unsuccessful in others. Often one or two persons assume the role of tension-relievers, and the group looks to them for help when the time arises. Sometimes a tension-reliever is a jokester—a person who is carefree, happy-go-lucky, and makes people laugh. But laughter is not always a clear sign of tension release but may even signify excessive tension. When members laugh at comments which are really not funny, they are probably exhibiting rather than releasing tension. Quick, abrupt, high-pitched laughter is generally a sign of tension rather than tension release. One group successfully relieved their primary tension through a member who constantly told jokes, often at her personal expense. But when secondary tension arose, her self-deprecating jokes were totally unsuccessful. In fact, the other members resented her carefree attitude and finally demanded that she take a more serious attitude toward their task. Thus, the behavior which dispelled primary tension was unsuccessful in coping with secondary tension, even in the same group.

Another tension-relieving role may be a mediator between two conflicting members. When secondary tension erupts from such an interpersonal conflict, the conciliator *who is respected by both the conflicting members* is a tension-reliever. Sometimes excessive tension is reduced by finding a scapegoat as a mediating agency. When tension arises from frustration over environmental or task pressures, that frustration must be vented at someone or something. In a classroom group, the instructor serves as a convenient scapegoat. In a business organization the "boss" becomes the outgroup "enemy." The successful scapegoat is generally outside the immediate group membership. Most important to the group, though, is not how they manage tension but whether they do.

The key to successful tension management is distressingly and deceptively simple. *The successful group confronts their social problems head-on.* More problems are created by avoiding or ignoring potential problems than by facing them squarely. Such overt action is rarely easy, however, and generally requires old-fashioned guts! But the social benefits are worth the momentary and perfectly normal reluctance. One member's diary, written immediately after a particularly productive group meeting, emphasizes the wisdom of confrontation:

But almost everyone got the hippie-stereotype impression of me. It goes to show, first impressions are really terrible, because everyone is so different than I first pegged them out to be. I told everyone exactly what I thought of them and they told me. I thought this would be a total disaster, and everyone would end up hating each other. But it brought us very close together, I think. This meeting is a great accomplishment for our group. Now I think we can start moving.

Whatever the social problem, the importance of confronting it head-on cannot be overestimated. Occasionally the group is in for a painful period of agonizing tension during this confrontation. But in the long run the group not only survives but becomes stronger. One classroom group provides a fantastic example of extreme measures used to confront a social problem centered in a single person. This example also demonstrates equally fantastic results which accrued in the group's socioemotional climate. This five-member group was composed of four women and one man. For a variety of reasons the man was considered a male chauvinist by the women members, a thorn in their side. They deeply resented what they considered to be his domineering behavior although they had not directly verbalized their resentment. At one climactic meeting they finally decided to let him know—clearly and forcefully. The following excerpts from the male member's paper analyzing his group most clearly illustrate what happened during the confrontation and its aftermath:

> Then there was the meeting when one of the members hit me with the comment, "Go to hell, you egotistical creep!" It was then that I began to realize the value of this class and how our group reacted. There was, of course, a great deal of tension that day. I was very nervous and uncomfortable. . . . In being blasted I, more than anyone else, I think, felt what a brutal force and what brutal pressure can fall on someone in the social dimension of a group when people begin to attack you.
> . . . It was exciting to have each member of the group become confident enough to bare his or her soul to the rest of the group.

A comment from another member of the group corroborates the positive effects of this extreme confrontation:

> My first reaction to Marilyn's "Tom, go to hell" was that it was uncalled for. I thought that that type or degree of honesty was not needed. However, it was exactly what was needed because it opened the door to real communication. We all became very sober and honest with each other. . . . By the end of the meeting my mind was so elated that I felt completely free of anxiety or pressure, and I felt very much at peace with myself and with the world.

Granted, not every confrontation will have such immediate and such positive effects. Nor will every confrontation be centered on a single member or even on a person at all. But avoiding potential social problems will have even less immediate and much less positive effects. Social problems do not go away if they are not solved. They simply remain and fester. It takes guts to confront social problems as squarely as this last group did. It is exceedingly difficult to cast off natural inhibitions so quickly and so completely. But, of course, most confrontations would not be nearly as extreme or painful either. The important point, again, is not the extreme measure used by the group to confront their problem but the fact that they did overtly and conscientiously decide to confront their problem.

But what of compromise as a solution? Surely problems are not always win-or-lose propositions. A group should be able to effect some sort of "golden mean." The spirit of compromise is healthy. No one should belittle the wisdom of the spirit of compromise. Nor should one assume that compromise is the cure for all social problems. Often compromise is a tactic used by a group to avoid facing their problems. The following excerpt from a classroom group's final self-analysis reflects this point:

> It was surprising that our first task was completed because we had competition within the group that became disruptive. In order to achieve the task we had to compromise and stop competing. . . . However, compromise never was the ultimate solution as we were to learn. Our group suffered from tension because we did compromise. The only thing our first compromise did was to produce a paper but leave the members with a sub-conscious feeling of "something is wrong." We concluded that compromise is an easy way of dismissing tensions that could go beyond the threshold—an escape from facing the ultimate questions that have to be answered for group survival.

In this group compromise was a substitute for the solution of their social problems. They compromised as the easy way out. Rather than facing up to their problems, they escaped from them through compromise. We must conclude, then, that compromise is a useful mechanism for tension management. But compromise should come *after* the group confronts their social problems and should not be used as a substitute for facing up to their problems.

In summary, there is one vitally important point to remember. The successful and socially healthy group is not characterized by an absence of social tension but, rather, by successful management of social tension. No group should expect or even hope for an absence of problems caused by social tension. Instead, they should expect social problems to occur, to confront those problems, and to develop mechanisms for their control. This means that the members must learn to overcome their own personal inhibitions, be honest, and require or demand the same behavior from other members. Such "good advice" is, of course, deceptively simple. It is more easily said than done. But a successful group requires not only time for development but also overt effort on the part of its members to make it a success. One student group encapsulated this "good advice" in a pithy slogan which may be worthy of repeating—"The group that fights together stays together!"

INFLUENCE OF COMMUNICATION

Although Chapters 6, 7, 8, and 9 include more specific discussion of communication in the small group, it is important to make several observations at this point about communication and the group's socioemotional climate. One important assumption underlying the viewpoint of group communication is that individuals possess the capacity of free will and free choice over their own behaviors. Every person, at least in our society, chooses to behave in his own way. But, paradoxical as it may seem, his behaviors are subject to numerous constraints. We are only vaguely aware of many of these constraints on our behavior, but we submit to them nonetheless. For example, we wear clothing in public rather than appear nude. We speak using a language with specific rules of syntax and semantics. Even though we may not be totally aware of them, we conform to a multitude of constraints on our behavior and do so willingly and freely. To live in a social environment is to conform to many constraints on our behavior.

A second assumption, which will be apparent later, is that every externally observable behavior is potentially communicative. Furthermore, all communication is externally observable as behavior. This assumption rules out of communication such phenomena as ESP or anything which cannot be perceived through one of our five senses. And what one thinks or feels is not communicative unless it can be inferred from sensory observation. Thus, we are using the terms "behavior" and "communication" almost interchangeably at times. For our purposes, all communication is behavior. You will notice the term "communicative behavior" appears in this book rather frequently. But the two words are used in conjunction as a form of emphasis more than anything else. In reality, the term "communicative behavior" is inherently redundant.

A third assumption concludes this preliminary discussion of communication. As a member of a social system, the individual chooses to constrain his behaviors and has no choice but to submit to behavioral constraints. This statement is so self-contradictory as to appear facetious, but it is vitally important to the functioning of communication and the interdependence of individuals within a social system. As one person communicates to another, he chooses to frame his message in a certain way in order to "manage the impressions" of the other person. And he has no choice but to do so. The other person has no choice but to respond and thus "manage the impressions" of the first person. Even ignoring the first message and responding with silence is a response which will serve to create an impression in the other's mind. As the cliché goes, "One cannot not communicate."

In the developing social system of a group, each member behaves, that is, communicates to his fellow members. Even though he remains silent, he is communicating to his fellow members who form some impression of him based on his noncontributing behavior. As interpersonal impressions grow stronger with additional communicative behavior, each member fits into a pattern of interlocked and integrated behaviors which constitute "the group." That is, each member chooses to constrain his own behaviors so that he fulfills a role in the group and conforms to the norms developed by the group. In short, group communication is inherently a pattern of behaviors which characterize that group. And that pattern of interpersonal behaviors is the perfectly natural and even inevitable outcome of group communication.

The LGD was selected for our purposes so that the individual's natural freedom of choice is given the widest latitude. To the extent that a group is not an LGD—that is, subject to constraints imposed on the group by some external authority and not by the group members themselves— the latitude of the individual's initial freedom of choice is narrowed. This chapter has discussed roles and norms as they emerge through group interaction rather than considering them purely as positions or standards imposed on the group before its interaction. In doing so, we can see the full impact of communication in the small group. In the LGD there is no distinction between formal and informal standards. They are one and the same.

In summary, then, a group's socioemotional climate exists in the form of externalized observable behaviors—communication. Each individual member's emotions or feelings are considered irrelevant to the social system as long as they are not visible through inference to the sensory perceptions of the other members. Only when a member communicates can he have any chance of influencing the perceptions of his fellow members. When one views the group in this manner, communicative behavior is not only *a* perspective from which to view a group's socioemotional climate; it is *the* perspective.

SUMMARY

There are several ways to view the socioemotional climate of a group. All deal in some way with a perception of the cohesiveness of a group. The most common method is to view the extent to which group members like each other. A second perspective involves the degree to which members are satisfied with their group experience. Similar to member satisfaction is the view of group identification—the extent to which members are committed to their membership and exhibit loyalty to the social system.

Developing the group's socioemotional climate may be regarded as a process of acculturation—in an LGD, the process of developing a group culture from scratch. Acculturation implies the existence of and conformity to certain specified and unspecified standards of behavior. One form of behavioral standards is the development of an interlocking network of roles which are performed or fulfilled by each member, second form of behavioral standards is the development of social norms. Both norms and roles in the LGD are largely idiosyncratic to the particular group. There is probably no role or norm which is universal to all groups unless it is the role of leader or the norm of reciprocity.

The socioemotional climate of a group is, to a great extent, dependent upon the social tension experienced by the group. Social tension is of two types—primary and secondary. Primary tension refers to the normal period of tension in early stages of group development caused by the absence of a social structure and normal inhibitions of members new to a developing social system. Secondary tension occurs during group interaction as disruptive periods in group routines of activity. Of the two types of tension, only secondary tension is generally a problem to a group's effective functioning.

Although some degree of social tension is inevitable and, in fact, vital to a successful group, tension may rise above a group's tolerance threshold and keep the group from functioning efficiently. A socially healthy group experiences frequent periods of social tension above their tolerance threshold and develops mechanisms for reducing tension to a tolerable level. Although devices used to reduce excessive tension vary widely and include anything that works, all devices seem to possess one attribute in common. Each device involves a direct confrontation of the social problem, facing it squarely without any attempt to avoid or ignore it.

Chapter 5

Leadership
and Status

Probably the most familiar of all social phenomena is the concept of leadership. Although not studied extensively until the last three or four decades, leadership has intrigued philosophers for centuries. How and why do people come to power? Why do people so zealously follow leaders such as Adolph Hitler? What do leaders do that nonleaders don't? What constitutes good or effective leadership?

It is amazing that so many people could study one phenomenon and gain such little understanding of it. The number of unanswered questions concerning leadership is staggering. The purpose of this chapter is to shed some light on leadership in a small group, specifically how leadership develops in the small decision-making group. Consistent with the perspective of communication and group process, this chapter deals with leadership as an emerging process precipitated by the interstructured communicative behaviors of all group members.

THE STATUS HIERARCHY

One of the earmarks of any social organization is the existence of a hierarchical order of status. Although the familiar caste system of India remains the most striking example of a large-scale social status hierarchy, no one would deny that our own country is divided into different social classes. Normally membership in a higher class involves money, but often family background and professional membership play key roles in determining one's status position. Those in the lower and middle classes strive for membership in a higher class, vicariously and realistically, by procuring symbols of a higher status—a big new automobile, a color television set, an expensive home in an exclusive section of town. We cling to the belief that any American may become President, but we know that the presidential chances of a person who is nonwhite, poor, or female are extremely small.

The status symbols in an LGD are not quite so clear. Certainly money doesn't seem to be an important factor. Generally the social classes—that is, the status hierarchy—of the small group is an order based on the ability to influence other group members. More specifically, high-status members in an LGD are perceived by other members as having provided the greatest assistance to the group's task accomplishment. If the *raison d'être* of the group is to accomplish some goal, the person or persons who help the group make progress toward that goal are rewarded with high-status positions.

ASCRIBED AND ACHIEVED STATUS

Status may or may not be earned by the individual. This point may be obvious, but in order to avoid any misunderstanding, it must be emphasized. The person who is born with the proverbial silver spoon in his mouth or on the other side of the proverbial tracks acquires his status position through an accident of birth. Such status may be said to be "ascribed" in that the individual has been given the status position through no fault of his own. On the other hand, a person may earn status by his own individual striving. A social group awards him status on the basis of his past behaviors in that group. Achieved status is the major concern of the LGD, of course, since no external authority impinges upon the ability of the group to develop its own social organization.

Often two status hierarchies—one based on ascribed status and one based on achieved status—exist side by side in the same social organization. A business organization, for example, has its own status hierarchy ascribed by the organization itself. But the workers in that organization may have developed their own status hierarchy which may not conform to that sanctioned by the organization. These two hierarchies comprise the "formal" and the "informal" structure of the organization. When the authority of the two hierarchies is in conflict, the ascribed status position of the formal structure is often second best.

The problem of ascribed and achieved status may exist in a classroom group if, for example, the instructor designates one of the members a leader. Whether the ascribed leader achieves the informal status of leader is wholly dependent on his behaviors during group interaction. Mortensen (1966) indicates that when the group meets for sustained interaction (more than one hour), assigning the leadership role exerts little influence on whether the assigned leader achieves group acceptance as leader. Apparently the small group assigns its highest status level to the person whom they feel has provided them with the most assistance in meeting their group goals. Therefore, the functioning status hierarchy in a small group is based on the behavior patterns of the members with minimal influence from some outgroup authority who assigns status levels.

STATUS LEVELS

Each group develops the number of levels in its status hierarchy as well as the degree to which one status level is separated from another. Of course, any hierarchy requires a minimum of two levels although three levels often, perhaps typically, occur in the LGD. The leader may be assumed to occupy one of the roles in the top status level with other roles ordered in comparison with his role. That is, the choice of leader is generally the first step in developing the status hierarchy. Once the group identifies their leader, they compare him with each of the other members' roles and assign each member to a corresponding status level. Other members may share the top status level with the leader, but rarely will another member's role be judged higher than the status of the leader's.

You will recall that status consensus was one of the dimensions of member satisfaction. Thus, a cohesive group will agree on which of their members occupy the top status level—leadership, at least. The development of a status hierarchy should not be confused with authoritarianism or antidemocratic methods, however. Some groups, who naturally admire the ideal of a democracy, would like to think that there are no status distinctions among their members. Such an attitude is not only unrealistic, it is utter nonsense! A status hierarchy is not incompatible with a democracy or with democratic methods. The fact that LGD members have the capacity to direct their own destiny (They have no choice but to do so.) implies a minidemocracy. The group members may or may not utilize authoritarian methods. But whether they do is their own choice. More importantly, a status hierarchy will exist in any group regardless of the extent to which the members employ democratic methods.

One final observation about the status levels also seems necessary. The existence of two or more levels in the hierarchy does not necessarily imply that some members are perceived to be of little value to the group. Indeed, the cohesive group typically values the contributions of every one of its members. But some members' contributions are perceived to be more helpful than others. Thus, they are assigned a higher status. Members in the second or third status level may also be high status in the eyes of their fellow group members. But relative to some other members, the second and third levels are simply not as high as the top level. The hierarchy of status levels, then, is a rank ordering of member roles relative to each other, but the roles are not judged according to some absolute standard or scale ranging from good to bad.

Leadership and Power

Several years ago I served on a committee charged with the task of selecting a chairman for our university department. Several of our initial meetings were devoted to defining the role of our chairman. We were unanimous in agreeing that we desired a departmental "chairman" rather than a departmental "head." In other words, we were agreed that we wanted leadership, but we did not want a dictator. The essential difference between chairman and head was apparently the degree of power at the disposal of the leader.

The concept of extreme power in the hands of a leader is not novel. Indeed, nearly five centuries ago Machiavelli conceived of a political power so strong that a ruler could use any means at his disposal to control the behavior of his followers. In fact, Machiavelli believed that such power was essential for a centralized government. Machiavelli's name today refers to the unscrupulous exercise of political power. And the term "Machiavellianism" has recently been employed in reference to an individual's ability or desire to dominate or control the behavior of another person during interaction.

It is important to distinguish between a "head" (for lack of a better term) and "leader." A head possesses the power to control the fate of others and thus has considerable power to coerce those under his leadership. A small group "head" would determine the goal of the group, give directions that must be obeyed willingly or unwillingly, and levy direct sanctions against nonfollowers. There would be considerable social distance between the head and his followers. In short, the relationship between a head and his followers is unidirectional. He can influence followers but is not susceptible to any influence from them.

The LGD, of course, has a "leader" rather than a head, in virtually every case. But a leader has power, too. The difference between headship and leadership is not the amount of power but the basis from which the power is derived. One common basis of power is to control resources which are needed or desired by others. Saudi Arabia, for example, possesses much more power than its size warrants because the country controls a vast quantity of oil which is needed and desired by all industrialized countries of the world. And when we think of powerful countries, we immediately think of those countries with the capacity of nuclear weapons. In short, power resides in the possession of some relatively scarce resource needed or desired by others. Such a concept of power is expressed in conventional wisdom by the adage, "In a country of the blind, the one-eyed man is king."

The LGD does not typically provide such a basis of power. While intelligence, for example, might be considered a personal resource, it is not something which can be transferred from one person to another or acquired by a person in the same sense of resources in the examples above. Nevertheless, the leader of the LGD does have a kind of power, even though its basis is not so easily defined. Unlike the unidirectional relationship between a "head" and his followers, the relationship between a "leader" and his followers is reciprocal. Consistent with the doctrine of interdependence, a leader leads at the discretion of his followers. That is, the basis for a leader's power is "consent of the governed." A leader may be deposed at any time. When he fails to satisfy his followers, the leader's basis of power is undermined. Hence, he ceases to lead. A basis of power, such as control of scarce resources, defines a leader in isolation, regardless of the will of other group members. Such a definition is contrary to the elements of process and interdependence inherent in the LGD. For our purposes, then, a leader is defined only in terms of his followers. To discuss leadership is to discuss followership. One cannot exist without the other.

A leader of an LGD is, of course, recognized by group members as the leader. Their recognition takes the form of deferential behavior directed toward him. That is, members accede to the leadership moves made by the leader. They accord the leader respect, and they generally like him. (We will return later to the subject of the leader as an object of liking.) Members perceive the leader to be aiding the group in making progress toward their group goals. Normally, such progress implies the leader's activity in aiding the group in accomplishing their task. Perhaps more important than any other definitive characteristic, the leader is the person who consistently acts like a leader by performing leadership acts.

The definition of leadership at this point is admittedly quite general, but it does provide a basic understanding of what constitutes leadership in the small decision-making group. A more precise description of why certain persons achieve leadership status is provided later.

PERSPECTIVES ON LEADERSHIP

The vast quantity of research and philosophical writings about leadership reveals considerable confusion. The reason for the confusion stems from the many varied perspectives used to view leadership. People commonly consider leadership to be embodied in a person occupying a given position in the group. Therefore, a leader is a person first and a position in a role network second. While this viewpoint is a common one, it may have hindered progress in discovering the nature of leadership. In order to provide the basis for this book's perspective on leadership and to enrich our understanding of this elusive phenomenon, an evaluative survey of the most common perspectives on leadership follows. Hollander and Julian (1969) also provide a concise summary of some common perspectives on group leadership.

Traits

Letters of reference to employers, universities, and scholarship/loan agencies often ask for evaluations of the applicant on selected personality characteristics. A common characteristic included in such lists is "leadership ability." The assumption underlying this characteristic is the belief that a leader is a unique individual possessing some innate ability which allows him to assume a leadership position in any social system. Further assumed is the belief that leaders are born and not made. Our conventional wisdom contains this same assumption in such well-worn phrases as "a natural leader" and "born to be a leader." It is not surprising, then, that the early approach to leadership searched for those individual characteristics or traits which leaders possess. Although not nearly as popular today, the traits approach still influences contemporary views on leadership.

The traits approach attempted to distinguish leaders from nonleaders on the basis of how they differed on personal characteristics. The very earliest research using the traits approach highlighted physical characteristics consistent with the notion that the childhood leader is the biggest bully on the block. Because of consistently fruitless efforts to discover distinctive physical characteristics of leaders, this perspective soon focused on the distinctive traits of a leader's personality. The results from the traits approach have been contradictory and disappointing. Many personality traits have, at one time or another, been linked to leadership, including such traits as dependability, intelligence, self-confidence, enthusiasm or dynamism, originality, responsibility, verbal facility, critical thinking ability, and creativity.

A list of such traits appears consistent with common sense. One would normally think that a leader should possess all these traits. But the traits approach to observing leadership has failed to achieve consistent results. Indeed, a leader of one group does not consistently achieve leadership in other groups. In fact, the leader of one group often cannot maintain his leadership even in the same group. The traits approach simply cannot account for the change of leadership in the same group.

Virtually no one today considers the traits approach a satisfactory explanation of leadership. In addition to the fact that no trait has been consistently associated with leadership, there are other reasons for finding this approach less than satisfactory. First of all, personality is an elusive phenomenon. No one has been able to determine successfully the specific components of personality. Because no one can directly perceive personality with his senses—cannot see, touch, hear, or taste it—one's personality cannot be reliably measured or observed. For example, it is not unusual for two people to disagree about another's personality. What one would consider a pleasing personality, another would find unpleasant. In short, while personality is often used as an overall impression, it is not reliable as a specific definition or observation. Viewing leadership from the traits approach does not render leadership less abstract.

A second reason for rejecting the traits approach distinguishes between achieving leadership and maintaining it. What one needs to gain leadership in a group may be quite different from what he needs to maintain leadership after he has achieved it. The successful leader of a revolutionary coup is often not successful as the leader of the newly established country. Although he may have excelled as a revolutionary leader, he may be a total failure as an establishment leader. The traits approach fails to account for the apparent difference between achieving and maintaining leadership.

Perhaps most important of all, the traits approach cannot differentiate between a good and a bad leader. What constitutes effective leadership as opposed to ineffective leadership? The traits approach goes only so far as to distinguish leaders from nonleaders and is inherently incapable of distinguishing good or effective leadership or drawing any sort of distinctions among leaders. With such a limited perspective, it is not surprising that the traits approach should be discarded as a useful approach for understanding leadership.

Styles

The traits approach to leadership attempts to distinguish leaders from nonleaders and to identify those personality traits which characterize persons who rise to leadership status. The styles approach proceeds from a different perspective. Leadership styles assume an a priori identification of the leader either through ascription or achievement and a general description of how the leader leads. This approach seeks to determine which style of leadership is best or most effective in a group by comparing one predetermined style with another.

The early research utilizing the styles perspective differentiated among three general styles of leadership. Those three styles were generalized descriptions of the relationship between the leader and his followers based on the leader's general pattern of behavior—democratic, autocratic, and laissez faire. The laissez faire style of leadership was soon discarded because it was so difficult to define. Essentially the hands-off policy indicated by a laissez faire style of leadership implies that the leader leads through not leading at all. Even on a common-sense level a laissez faire style of leadership is an anomaly. Nonleadership is viewed as leadership. Therefore, only two leadership styles are typically recognized today—democratic and autocratic.

Numerous studies have compared democratic and autocratic styles of group leadership. Those in business management commonly refer to the two styles as participatory and supervisory management styles. Unfortunately, because the two styles are considered diametrically opposed to each other, the comparisons between them are not always realistic. Typically an extremely democratic style is compared with an extremely autocratic style. That is, the democratic leader is totally unselfish, seeks group participation at all times, and consistently functions in the best interest of the group as a whole. The democratic leader tends to overemphasize the socioemotional dimension of the group. On the other hand, most comparisons require the autocratic leader to behave with an absolute minimum of group participation, give blatant orders, and work for highly selfish goals. The autocratic leader, then, overemphasizes the task dimension of the group. Realistically, of course, there are many leadership styles that exist between these two extremes. And a single leader may even be democratic at times and autocratic at other times.

Past comparisons, however, have discovered some differences between groups functioning under each of the two styles. For example, the group with a democratic leader typically experiences more member satisfaction, while the group with an autocratic leader is more efficient and more productive—particularly when productivity is measured on the basis of efficiency (for example, fewer errors). But the difference between groups tends to diminish over time as the group members accustom themselves to the style of their leader. Since the task and social dimensions are interdependent, the success experienced in one dimension affects success in the other. That is, because members experience greater member satisfaction with a democratic leader, they will tend to work harder as a result and increase their productivity. And because groups are highly efficient and productive under an autocratic leader, the members experience greater pride in their achievements—hence, an increase in member satisfaction.

The styles approach also is not a satisfactory perspective from which to view leadership in a small decision-making group. It is intuitively obvious that one style is not most desirable or most effective for all groups and all situations. For example, a military leader in battle and an airplane pilot in a storm are autocratic leaders and undoubtedly should be. When the going is rough, neither of these two leaders can stop to take a vote. Rather, they give orders which must be followed immediately and without hesitation. Naturally, in less trying situations the pilot or the military leader is often more democratic in his style of leadership.

Perhaps the greatest problem of the styles approach to leadership is the unduly nebulous nature of the autocratic style. Since we live in a democratic society, we would like to believe that a democratic leader is superior to an autocratic style. But certainly the autocratic leader is not inherently evil. What about the benevolent dictator? His methods may be autocratic, but he consistently functions in the best interests of the group, which is also characteristic of the democratic leader. He may consistently seek the opinions and advice of other members while still maintaining his autocratic power. While we tend to see democratic and autocratic styles of leadership in opposition, the distinction between the two, as well as the influence of the styles on the group, is not always clear cut.

Situations

Due to the inability of the traits and styles approaches to provide robust explanations of group leadership, many have turned to other perspectives. Today the situational approach is by far the most popular and common perspective of group leadership. The situational perspective describes the person who rises to the leadership position with emphasis on discovering the appropriate person for the appropriate situation. Less consideration is given to what the leader does or what he needs to do for effective group functioning.

Utilizing the situational approach to group leadership requires a thorough description of the group situation. Although a comprehensive description of a situation is not now available, some variables have often been associated with the situational perspective. Perhaps the most common ingredient of the situation is the particular combination of personality traits of the group members, their level of interest in the task, their motivation, and so forth. Then, too, the nature of the task is often believed to be an ingredient of the situation which requires a particular kind of leader. Other less common situational variables include factors of the physical setting. For example, sitting at the head of a table has been associated with leadership in our culture, although seating arrangements have not proved to be highly successful as indicators of leadership. And the size of the group has had some bearing on leadership. Obviously, as the group increases in size, the visibility of each individual member becomes more of a problem. On the other hand, charismatic leadership has been closely associated with very large groups and a corresponding increase in social distance between a leader and his followers.

At first glance, the situational approach to group leadership appears to solve most of the problems associated with the traits and styles perspectives. But the situational perspective is also troublesome. There are few, if any, general principles to direct a prospective group leader on what he should or can do in a given situation. Of course, there are many lists of "dos" and "don'ts" to guide prospective leaders, but such lists have not proved very successful. Then, too, no comprehensive list of situational ingredients now exists. Even compiling such a list may be quite impossible. Among even those variables which have been observed to exist within the situation, there is no way of determining which ingredients provide the greatest impact on the situation.

Perhaps most importantly, the situational perspective provides little assistance in furthering our knowledge of group leadership. Rather than providing guidelines of how and what a group member should do or can do to exercise influence on other group members, the situational perspective instead provides general advice of adapting the person to the situation, whatever it happens to be. Rather than discovering what critical behaviors are effective in leading a group as it varies from situation to situation, the situational approach can only say, "It depends on the situation." In short, the situational perspective of group leadership may be a compromise between the traits and the styles approaches, but it seems to be little more than a "cop-out" in order to explain the inexplicable.

Functions

All the above perspectives on group leadership—traits, styles, situations—have one element in common. Each assumes that leadership is centered in the *person* who occupies the leadership position in the group's network of roles. The functions perspective shifts the point of emphasis from the person to the communicative *behaviors* performed. While the functions approach is certainly not new—in fact, this approach to leadership has been around for over thirty years—no consistent search for leadership functions has developed over the years. The functions perspective has never achieved the significance or popularity enjoyed by each of the other three perspectives at one time or another. One reason for this lack of popularity may be a confusion over what is meant by functions. While some have considered group functions to be general principles essential to group operation, others discuss functions as specific behaviors capable of being performed by an individual.

The view of functions as general principles necessary for maintaining the group fails to serve our purposes and is not congruent with the perspective of communication and group process. The concept of group functions becomes diluted through overgeneralizing. Most group functions are "good advice" principles with insufficient practicability. For example, some commonly listed group functions include: (1) to advance the purpose of the group, (2) to inspire greater activity among members, (3) to administer procedural matters, and (4) to build group cohesiveness. Essentially, these group functions imply some sort of influence which achieves desired results such as greater cohesiveness, increased productivity, or greater group unity. Group functions, then, are little more than desired goals achieved rather than specific communicative behaviors which help to achieve these goals.

Although there is no single acceptable list of individual functions—that is, communicative behaviors—several suggested lists indicate some individual behaviors which have been associated with leadership in the past. Cartwright and Zander (1968, p. 306), for example, distinguish between group functions and individual functions and provide such a list:

> It appears that most group objectives can be subsumed under one of two headings: (a) the achievement of some specific group goal and (b) the maintenance or strengthening of the group itself. Examples of member behaviors that serve functions of *goal achievement* are "initiates action," "keeps members' attention on the goal," "clarifies the issue," "develops a procedural plan," "evaluates the quality of work done," and "makes expert information available." Examples of behaviors that serve functions of *group maintenance* are "keeps interpersonal relations pleasant," "arbitrates

disputes," "provides encouragement," "gives the minority a chance to be heard," "stimulates self-direction," and "increases the interdependence among members."

It should be apparent that not all functions included in Cartwright and Zander's list are satisfactory. Some functions are so blatantly abstract as to preclude virtually any practical application. What type of behavior, for example, "increases the interdependence among members"? Perhaps more significantly, Cartwright and Zander separate functions into two categories—task functions and social functions—and consequently deny the interdependence of these two dimensions of group process. But the list does include some behaviors which are meaningful. For example, "initiates action," "clarifies the issue," "evaluates the quality of work done," and "provides encouragement" are some specific behavioral functions which may be practicably applied by the prospective group leader.

Mortensen (1966) devised five categories of individual behaviors which he labeled "attempted leadership." Those five categories include "introducing and formulating goals, tasks, procedures," "eliciting communication from other group members," "delegating, directing action," "showing consideration for group activity," and "integrating and summarizing group activity." These five categories are also not very practicable, but they do imply several characteristics of leadership behaviors. For example, Mortensen conceives of a leader as initiating proposals for action, asking focused questions, and summarizing group activity. These functions are also reflected in Cartwright and Zander's list.

Hugh C. Russell (1970) discovered four dimensions of a leader's communicative behaviors. Those dimensions include "goal facilitation," "emotional control," "objectivity," and "communication skill." These dimensions indicate that a leader directs the group toward the group goal, attempts to reduce tension and resolve conflicts, contributes balanced information, and possesses the qualities of a skillful speaker. Unfortunately, Russell's list of dimensions does not attempt to specify those behaviors which exercise influence or which a leader specifically uses in order to exert leadership. He does not, for example, specify a behavior which could reduce tension or resolve conflict. These dimensions are only descriptive characteristics of the totality of a leader's behavior—not types of communicative behaviors themselves.

In sum, the bulk of these lists of leadership functions do indicate some specific behaviors associated with leadership. Moreover, the functions appear to emphasize those behaviors which facilitate group task accomplishment. A more specific list of behaviors which comprises all the functions performed by a leader is not yet available, although a partial list is apparent and may be used as a springboard for further consideration. Certainly the performance of appropriate leadership functions requires a social awareness of what function needs to be performed, when it needs performing, and the ability to perform it. Later chapters should provide more specific assistance in determining the appropriate times.

The functions perspective on leadership is not without its shortcomings, however. While the approach itself has vast potential, the state of knowledge about leadership functions is deplorably small. In the first place, the functions of leadership now being used are too global and not easily applied on a practical basis. Too often the list of functions reflects the perceptions of the observer or the results of the act rather than the central descriptive characteristics of the act itself. Then, too, every past effort to discover leadership functions has attempted to describe communicative behaviors or their consequences in isolation without viewing leadership acts within the interstructured sequence of group interaction. What type of act precedes and follows a leadership act? Perhaps the leadership act can be defined as a leadership function only in terms of what act precedes and follows it. If leadership involves a reciprocal relationship of leader and follower, the behavior of the leader is probably meaningless when isolated from the behaviors of the followers. Thus, leadership functions should reflect the interdependence of the communicative behaviors performed by both leader and followers during the process of group interaction.

Some Specialized Perspectives

Several approaches to leadership do not correspond clearly with one of the four major perspectives. The following approaches do not attempt a full-fledged description of leadership but consider only applications or descriptions of leadership under special circumstances. As such, they are not complete perspectives of leadership and only emphasize selected aspects of leadership in small groups.

The Contingency Model of Leader Effectiveness Fiedler (1964) has proposed a model which attempts to estimate the effectiveness of small group leadership. He labels this model the "contingency model" and bases it on ASo/LPC scores of leaders who respond to two paper-and-pencil tests. One of these tests attempts to measure the "assumed similarity of opposites" (ASo) and asks the leader to evaluate his "least preferred coworker" (LPC) and his most preferred coworker. When the leader's evaluations of these two fellow group members are similar, his

ASo score is high. The second test measures the leader's evaluation of his least preferred coworker. The higher he rates his fellow group member whom he likes least, the higher is his LPC score. The scores on these two tests have been found to correlate very highly. Thus, the scores from the two tests are used almost interchangeably as a single ASo/LPC score.

In regard to leaders' behavior, high ASo/LPC leaders have been found to be socially oriented and generally lead rather cohesive groups. Conversely, low ASo/LPC leaders are task oriented, and group cohesiveness often declines (Gruenfeld et al., 1969). Actually, ASo/LPC scores may be more a measure of group cohesiveness than an insight into leadership. At best, the contingency model indicates what type of person most appropriately occupies the leadership role in given situations. For example, low ASo/LPC leaders are most desirable when the situation is highly favorable or highly unfavorable for the leader. Low ASo/LPC leaders can allegedly function with high task motivation under extreme conditions and get the task accomplished. High ASo/LPC leaders are most appropriate when the situation is moderately favorable or moderately unfavorable. Apparently their social orientation allows the group to function efficiently when the situation is not so extreme. For this reason the contingency model is often associated with the situational perspective of leadership.

The contingency model has been shown to be applicable in a wide variety of groups engaged in a variety of tasks. But Fiedler also views leadership as a person occupying a position in a network of roles. His model is a unique blend of traits (The ASo/LPC score is almost a trait of the personality.), styles, and situational perspectives. But the model still provides little insight into what a leader does or can do in given situations. Appropriately, both high and low ASo/LPC leaders have been observed to be successful in similar conditions (Hill, 1969). In short, the model ignores communicative behaviors. Given the perspective of communication and the group process, the contingency model is not very helpful.

Dual Leadership—Task and Social With the exception of the functions approach, all perspectives on leadership have considered leadership as a role filled by a single individual. Bales and Slater (1955) discovered through the use of Bales's Interaction Process Analysis (IPA) that leadership duties are often divided between two group members. Consistent with the IPA's separation of behaviors into task-oriented and socially oriented behaviors, the authors discovered that the leadership role was similarly divided between a task specialist and a socioemotional specialist. That is, most of the acts of the task specialist are contained in the task categories, and most of the acts of the socioemotional specialist fall into the socioemotional categories.

Bales and Slater discovered further that the task specialist was rated high by his fellow members in areas instrumental to task accomplishment, but he was not well liked. On the other hand, the socioemotional specialist was rated high on liking scales. These discoveries led to the hypothesis that small groups typically have two members who divide the leadership role between task specialties and socioemotional specialties. Occasionally one person performs both task and socioemotional specialties and is well liked by other members. Bales and Slater attribute this occurrence to the presence in the group of an extraordinarily capable individual, sometimes called the "great man" model of leadership.

The dual presence of a task leader and a social leader is intuitively uncomfortable for those who believe the task and social dimensions of a group are inseparably interdependent. As a result, many others—for example, Verba (1961) and Turk (1961)—sought alternative explanations to Bales and Slater's duality of the leadership role. Stephen R. Wilson (1970), along with the others, argues strongly and credibly that the alleged dual leader phenomenon is a function of the members' low interest or low involvement in the group's task. That is, when members are involved or interested in what the group is trying to accomplish, no dual leadership occurs. Wilson argues that the single leader occurs, not due to the presence of any "great man," but because leadership is typically not divided between task and socioemotional specialties.

Wilson explains that group members, whatever their level of involvement in the group task, perceive task competence in a fellow member and will naturally consider him to be a leader. And members will also expect this competent individual to be rather directive and assertive. (Recall that assertiveness is a descriptive characteristic associated with a leader's communicative behavior.) But group members will place a value on the leader's directiveness proportional to their level of involvement in the group task. If members are involved and find task performance desirable and even necessary, they not only expect directiveness from the competent leader but value it highly since it aids the group's progress toward their goal. If the members are uninvolved, they resent directive behavior of the leader and certainly don't value progress toward a group goal which they consider unimportant or irrelevant.

The uninvolved member realizes he is captive in an unpleasant situation and wishes to make it as least unpleasant as possible. He certainly will not like the directive leader who is trying to urge him to accomplish some "unimportant" task. On the other hand, the uninvolved member will tend to like the person who is also not interested in the task but consistently behaves in the social categories and tries to make the social experience as pleasant as possible. Hence, the uninvolved member divides "leadership" into two specialties—the task leader whom he does not appreciate and the social leader whom he does appreciate. The group's "real" task when members are uninvolved is maintaining social pleasantness, and the social leader is their only "real" leader. When members are involved, however, the task leader is their only "real" leader.

Bales and Slater are highly susceptible to the criticism of Wilson and others since they observed the phenomenon of dual leadership almost exclusively in research laboratory groups. Nearly all these groups were composed of "captive" members, typically university undergraduates who were fulfilling some class requirement. On the other hand, most groups in the "real world" have been formed because their members experienced some common problem or reason for joining a group effort. If members of a typical "real world" group were uninvolved, they would not maintain their membership in that group. Certainly accomplishing an unimportant group goal would not be sufficient cause for their remaining in the group. Therefore, the phenomenon of dual leadership—a task specialist and a socioemotional specialist—is probably an artifact of the captive group but probably not typical of groups in the "real world." Thus, for the purposes of this book, dual leadership is quite insignificant. Later discussions assume that a small group typically has only one leader.

ON CHOOSING THE FUNCTIONS PERSPECTIVE

It is no secret that the bias of the author favors the functions perspective. Indeed, the overall perspective of communication and group process which underlies this book demands the functions perspective of leadership. In other words, group leadership is a process in which communicative behaviors associated with leadership are performed by a group member or members. Those behaviors, then, develop the pattern of leadership which characterizes that decision-making group. If leadership is a process, it cannot be viewed as a personal quality possessed by some individuals and not present in others. Nor can leadership be viewed simply as a structural position occupied by some person within a network of roles. Leadership develops through time as group members interact with each other. And the interaction patterns of the group members eventually reflect leader-follower relationships among members.

The problem of identifying leadership acts has not been completely solved. In fact, the "cop-out" of the situational perspective is not totally absent from the present treatment of leadership. Although the explanation should be more explicit in the later description of the leadership emergence process, the basic axiom identifying a leadership act is appropriateness within a given interaction sequence. That is, what may be a leadership act at one time during the group's interaction may be quite inappropriate at another time. If this explanation sounds similar to the situational perspective of leadership, it is at least different to the extent that it defines all ingredients of the situation exclusively within the interaction patterns of the members' communicative behaviors.

Shifting the focus of leadership from the person to his communicative behaviors, the functions approach no longer implies that leadership acts are performed only by a single individual. Typically members of a decision-making group designate a single individual as their leader in that the bulk of the leadership acts are generally performed by a single individual. But it would not be extraordinary if several persons perform the leadership functions and, hence, provide the group with shared leadership. But shared leadership in no way implies that one person is a task specialist while the other is a socioemotional specialist. Rather, inherently implying the interdependence of the two dimensions, group leadership functions are shared in that several members perform leadership functions without partitioning their leadership responsibilities into neat pigeonholes.

The functions approach also allows for and serves to explain how leadership changes from one person to another within the same group or in different situations. Mortensen (1966) discovered that some leaders consistently performed leadership behaviors throughout all periods of the group's interaction and, hence, maintained their leadership positions. Others, however, noticeably declined in their attempted leadership acts, thereby indicating their fall from leadership status. As the deposed leader decreased his performance of attempted leadership acts, another member or members apparently performed those acts and took his place as leader.

Finally, the functions approach allows for the eventual discovery of those functions which are characteristic of a good leader or an effective leader. Conversely, it will be possible to discover the functions indicating poor or ineffective leadership. None of the other perspectives is capable of defining or characterizing the qualities of effective leadership. To do so requires evaluating what the leader actually does. Hence, the functions perspective is necessary in order to be able to evaluate leadership behaviors.

LEADERSHIP EMERGENCE

To reiterate an earlier point, this book views group leadership as achieved status rather than ascribed leadership status. In the event that a leader is appointed through some authority outside the group, the process of leadership emergence applies to the emergence of the informal leader. This view of leadership assumes that "true" small-group leadership is always achieved—not ascribed. Moreover, leadership is always achieved gradually over time and is therefore viewed as a process. Because the leader achieves his status gradually, the process bears the label "leadership emergence."

The Process—Elimination of Contenders

A common view of leadership depicts a leader achieving status by somehow rising above all the others by demonstrating superior abilities or behaviors. According to this view, leadership is a process of a leader's excelling all others in a struggle to rise to the status of leadership. Apparently, then, all members start out at the bottom of the status ladder and attempt to work their way up. Such a view, however, may be the reverse of the actual process of leadership emergence. The process apparently begins with all members contending for the leadership role. As the process continues, members drop out of contention, one by one, until only one contender remains. He then achieves group recognition as leader. The process of leadership emergence, then, is a process of elimination.

John Geier (1967) indicates that typically all members actively desire and seek leadership status. While this may be quite true, many people would deny a conscious attempt to contend for leadership. But it is really quite irrelevant whether members consciously desire to be leader. The fact is that they have no choice. In an LGD all members are potential candidates for leader. No member can deny his own candidacy whether he wants to or not. Indeed, every member campaigns for leadership status every time he communicates. And remember that one cannot *not* communicate. Therefore, there is no way to disavow one's candidacy for leadership in the LGD.

A Hypothetical Model of Leader Emergence

Leader emergence occurs over a period of time. As a process of elimination, certain members are eliminated at various stages in the group's continuing interaction. The stages of the following hypothetical model, along with its variations and special problems, are adapted from the research of Geier (1967), Charles Larson (1969), and personal observation of classroom groups and member diaries. Before discussing this model, the reader will note the use of a five-member group. While five members may be the optimum size for a small group, the required size of the small group is a trivial point of discussion. The model should apply to any small group regardless of its size.

Figure 8 indicates the presence of three stages in the group process of leader emergence. In Stage One, Member E is eliminated from contention. In Stage Two, Members B and D are eliminated, and in Stage Three only Member A remains in contention thereby achieving the status of group leader. Geier (1967) indicates that in the initial stages of group interaction some members (epitomized in Figure 8 by Member E) reveal themselves to be uninformed or excessively rigid in their beliefs. Some members just do not contribute much to the group interaction. They may be overly shy or simply uninvolved in the group task. For whatever reason they are significantly less active than other members and drop from leader contention because of nonparticipation. Stage One is usually brief. Nonparticipators are quickly recognized by other group members and just as quickly eliminated as leader contenders.

During Stage Two several members are strengthened in their bids for leadership status by gaining the support of other members to support their candidacies. Thus, Members A and C remain contenders for group leadership while Members B and D drop out of personal contention and serve as lieutenants of A and C, respectively. As a lieutenant, each becomes less an initiator of action and more a supporter of proposals initiated by one of the contenders. In Stage Two, two opposing factions or coalitions develop around each of the remaining contenders. Stage Two is typically a lengthy phase and often involves some verbal bloodletting. But as Stage Two comes to an end, one of the contenders loses his bid for leadership and leaves the remaining contender alone at the top. Geier (1967) indicates that the member who characteristically drops from contention during Stage Two tends to be overly directive and uses offensive verbalization, such as stilted language or incessant talking.

Stage Three concludes the process of leader emergence as Member A remains the sole contender after the demise of Member C. Member E may reenter the emergence process by supporting Member A, thereby swinging the balance of power to the A-B coalition. Realistically, however, Member E's support is not particularly significant, particularly if he continues to be a low participating member during Stage Two. If, on the other hand, Member E takes a more active role in group interaction, his support is wooed by Members A and C during Stage Two. Then his decision to side with one or the other is a crucial factor in the final emergence of Member A. Of course, Member C could also drop out of contention if he were to lose the support of Member D as a lieutenant, particularly if Member C is overly directive and verbally offensive as

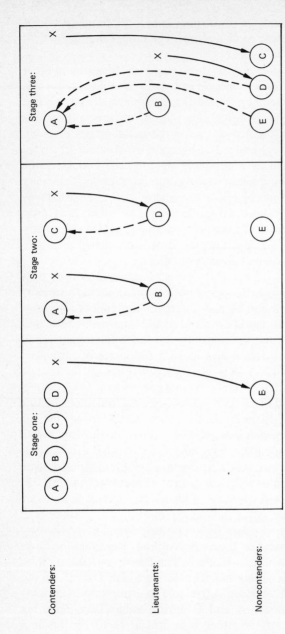

Figure 8 The basic model of leader emergence.

perceived by his lieutenant. Member D could easily shift the balance of power by transferring his allegiance and support to Member A.

Figure 8 represents a basic model from which many variations might occur. For example, successful leader emergence may involve only two stages in which only one contender picks up a lieutenant, and all other members jump on his bandwagon. This variation is not at all uncommon and signifies a socially painless process of leader emergence. It evolves very quickly and allows time for the group members to develop their status hierarchy and level of cohesiveness quickly and generally satisfactorily.

Another variation of leader emergence involves the early emergence of a group leader who is deposed as group leader, leaving the group once again in a leaderless situation. The process of leader emergence would then recycle back to the beginning of Stage Two and begin all over again. Unless the nonparticipating member has abruptly increased his level of participation and involvement, he remains out of leadership contention. The deposed group leader could even regain his leadership status, but he would undoubtedly have more difficulty the second time around.

A third variation of successful leader emergence involves the absence of Stage Three. In this case two or more members share the leadership functions and are recognized equally as leaders. While shared leadership is not extraordinary, neither is it the typical case. One can generally expect a single individual to emerge eventually as the leader of a small decision-making group.

After a contender has successfully emerged as leader, the group typically experiences an abrupt release of tension. Without a consensus among group members on their top status level, a group generally functions somewhat haphazardly and in a state of relatively high secondary tension. As soon as their doubts are dispelled concerning leadership, they quickly release a great deal of secondary tension. The group then experiences an abrupt rise in member satisfaction—hence, greater group cohesiveness. This is not to say that the group is suddenly a highly cohesive group, but status consensus is one prerequisite for member satisfaction. With that hurdle out of the way, the group is capable of developing a relatively high level of cohesiveness and, correspondingly, a high level of productivity.

With the emergence of the leader, the status levels in the group's hierarchy typically fall quickly into place. The successful group generally accords the losing contender a high status position equal to or slightly lower than the status level of the leader. Thus, three status levels often appear after the completion of the three-stage model of leader emergence. The top status level is occupied by Member A (and possibly Member C).

The second level includes Members B and D (or possibly C). Member E would be in the third status level. In his capacity of shifting the balance of power to Member A, though, Member E might very well achieve higher status—perhaps in the second level. If this were the case, the group would have only two status levels. A five-member group will typically include three status levels but may possess only two status levels. Significantly, the process of leader emergence involves not only the selection of a leader but the development of the group's entire status hierarchy.

Special Problems of Leader Emergence

The basic model of leader emergence should not, of course, be considered the unwavering rule for leader emergence. Some variations have already been mentioned. Each dealt with successful leader emergence and a quasi-methodical process of elimination. It is not unusual, though, for the process to be less methodical and less successful. Although the following deviations from the model are not common, they are worth noting and are considered "problems" rather than minor variations. Each problem is considered a special "case" involving a particular problem which any group may encounter during its own process of leader emergence.

The Case of the Leaderless Group The discussion of leader emergence has assumed up to this point that the process of leader emergence is always successful. Some groups, however, may struggle indefinitely over their status hierarchy and never satisfactorily solve their leadership problem. Usually a group which fails to develop a status hierarchy remains a collection of individuals who are unsuccessful in developing groupness. Very rarely is a group able to maintain itself without a successful process of leader emergence and a fairly well-established hierarchy of social strata.

A group may continue to be leaderless if the process of leader emergence is still continuing when the group ceases to exist. It is often the case that the quarter or semester ends while the classroom group is still in the process of developing its status hierarchy. Such a group should not be considered unsuccessful. Their process of group development might be slower than desired. But one must assume that were the group to have more time for the process to continue, they would successfully develop group leadership and subsequent status hierarchy.

The Case of the Temporary Leader During the struggle between the leader contenders in Stage Two, a group may be unable to resolve their leadership problem by moving to Stage Three. The group is in a state of limbo during this period while the leadership identity remains un-resolved. This period is typically characterized by a rather high level of secondary tension. If the group simply cannot function at this level of tension, the members will attempt a compromise in order to release the tension. Thus, a noncontending member will be accorded leadership status so that the group can progress.

The noncontender who is granted leadership status must be considered a temporary leader. He is generally accepted by the contenders because he is a relatively weak participator and, therefore, not a significant threat to their leadership bids. But like most compromises, the solution is typically a temporary one. The compromise leader will find it difficult to sustain his leadership status, particularly if he remains uninformed or rigid and a low participator—those same behaviors which eliminated him from contention during Stage One. An abrupt change in his behaviors would increase his chances for maintaining his leadership status. Otherwise, the group will eventually return to Stage Two and the yet unresolved problem of leadership contention.

The Case of the Catalytic Role Often a nonleader's role is crucial to a group's process of leader emergence. A particular member may or may not be a strong leader contender, but his behaviors indicate that he fulfills a role which determines the group's development of its status hierarchy.

Tom in the group described in Chapter 4 fulfilled such a catalytic role. Tom was definitely a leader contender by virtue of his behaviors, but the other members of his group (all women) were acceding to his leadership moves even though they resented them as being overly directive. A second member had gained a lieutenant during Stage Two and was still in contention for leadership with Tom who, oddly enough, remained in contention without a lieutenant.

Tom's role was catalytic for his group because they were not functioning efficiently with him as a directive leader contender. When his fellow members confronted him and dropped him from contention, Tom's role was clearly decided as a top status level member but definitely not the leader. Other members valued his contributions but were unwilling to assume followership status in relation to him. When Tom's role was established, the other roles including the leader and the remainder of the entire status hierarchy fell quickly into place with a dramatic rise in cohesiveness and productivity.

A common catalytic role is that of the problem member—for one reason or another, the "oddball" in the group. The problem member generally has not committed himself to the group and consistently causes trouble for the rest of the group members by not doing his share of the work, consistently criticizing other members, continually arguing against decisions reached by other group members, and generally assigning low value to the group and the other members, "bad-mouthing" both.

One member in a classroom group completed a sociometric questionnaire at midterm and revealed herself as a true problem member. For example, in response to a question asking which member in the group she liked most, she wrote, "None of them!" Her response to a question asking which member she liked least was "All of them!" Her role was obviously a problem that the group simply had to control.

The member who succeeds in controlling the problem member may abruptly rise to leadership status. In this particular classroom group, one girl made an overt effort to handle the problem member both during and outside group meetings. On several occasions she talked to the problem member alone, bought her Cokes in the Union, and generally went out of her way to make the problem member feel more a part of the group. While the problem member never did become a high-status member wildly enthusiastic about the group goals, she did cease to be a problem for the group. And the member who solved that problem for the group eventually became their leader.

Member E in the basic model of leader emergence may also perform a catalytic role if his support decides between the leadership contention of Members A and C. In fact, the member who casts the deciding vote on any crucial question is invariably catalytic for the group. If one member consistently fulfills the role as ultimate decider, that member is a catalyst for the normal functioning of the group. On the other hand, a member such as E is probably less committed to the group and therefore less active in group interaction. His record of reticent behavior diminishes the importance of his subsequent contributions. Group members must come to expect the deciding vote from a member if he is to perform a catalytic role in the process of group development. Otherwise, his influence as a catalyst is probably short-lived.

Behaviors of Emergent Leaders

Our present state of knowledge does not allow a thorough and specific definition of the communicative behaviors leading to successful leader emergence. But emergent leaders have been associated with certain types of communicative acts. Geier (1967), for example, pinpoints some kinds of communicative behaviors which characterize those members who are eliminated from leadership contention. Those negative behaviors include nonparticipation, uninformed contributions, and a rigidly argumentative stance in Stage One; overly directive comments and offensive verbalization including stilted language or incessant talking during Stage Two. One might appropriately infer from Geier's discoveries that the emergent leader avoids these types of communicative behaviors during each specific stage of leader emergence. But to know what the emergent leader does not communicate provides only scant assistance in discovering what an emergent leader does communicate. Hence, Geier's negative behaviors are helpful but certainly not sufficient to describe the communicative behaviors of emergent leaders.

Because it is so obvious that it might be overlooked, one absolutely requisite behavior for successful leader emergence must be emphasized. That requisite is verbal activity itself. In the LGD the member who does not "campaign" for leadership by contributing to group interaction has virtually no chance to achieve leadership status. While the emergent leader is not necessarily the member who talks the most, he is among the high participators (Morris and Hackman, 1969). The emergent leader is virtually never one of the low contributors to group interaction.

In addition to mere quantity of verbal activity, the nonverbal quality of the leader's contributions appears to be important as well. The evidence that an emergent leader is a skillful communicator is indisputable. That is, an emergent leader is fluent in delivering his contributions. He expresses his thoughts articulately. Furthermore, the leader's participation is forceful and dynamic. His dynamism is probably a nonverbal indication of his interest or involvement in the group task. Leadership, though, is not at all ability to win men's minds through glibness of vocal delivery. Quite the contrary, communicative skill is grossly insufficient, by itself, to achieve any status and maintain it for any length of time. Nevertheless, an inarticulate spokesman is at a disadvantage regardless of the apparent value of the cause he advocates. The leader is not necessarily the most skillful communicator in the group, but apparently he is among those members who are articulate and dynamic in their communicative skills.

Charles Larson (1969) discovered that the emergent leader consistently initiates more themes during group interaction than nonleaders. Not only does the leader initiate more total themes, but he consistently initiates more themes throughout every stage of group interaction. The consistency in initiating themes may be a more vital aspect of the leader's behavior than merely the quantity of themes he initiates. If members come to expect the leader to be an initiator, they will look to him throughout their interaction to serve that function. On the other hand, an emergent leader has responsibilities to the group after he has gained leadership status, too. Hence, one might infer that the leader must continue to be an initiator in order to maintain his leadership position. Otherwise, the other members might depose him and look elsewhere for a member to serve as their leader.

The communicative behaviors of an emergent leader also include seeking comments. That is, the emergent leader actively and overtly seeks the information and opinions of the other members. Such comments are particularly frequent and important in the early and intermediate stages of a group's task performance. The leader does not behave as though he has no opinions of his own. Rather, he is interested in the opinions of others and in procuring as much information as possible so that the group can reach an intelligent and informed decision. These behaviors which seek opinions and information from other members are, unlike initiating comments, not consistently employed by the emergent leader throughout the group interaction. As members of the group approach consensus, seeking additional information and opinions is unproductive and even irrelevant. Therefore, the emergent leader uses "seeking comments" frequently only when group consensus is not apparent.

Some conventional wisdom asserts that a true leader does not attempt to impress his opinions on other members of his group. Underlying this alleged wisdom is the assumption that members resent being told what they should do and that the leader should be unselfish so that he overtly avoids attempting to persuade others to his own point of view. Nothing could be farther from the truth. The leader provides significant assistance to the group in their progress toward fulfilling their goals. He cannot do so without expressing his opinions and supporting them. Like seeking comments, however, the leader does not take a strong stand throughout group interaction. While he is seeking opinions of others initially, the leader does not express strong opinions. In fact, rigidity in Stage One of the model of leader emergence results in eliminating members from contention. But from the intermediate stage on, the emergent leader takes stands on issues and defends them. Having strong opinions may be a negative virtue early in group interaction, but it is vitally important for successful leader emergence later.

While it is obvious that the emergent leader does express his own position on substantive matters, his positions proceed from an informed and objective basis. Recalling that the emergent leader also contributes many comments which seek opinions and information from others, his past behavior provides the basis for his informed and objective stance. Therefore it is imperative that an emergent leader both seek opinions from others and express his own opinions. He does not do one or the other but both, encouraging a spirit of free exchange of ideas among all members. Everyone has a right to his opinion and the freedom, even the responsibility, to express it. Moreover, the leader must have an opinion, too, or he will be rejected as a wishy-washy member without a mind of his own.

It is no secret that this list of behaviors associated with emergent leadership is far from a thorough description of leader functions. However, the present state of knowledge concerning leader behaviors does not allow for a more precise or more complete list. While some behaviors, such as clarifying and summarizing, have occasionally been linked with leadership functions, the evidence supporting their inclusion in this list is too spotty and contradictory. But several research projects are now underway at several universities to provide more specific information about the communicative behaviors of emergent leaders. When these projects are completed, a specific description of a leader's behaviors and how they fit into the overall pattern of group interaction should be available.

Legitimacy and Leader Emergence

Although the LGD should preclude the influence of legitimate bases of leadership, the influence of some varieties of legitimacy in the LGD should not be overlooked. The principle of legitimacy is generally defined as prescribed or ascribed approval of norms, values, roles, or other behavioral standards. Typically an organization endows certain roles with legitimate status by prescribing a formal status hierarchy independent of the persons who occupy positions in that status hierarchy. For example, a colonel in the armed forces has legitimate authority of leadership over all those of lower rank by virtue of the rank given to him by the organization itself and not necessarily because of any achieved informal status. A familiar theme of war movies is a story of veteran soldiers who resent the leadership of a young "ninety-day wonder" second lieutenant who does not have the experience or achievements of some of his followers of lesser rank. But nevertheless, the veterans formally recognize his authority due to his legitimate rank of commissioned officer.

Normally, legitimacy refers to formal recognition of approval by some external agency which has authority over the group. In a "true" LGD, no such agency exists outside the group. But a "true" LGD is very rare. In a university classroom the instructor and the values of the student culture both exert an impact on the classroom LGD. Some members may have legitimate approval of their roles by virtue of the instructor's designation or campus-wide status as a BMOC. Such quasi-legitimate recognition may endow the member with some vestige of formal leadership. He then must earn informal recognition of his leadership status during the process of leader emergence.

Legitimacy exerts little direct influence on the LGD, but the group itself manufactures its own symbols of legitimate recognition. Certain symbols of authority are endorsed with a kind of legitimate approval, and the member who possesses one or more of these symbols takes on the aura of legitimate recognition of authority. Numerous examples of such symbols may be found in a classroom LGD. Some instructors ask classroom groups to record their interaction during each meeting on audiotape recorders. The member who takes possession of the tape recorder, adjusts the microphone, and controls its operation possesses a symbol of authority. It is not uncommon for members who are contending for leadership to fight over the right to possess this authority symbol.

One classroom group using transistor cassette recorders encountered a problem in operating the machinery. For some reason it did not work properly, and the member who had habitually taken charge of it was unable to get the recorder working. Another member who conveniently owned a similar recorder easily spotted the trouble and fixed it. His leadership contention received a big impetus with this seemingly unrelated act. His fellow members insisted that he take charge of the group's cassette recorder in subsequent meetings. He did and later emerged as the group's recognized leader.

Often groups sit around a rectangular table, and leader contenders race to their meeting room in order to be able to sit in the chair at the head of the table. One classroom group typically held their meetings in an instructor's office with the alleged seat of authority the instructor's swivel chair behind his desk. Perhaps not coincidentally, the group's emergent leader turned out to be the member who consistently occupied the swivel chair during group meetings. He admitted afterward that he initially wanted to sit in that chair because it was the most comfortable chair in the room. He also expressed having been surprised on several occasions when he arrived late for a group meeting to discover that the other members had left the swivel chair vacant for him. He believed that seat was a symbol of his leadership authority apparently recognized, perhaps at a low level of awareness, by his fellow group members.

Another classroom group's emergent leader was the sole member of the group who took notes during group discussions. As a result of his trusty legal pad, he was always an expert on what the group had decided and accomplished during past meetings and was able to organize their future activity. He often referred to his legal pad, and was consistently asked by other members what was written on it. For him and his group that legal pad became a legitimate symbol of authority.

But a legitimate symbol of authority need not be a physical object. Often an activity by a group member receives formal recognition by the group and takes on legitimacy by itself. One group often met outside class hours at the apartment of one of the members. She became the hostess of the group meetings, served them coffee and pop, potato chips and snacks, and enveloped herself in the legitimacy of being the authority in her own apartment. She was recognized as the emergent leader—quickly and painlessly.

A common activity which achieves legitimate recognition in the classroom group involves collecting, organizing, and typing contributions of members to form the final group document which is handed to the instructor as a class requirement. The person who types that report often acquires formal recognition for his efforts and gains some legitimate recognition of his leadership bid. Rarely is such an activity unrewarded by the group.

Although there are many more examples of manufactured legitimacy in the LGD, all cases have one ingredient in common. Whether a physical object or an activity, the legitimate symbol of authority is associated with a single person who has assisted the group in making progress toward their group goal. The symbol is not prescribed by some outgroup authority but receives formal and relatively permanent recognition by the group members themselves. While not a complete description of the process of leader emergence, instances and symbols of manufactured legitimacy do influence the process and highlight a person who is contending for leader. The combination of communicative behaviors and symbols of manufactured legitimacy allows the group or an outside observer the opportunity to perceive the process of leader emergence in operation.

SUMMARY

Perhaps the most pervasive element of social systems is the existence of leadership and a status hierarchy. In the LGD, roles fall into several hierarchical levels, typically two or three, proportional to the contribution by the member aiding the group to achieve their group goals. In an LGD each member achieves his status level through his communicative behaviors rather than being given status by some outgroup authority. A group typically has two or three status levels. The leader's status is based on a reciprocal influence of leader and follower—an interdependence among the communicating members in the LGD.

Several perspectives of viewing leadership have been popularly employed in the past. They include the traits, styles, situational, and functions approaches to group leadership. The functions perspective, unlike any of the other three, focuses on the communicative behaviors of individual members which contribute to group progress. This perspective deemphasizes leadership as the person who occupies a given position in a network of roles. Because there have been so few studies of leadership utilizing the functions perspective, no comprehensive list of communicative behaviors associated with leadership yet exists. But a partial list of behaviors is available.

Employing the functions perspective, leadership is viewed as a process whereby a group leader achieves his status gradually over time as a direct result of group interaction patterns. That process, termed "leader emergence," may generally be described as a process of elimination in which each member is a contender for leadership, but all are eliminated, one by one, until a single person remains and is recognized as group leader.

A basic model of leader emergence hypothesizes three stages of elimination. In Stage One, uninformed, low-participating members are eliminated. In Stage Two, two or more contenders emerge by gaining lieutenants who support their leadership contention. Those contenders eliminated in Stage Two typically are overly directive and use offensive verbalization so that Stage Three includes only one remaining contender who achieves recognition as leader. Several variations from this basic model are possible in a particular small group.

Behaviors associated with emergent leaders include: verbal activity, communicative skill, consistent initiating of themes, seeking opinions and information in early and intermediate stages of group development, opinion stating and attempts to persuade other members in intermediate and later stages of group development, and an informed and objective argumentative stance.

The LGD also manufactures formal symbols of legitimacy in group interaction. Such symbols, which may be physical objects or member activity, are associated with a particular member and with the formal authority of leadership, although they may vary from group to group.

Chapter 6

Social Conflict
and Deviance

The past decade and a half has witnessed numerous instances of social conflict and deviant behavior within our society. Many believe the recent upsurge of minority dissent is unparalleled in our history. But dissent has been present since our system was founded. Many eligible young men resisted the draft during the Vietnam war, but draft resistance has been prevalent since the first Selective Service during the Spanish-American War. Hundreds of thousands of protesters marched on Washington, D. C., several times during the decade of the 1960s, but so did veterans of World War One forty years before. The civil disobedience of Martin Luther King, Jr., and the Berrigan brothers led to their imprisonment just like Henry David Thoreau, Eugene Debs, and countless labor organizers during the early struggles of the labor movement in the United States.

Some historians have compared recent dissent with that of the colonists in pre-Revolutionary War years. The comparison seems appropriate. Many campus and urban protests in recent years wantonly destroyed private property. But the tea thrown into the Boston harbor by pseudo-Indians was also property which those colonist-protesters did not own. Soldiers fired on private citizens on the campus of Kent State as did British soldiers on the Boston Commons nearly two centuries before.

The common but erroneous belief is that protests such as those during the 1968 Democratic Party convention and on university campuses are unique to the present. Many also believe that such social conflict is detrimental and reflects some failure within our culture. Others believe that social conflict is symptomatic of a healthy society. The truth, as in most cases, undoubtedly lies somewhere between the two extreme positions. The preceding examples of social conflict are not intended to prove that current social dissent is heroic or necessary. Nor are the historical comparisons intended to degrade yesterday's heroes.

Obviously some conflict within a social system is detrimental, just as some conflict is beneficial. The point to be emphasized is that social conflict, both good and bad, is normal and a recurring phenomenon of our social system throughout its history. Moreover, social conflict has been normal in the functioning of every social system throughout the history of human civilizations.

CONFORMITY

Man as a conformist with no apparent will of his own is a theme familiar to all. The "man in the gray flannel suit" became famous as the stereotype of middle-class Americans. Pete Seeger immortalized the middle-class suburbanite in song with his "Little Boxes," referring to rows and rows of look-alike suburban houses all made of "ticky-tacky." To a great extent Archie Bunker epitomizes the intellectual conformity of the middle American who drinks beer, watches television, and steadfastly believes all the hackneyed clichés and stereotypes. He believes with such unthinking, jingoistic fervor that he becomes a pathetically humorous character.

Certain segments of any society rebel against conformity pressures imposed by the social system and use the larger system as a negative model for their behavior. In the 1950s these social dropouts were given the name "beatniks." During the 1960s the rebellious minority became known as "hippies." But because the larger society is a negative model for their behavior, their acts of anticonformity developed a subculture with its own highly rigid rules of conformity.

One element is basic in every social system, large or small—conformity. The identity of any social system, including a small group, includes the evolution of certain behavioral standards, such as roles, norms, and values. Those constraints which identify members of the social system result in conformity among members. As long as man is a social animal, he cannot avoid conforming to some social standards.

The Nature of Conformity

The nature of conformity normally brings to mind a group of people displaying uniform behaviors. But mere uniformity of behavior does not necessarily imply the existence of conformity. One obvious requisite of conformity is social pressure, although some uniformities are present in our society without any overt social pressure. For example, nearly everyone believes that the earth rotates on its axis, but this belief is not the result of any social pressure. Rather, the fact of the earth's rotation has gained so much validity that it is almost universally accepted. Certainly belief in such a fact is not the result of social pressure but of individual acceptance.

Many uniform behaviors are subject to social influence but are not realistically the product of conformity. Social influence leads us to live in houses, wear clothes, and go to school or to a job. But these behaviors may be more appropriately called conventional behaviors. They are performed without ever considering other viable alternatives. People who willingly violate conventions may be eccentric or unconventional, but they are hardly deviates.

One ingredient is missing in the foregoing examples—conflict. Human beings conform because they are confronted with two or more courses of action, each with relatively specific consequences. The individual then chooses among his alternative courses of actions, and his choice is governed by the desire to avoid the unpleasantness of social pressure. Men today wear their hair long to avoid being labeled old-fashioned. For the same reason, women would not wear a hoop skirt with multiple crinoline petticoats today. Today the fashion of clothing is losing much of its conformity pressures, but there are still limits beyond which most people do not venture.

Simple conformity is defined as merely adopting certain standards of behaviors. Nor is the presence of uniformity of behaviors, even due to social influence, a sufficient indicator of conformity. When social behaviors are uniform because individuals decided among several conflicting alternatives and resolved that conflict by yielding to the balance of positive and negative social consequences of a particular behavior, then conformity is present. Without conflict among alternative behavioral choices, an individual cannot be said to be conforming.

To explain conformity is also to explain deviance or instances of nonconformity. Deviance is behavior based on conflict among alternative behavioral choices in which the conflict is resolved contrary to social expectations. That is, deviant behavior violates the expectations of the social system by contradicting the behavior expected of each member. Thus, the deviate subjects himself to the unpleasant social consequences of that behavior. He expects to receive influence attempts from other members of the social system—influence directed at him for the purpose of modifying his behavior consistent with social expectations.

Conformity Pressures in Small Groups

The intimate, face-to-face relationship in a small group provides this social system with the ability to exert extraordinary social pressure on the deviate—that is, the nonconformist. While a single individual may lose himself in the large and impersonal social system of a metropolitan city, every individual member of a small group is always visible to all others. Any deviating behavior is immediately recognized and easily attributed to one of the members. It has been said that the rigidly bureaucratic organization excels all other social systems in exerting conformity pressures on its members—except for the informal small group. The potential for extreme social pressure in a small group cannot be overestimated.

The classic series of experiments by Solomon Asch (1951, 1955, 1956) proved beyond any doubt that an individual can seldom withstand the social pressures to conform. When the single member is alone in opposition to a unanimous majority, he will frequently modify his belief or judgment to conform to that of the majority. And he will conform even when the majority opinion is blatantly false. Whether the individual knows the majority is incorrect or whether the majority overtly exerts influence is, for the most part, irrelevant. The lone deviate generally conforms despite the conditions.

The pressures on the individual to conform are apparently greater when no single correct decision or solution is available. That is, the truth or reality of the decision can be validated only by achieving consensus within the social system. You will recall that such a decision situation is the group task. Thus, when the group is engaged in performing a task appropriate for a group, the social pressures toward conformity are most extreme. When social agreement is the sole means for validating one's opinion or belief, conformity pressures are greatest.

Not every member of a small group is a weak-willed automaton. Several circumstances serve to strengthen the deviate to resist the majority's social pressure. If the deviate publicly commits himself to his position before becoming aware of the prevailing position of the unanimous majority, he tends to resist modifying that position (Gerard, 1964). A prior public commitment to a position tends to provide the deviate with strength to resist social influence away from that position.

Even stronger than public commitment is the presence of a second deviate as a confederate (Allen and Levine, 1969). If the only method for validating one's position is social agreement, the presence of a second member who agrees provides some measure of validation. With each of the two deviating members providing social support for the other, the deviate is no longer alone against a unanimous majority but is a member of a unanimous minority subgroup, no matter how small. With social support the deviate secures social strength to withstand the influence from the majority members.

The social pressures toward conforming behavior in a small group are extraordinarily severe. Yet deviance is a very common phenomenon within group interaction. The member who deviates apparently possesses a strong commitment to his position. His involvement in the task is evidently quite high, or he would not subject himself to such social pressures. Without involvement or commitment, the member would either conform or remain silent. The deviate, then, is not necessarily a troublemaker who doesn't care about the group. He may be a member deeply involved in accomplishing the group task but in disagreement about how it should be done.

MUCH CONFLICT ABOUT SOCIAL CONFLICT

Many sociologists view a social system as a delicate balance of opposing forces—forces which threaten to disrupt the system and forces which maintain the system. According to this view, a social system is perpetually in a state of conflict which may at any time tip toward the disruptive forces and destroy the system.

The perspective of this book—communication and the group process with emphasis on interdependence—is not consistent with viewing the system as a balance of opposing forces. The process viewpoint assumes that such forces, if they exist, are interdependent so that they cannot be separated or in opposition to each other. For example, "temperature" is hardly an arithmetic difference between forces of heat and forces of cold. If it were, one would be comfortable if he held a block of ice in one hand and a burning coal in the other. Temperature is a single reading and not a balance of two readings—one high and one low.

It is important to know that not all experts agree on the nature of social conflict, its effects, or its solution. Understanding social conflict from the communicative process perspective requires an understanding of the varied and often conflicting views of social conflict.

Intrapersonal—Interpersonal—Intergroup

To understand the nature of social conflict, one must first identify who or what is in conflict. Probably the most common view of social conflict is intergroup conflict, that is, conflict between opposing social systems. Intergroup conflict involves conflict between groups or societies rather than between single individuals. Intergroup conflict embodies labor-management relations, particularly during periods of contract negotiations, as well as conflicts between nations. When an individual human being is involved in intergroup conflict, he does not participate as an individual entity but as a representative of an entire social system.

Although intergroup conflict is a fascinating area of concern and even though some examples will be drawn from intergroup conflict, this type of social conflict does not satisfactorily suit the purposes of this book. Since our purpose is to understand the communicative process which characterizes group decision making, intergroup conflict is not highly pertinent.

Intrapersonal conflict, as the term implies, involves the psychological conflict that rages within a single individual. The intrapersonal view alleges the existence of opposing forces within the individual's mind which determine his actions, beliefs, and values. Numerous balance theories attempt to explain individual behavior through intrapersonal conflict. They include cognitive dissonance theory, congruity theory, equity theory, exchange theory, and consistency theory, among others. Leonard C. Hawes (1969) has also explained member satisfaction within a small group through the concept of ambivalence—a balance of internal forces which attract or repel his relationship to the group.

But intrapersonal conflict does not serve the purposes of this book either. In the first place, internalized conflict cannot be directly observed through communicative behaviors and may or may not be indirectly reflected in group interaction. Then, too, intrapersonal conflict utilizes the psychological makeup of the individual as the basis for understanding the small group rather than the process of interaction based on the interstructured communicative behaviors of all members.

Interpersonal conflict is most pertinent to the perspective of communication and the group process. But interpersonal conflict, for our purposes, does not necessarily imply a personality conflict between individuals. Quite the contrary, interpersonal conflict is defined solely in terms of interact patterns. Thus, interpersonal conflict is directly observable through sequences of communicative behaviors performed by members of the group. Personalities of individual members are not considered in conflict; behaviors performed by two or more members conflict with each other.

Affective—Substantive

A second view of social conflict considers the basis of that conflict—whether conflicting issues are affective or substantive. Typically, in reference to interpersonal conflict, affective conflict implies emotional clashes between individuals within a social system, generally over procedural or how-to-do-it problems. Such conflict does not ordinarily stem from a disagreement on opinions or beliefs but from a struggle based on selfish or personal issues. Substantive conflict, on the other hand, involves an intellectual opposition of group members on the content of ideas or issues pertinent to the group task.

Since social conflict and deviance are considered a single phenomenon in group interaction, the affective-substantive differentiation of conflict may also be called "role deviation" and "opinion deviation." While an opinion deviate disagrees with other group members on the content of ideas, a role deviate is a type of person who is not desired by other group members. One member of a student group found herself as a role deviate in her group. She received low sociometric rankings from nearly all her fellow group members. Concerned, she asked her fellow group members, "Why?" Her diary immediately following that group meeting describes the reactions of her fellow group members:

> They also said that they had projected me as being the type of person I played in class; they projected that role as being my true personality. . . . Now that they know me a little better, they could see I wasn't "Susie," a dominating woman, but "Susan"—a different individual altogether.

Role deviation and opinion deviation differ significantly in their impact on group interaction. Sampson and Brandon (1964) indicate that other group members increase their interaction with an opinion deviate and exert pressure on him to conform to their majority opinion. But the group virtually ignores the role deviate, apparently perceiving him as a hopeless case not worthy of conformity pressure. A social system tends to view deviance either as a behavior apart from the individual personality of the deviate or as a personality trait of the individual. As a behavior, deviance affects the group process of interaction and, thus, is central to the perspective of this book. Because the role deviate does not significantly affect the group's interaction patterns, he is considered irrelevant.

The opinion deviate is tolerated and perhaps even admired by his fellow members. After all, we have been taught from childhood that rationality and independence are virtues in our society. We are urged to be masters of our own fate, to make up our own minds. "Know thyself" is the Socratic advice. Advertising campaigns appeal to our rational independence by urging us to buy the product which gets us away from the crowd. The virtue of rationality and independence is often reflected in adolescents' rejecting their parents' ideas and beliefs. Their parents, often to their chagrin, had experienced the ultimate success in teaching one of our cardinal social virtues.

Lewis Coser (1956, pp. 48–55) distinguishes between realistic and nonrealistic conflict, which appears to be another dimension of affective-substantive conflict. According to Coser, realistic conflict is a means to an end—deviating behavior to further the group's progress toward their goal. But nonrealistic conflict is an end in itself not directly associated with any goal. For example, a worker may go out on strike against his employer because he sees the strike as a means to gain higher wages and better working conditions. But another worker may engage even in the same strike because of some oedipal hatred of his employer. This displaced father-hatred could as easily be directed against any authority figure. The point is that the person who performs deviant behavior as a means to achieve some goal is said to be engaged in realistic conflict.

The view of conflict which best serves the purposes of this book is, of course, substantive conflict—that conflict expressed as deviant behavior in intellectual opposition to ideas or issues associated with the group task or goals. Substantive conflict is realistic to the extent that it serves as a means toward accomplishing some goal.

Destructive—Constructive

More than any other single area of social conflict, there is probably more disagreement over the effects of conflict on the social system. One school of thought seems to view conflict as inherently undesirable since it inevitably leads to disruption of the social system. An opposing view considers social conflict essential to the effective functioning of every social system. It is intuitively obvious that neither view is absolutely accurate. Some conflict and deviance disrupts the system while other instances of conflict and deviance are beneficial to the system. Discriminating between the two kinds, however, is no simple task.

Many functions of the social system of the United States are predicated on the existence of conflict. Our economic subsystem of free enterprise assumes conflict and free competition among producers and retailers for the consumer dollar. The basis of our political system is the free and open marketplace of ideas in which societal values gain social consensus. Candidates for political office air conflicting views on the issue during the course of a political campaign. Our judicial system is based on the adversary system in which the accuser confronts the accused. Many of our recreational activities include games based on conflict—football, tennis, handball, chess, Monopoly, among others. Conflict is undoubtedly an integral part of our nation-society.

But despite the pervasive influence of social conflict in our society, most Americans are ambivalent about many forms of social conflict. Probably the best example is the right of minority dissent, constitutionally assured in the Bill of Rights. Freedom of speech is one of our most cherished national values, epitomized in such adages as, "I may disagree with what you say but shall defend to the death your right to say it!" National opinion polls have reaffirmed that nearly all Americans steadfastly uphold the freedom of speech of all Americans—majority and minority. But those same Americans, the polls tell us, would refuse to allow a professed Communist to express his political views in a public lecture. Battles over censorship laws are common in our social system. Apparently not all members of our society consider all realistic and substantive conflict or opinion deviation to be constructive. Indeed, many people consider much substantive conflict highly destructive.

A social system is too often viewed as an abstract ideal—a system of pure cooperation—so that any deviance must be unnatural. If a social system is idealized, then members of the system are constrained to strive for the perfection of pure cooperation. Any deviant behavior, then, is construed as a failure of the social system and must therefore be eradicated. The typically short-sighted view of common sense would have us believe that a "perfect" social system is worth striving for. But as we shall hopefully illustrate, the "perfect" social system free from conflict and deviance is doomed to failure because of its inherent inflexibility, its inability to cope with environmental stresses, its lack of capacity for growth and progress.

Assuming the idealized social system and the corollary that social conflict is inherently destructive leads to an incredibly naïve outlook on social conflict believed by many members of our nation-system. Too often, realistic conflict is camouflaged and dissenting views suppressed so that our social system masquerades as an absolutely perfect and ideal system, without fault or information to the contrary. But perfection is hardly possible in human beings or in man-made creations. Our nation's heroes had faults just as every other human being has had from the beginning of time. But most importantly, the consistent effort to accentuate the positive while eliminating the negative makes us naïve about social conflict and more susceptible to dissenting views.

Most of our nation was shocked when some United States soldiers elected to remain with their Communist Chinese captors at the close of the Korean war rather than return to their homeland. Many people reacted by advocating stronger teaching of only the positive aspects of our society. Others advocated a greater emphasis on comparative politics—to show the realistic faults and virtues of all political systems—so that our citizens could be fully aware of all alternatives. Indeed, all of us probably believe that our system would fare well in such a comparison. At least we would no longer be naïve and uninformed about social conflict and deviance.

The positive side of social conflict is represented by the functionalists—George Simmel (1955), Lewis Coser (1956), and Talcott Parsons (1951), among others. The functionalists do not deny that some social conflict disrupts the functioning of a social system and is therefore destructive. But the functionalists do emphasize the socially constructive functions of conflict and advocate an understanding of social conflict so that the social system is able to take advantage of its positive aspects. Some of the positive functions performed by social conflict are included later in this chapter.

Reactions to Social Conflict

The typical reaction to social conflict is to search for ways to resolve it, that is, to get rid of it. At the very least, according to this view, conflict must be controlled so that it doesn't get out of hand. Naturally, some conflict must be resolved or controlled because it is potentially destructive. Destructive conflict, unchecked, would lead ultimately to dissolution of the system itself. Hence, methods of conflict resolution are essential for instances of destructive conflict. Modes of conflict resolution include such devices as compromise, bargaining, appeasement, negotiation, and mediation.

Occasionally cure-all "formula" solutions are offered as substitutes for genuine methods of conflict resolution. Such formulas are usually not realistic and stem from a grossly oversimplified view of social conflict. One such formula answer is "more cooperation." If cooperation were so simple, the conflict would not have to be resolved in the first place. A more commonly suggested formula which is offered to solve virtually any social conflict is "more communication" or "opening channels of communication." If there is no communication at all between conflicting parties, which is rarely the case, then some communication is obviously called for. But communication inherently assumes specific forms, such as negotiation. "More communication" is meaningless. If present communication is ineffective, increasing the "amount" does not render communication suddenly more effective. More often, "more communication" is suggested as a substitute for any real effort to resolve conflicts. Such a "formula" stems from an overly naïve and grossly inadequate understanding of the nature of the communication process. The nonsensical nature of such a formula solution should be apparent in ensuing chapters.

When parties in conflict cannot satisfactorily resolve their conflict, they search for modes of controlling that conflict. One common and often effective means of controlling conflict, particularly intergroup conflict, is "encapsulation." Conflict which is encapsulated does not cease to exist. Rather, conflict continues under the governance of an agreed-upon set of rules. In international conflict, for example, we refer to the "cold war" between the United States, the Soviet Union, and the People's Republic of China. The cold war is the euphemism for international conflict which has been encapsulated within the rules of international diplomacy—embassies in each country, exchanges of diplomatic notes, treaties limiting nuclear testing, talks and treaties on arms limitations, trade agreements involving nonstrategic materials, reciprocal visits by high-ranking dignitaries. All conflicting nations agree to the rules and thereby control the conflict between their countries without attempting to resolve it.

Even wars are encapsulated, in part, by certain international "rules" of warfare such as those of the Geneva Convention and the Geneva Accords. Thus, even armed conflict with the avowed purpose of annihilating the enemy nation is governed by rules and therefore encapsulated. Encapsulation of conflict is a common ingredient of international relations.

The belief that conflict must be resolved or controlled is consistent with the view that conflict is inherently destructive. But resolution and control are inappropriate reactions for numerous instances of social conflict—particularly social conflict which serves socially positive functions. In fact, such conflict should even be encouraged and utilized to further the system's progress toward its desired goals. Utilizing social conflict in the best interests of the system requires a thorough understanding of the phenomenon itself and the ability to manage conflict in order to benefit from its positive aspects.

For the purpose of understanding the process of small group decision making, our primary interest is social conflict which is interpersonal, substantive, and constructive. Our goal is to understand social conflict and deviance as a process and to manage it constructively to the benefit of the group. This view does not deny destructive forms of conflict, but it does emphasize a view of conflict which is too often overlooked. While instances of destructive conflict do not typically exert significant impact on the general process of group interaction, constructive conflict plays an instrumental role in shaping the process of group interaction. Such conflict is vitally important, then, to the purposes of this book.

FUNCTIONS OF SOCIAL CONFLICT AND DEVIANCE

According to one of the foremost functionalists, Georg Simmel (1955, p. 13), conflict is inevitably a "form of sociation." It is impossible to have social conflict without interaction among the parties in conflict, and interaction is certainly a form of sociation. Simmel says of social conflict, ". . . it is a way of achieving some kind of unity, even if it be through the annihilation of one of the conflicting parties." Although the reference to annihilation may be with tongue in cheek, it is indisputable that social conflict cannot exist with an isolated individual. Certainly conflict is a distinct type of interaction between at least two persons. And interaction is one of the basic requisites of a social system. One can only conclude that anything which encourages interaction must be a potentially positive force in the development of a social system. It is on this deceptively simple assumption that the positive social functions of conflict are based.

Influence on Cohesiveness

Social conflict breeds not only social interaction but increased involvement. If a member is apathetic toward the group and toward the worth of the group task, he has little reason to engage in the painful process of social conflict. Moreover, the virtual absence of social conflict in group interaction is a trustworthy indication of low involvement or commitment on the part of group members. If the group develops even a moderate level of cohesiveness, its members will engage in rather frequent, though not extended, periods of social conflict. Thus, the natural development of group cohesiveness presupposes social conflict. In this sense, social conflict is not only desirable for the development of groupness, it is quite inevitable and should be expected as part of the *normal* sequence of group interaction.

Of course, social conflict, if it is to be beneficial to group cohesiveness, must not be perceived as threatening the group's social fabric. Substantive conflict serves to precipitate secondary tension. Therefore, the successful group develops mechanisms for managing social conflict as it arises. And a history of successful conflict management builds group cohesiveness.

Lest the term "conflict management" be misinterpreted, it is important to note that the group does not necessarily resolve the conflict or even control it through limiting its boundaries. Conflict management refers solely to the interaction sequences developed by a group to deal with social conflict and which the group consistently uses when social conflict occurs. Generally conflict management implies that social conflict will definitely occur again although probably in slightly different form. The normal process of conflict management to be discussed in later chapters is part of the process of decision modification.

Social conflict also aids group cohesiveness by providing an outlet for hostility. According to Theodorson (1962), a group must discover methods for venting hostility in order to gain and maintain even a moderate degree of cohesiveness. If the group develops norms which do not permit the expression of hostility, then the group members become either apathetic or dropouts as their deep-rooted negative feelings become ingrained. As group members shed their inhibitions about expressing negative feelings, they develop stronger ties to their group membership. One student group member, after a particularly fruitful meeting, experienced just such a reaction. Her diary contains her sentiments about what occurred during that meeting:

> We began to function as a group! Each of the individuals in the group expressed their feelings. Before really talking about our topic, we only had some "small" talk. . . . There were real differences of opinion. . . . Group became more cohesive.
> I began to think of myself as a member of the group. I felt more at ease with the members in my group to the extent that I felt free to disagree.

The more inhibited the group members in expressing their feelings, the greater the frustration they experience due to their suppressed conflict. And frustration leads directly to secondary tension. Thus, social conflict may actually serve as a form of releasing social tension.

Conflict performs a catalytic function in developing the social organization of the group. North, Koch, and Zinnes (1960) emphasize the role of conflict in increasing a group's social organization, particularly the interdependence of group members. Dentler and Erikson (1959) go further to say that groups actually induce, permit, and sustain deviant behaviors of members in order to develop a social organization. Deviant behaviors allow the group members to identify and strengthen their norms and other behavioral standards. In terms of an analogy, a law on the books which is never violated and hence never enforced soon loses its strength and visibility as a law. It becomes a "blue law" without any impact on governing the behavior of the society's members.

The deviate also allows the group to focus on a concern common to all members—the deviate himself—about whom something must be done.

Since the deviate is of concern to the group as a whole and not each member individually, the group's visibility becomes greater than each individual's self.

For these reasons, then, a group induces deviant behavior from one of its members when deviance does not occur through the initiative of one of the members. In order to maintain group solidarity and organization, the successful group not only permits deviant behavior but ensures that deviant behavior is evident in the group interaction. The group is in trouble when members avoid or ignore deviant behavior. Recall that the socially successful group learns to confront problems head-on by recognizing deviant behavior and doing something about it. It may be said now with some certainty that the cohesive group thrives on social conflict—or in more memorable words, "The group that fights together stays together!"

Influence on Productivity

Since this book deals with group decision making, its major concern is substantive conflict—intellectual opposition over ideas and issues. It seems paradoxical that a group whose members continually argue over ideas and issues can be very productive. But group productivity is measured in terms of the quality of its decisions and not by its efficient use of time. Obviously a group with substantive social conflict will utilize more time making decisions than a group without any conflict. But efficient utilization of time is not a characteristic of the group process anyway.

Substantive conflict leads directly to consensus owing to increased involvement of group members with their task performance. Thomas Beisecker (1969) discovered that as conflict over issues increases, group members tend to concentrate greater effort on those issues in order to bring about solutions. Hoffman, Harburg, and Maier (1962) discovered that conflict over ideas causes groups to search for more alternatives and thereby improve the quality of their group decisions. Conflict, then, serves as a stimulus to critical thinking and stimulates members to test their ideas. It logically follows that the issues which precipitate social conflict exert the greatest influence on the decisions which eventually achieve group consensus. And since those issues have survived the critical tests of ideational conflict, the decisions are probably of higher quality.

All members of the group benefit from the critical exchange of ideas. Committed members who engage in substantive conflict quite obviously receive the benefits of stimulated critical faculties. The undecided members, the low participators, also gain information necessary to commitment through observing the committed members "fighting it out." The principle also is present in a political campaign. Uncommitted voters apparently make their decisions after hearing the partisan voters air all sides of the issues.

One student member of a classroom group maintained that she played the role of a deviate in her group for just this reason—to stimulate the uninvolved members of her group. She analyzes her own role in the following excerpt from one of her diaries:

> I am the negative force in the group, i.e., I *can't* agree with everything that is being said. Other members in the group don't agree with decisions but are *too polite to say anything!* I voiced my opinion both for the silent majority and myself. Also, it was a means of manipulation to get things rolling. It worked! Without this, nothing would have been accomplished. The group members agreed with me after some discussion.

One of the problems that haunts every real-life decision-making group is the possibility of superficial or false consensus. That is, members agree on the final decisions but remain uncommitted to them. Hence, the decisions are never put into effect or are implemented only halfheartedly and consequently fail. Riecken (1952) found quite the opposite with decisions reached after uninhibited social conflict. Phillips and Erickson (1970, p. 77) also assert, "Once the public conflict has been played out in a democratic group and a consensus of policy and action has been derived there is a strong personal commitment on the part of the members that motivates them to act legitimately to implement group decisions rather than to subvert them." If members are committed enough to sustain social conflict over issues, they should remain committed once consensus is achieved. Superficial or false consensus is more apt to result from suppressed conflict than from expressed conflict.

One final note on the influence of social conflict and deviance on productivity concerns the "assembly effect"—the nonsummativity of group members which distinguishes group decision making from that of its individual members working alone. Social conflict is one of those group elements which a decision-making individual is inherently incapable of replicating. Quite assuredly, social conflict—particularly realistic substantive conflict—contributes to the assembly effect. Without it, the group decision-making effort adds nothing to a lone individual performing the same decision-making task.

Influence on Social Growth and Change

Viewing a social system from a process focus highlights the perpetual change which every social system undergoes through time. Our nation-system, for example, has experienced phenomenal growth and change within the brief two centuries of its existence. As conditions within and without the system change over a period of time, the social system adapts to those changes if it is to continue to exist. If any system is to keep up with the times, it cannot stagnate. Progress is essential. And progress can occur only through innovation. And innovation is, by definition, deviant from the traditional norms of the past.

Social growth and change are usually explained through the concept of feedback—a concept borrowed from the field of cybernetics. Although feedback in group interaction will be explained and illustrated more fully in later chapters, a few of its basic principles are appropriate at this time. The term "feedback" is common to nearly everyone's vocabulary. Unfortunately we typically use the term to refer to a simple response or reaction. A says something to B, after which B smiles and nods his head. We typically consider B's smile and head-nodding as "feedback" to A's initial comment. But a mere reaction should not be confused with the concept of feedback as it functions in the process of human communication.

Feedback is not simply a knee-jerk reflex to some antecedent stimulus. In fact, feedback is not a single act at all. Rather, feedback is a self-reflexive process initiated by some deviant behavior. The deviant behavior sets in motion a sequence of behaviors, each of which stimulates the next behavior in the sequence until the sequence closes its cycle by exerting influence on the original source of the deviant behavior. Thus, feedback is inherently a self-reflexive cycle or loop—self-reflexive because the deviant action exerts influence on itself through direct influence on each link in the chain of events contained in the cycle.

Feedback loops are of two varieties—positive and negative. Negative feedback is a self-reflexive process which counteracts deviant behavior. The standard illustration of negative feedback is the analogy of the thermostat. As the temperature in a room deviates from its normal range by falling below the optimum presetting, it sets into motion the negative feedback loop. First, the temperature causes the thermocouple to close, which in turn causes the fuel supply in the furnace to flow and ignite, which in turn causes the fan to blow, which in turn forces heated air into the heat ducts, which in turn causes the temperature in the room to rise. Note that the cause of the rise in room temperature is actually the original drop in the room temperature—thus, the self-reflexive nature of feedback. Note also that the downward deviation in room temperature was counteracted—hence, negative feedback. Negative feedback, then, serves to counteract deviant behavior in a system and keep the system operating within a relatively narrow range of "normal" behaviors.

Positive feedback is simply the opposite of negative feedback. The positive feedback loop initiated by deviant behavior sets into motion a cycle which reflects back on the deviant behavior by amplifying it and causing even greater deviance. The urbanization process of our cities illustrates too graphically the amplification of deviation through positive feedback. That is, farmers occupy a rural area and create a demand for services such as machinery repair, sale of agricultural products, groceries, a post office, medical care, and so forth. Soon a small village blooms in the middle of the rural area. Soon a company builds a small factory near the town because of the available supply of labor. More people move to the town in order to secure jobs at the factory. With more people available for work, the market for more services is larger, so more stores selling consumer goods are necessary. Shopping centers and more factories are built as more people move to the city. The small town booms to form a large megalopolis. Each deviation from the originally rural area stimulated more and more deviation in a classic illustration of positive feedback.

The international arms race is another classic example of positive feedback loops. The spiraling arms race has an extraordinary amplification of innovations in weapons development leading from the invention of gunpowder to dynamite, to the atomic bomb, the hydrogen bomb, the cobalt bomb, to the ICBM and MIRV, ad infinitum.

Progress, growth, and change in a social system can occur only through amplifying deviant behavior *via* positive feedback cycles. Naturally the social system must devise methods to manage positive feedback, along with progress, growth, and change, or the deviation gets out of hand. Urbanization may symbolize much progress in our nation, but unmanaged urbanization has created serious problems which we have only recently faced. The severity of these problems, such as air and water pollution, urban decay and blight, urban crime, inadequate civic services, overpopulation, has prompted the observation that a megalopolis such as New York City may be totally ungovernable. Nations, too, have recently agreed to set limits on the spiraling arms race through treaties and multilateral agreements. And arms limitation talks between the powerful nations of the world continue at the present time.

Progress and change in a social system are both desirable and essential for the survival of that system. But the system must learn to manage progress and change so that the benefits from progress can be realized. Management of social change leads to the development of new negative feedback cycles and strengthening of old negative feedback cycles allowing progress to occur gradually in manageable proportions and speed. That our society has not successfully managed progress in recent years is ingeniously portrayed by Alvin Toffler in his book *Future Shock,* in which he illustrates how we are actually living in the future while intellectually remaining in the present. Changes have simply been too frequent and too fast.

The normal process of managing conflict and deviance in a small group through positive and negative feedback loops is a focus of future chapters. For now it is sufficient to postulate that innovation, progress, and change in a social system require the existence of social conflict and deviant behavior. Moreover, the successful social system develops both appropriate positive and appropriate negative feedback mechanisms in order to manage social progress for the mutual benefit of all members of the system.

THE "NORM" OF CONFLICT AND DEVIANCE

To call social conflict and deviance a "norm" appears to be a contradiction in terms. Deviant behavior is by definition contrary to group norms. But the perspective of group process must not be ignored. To view conflict and deviance as either constructive or destructive is to consider only the effects of conflict and to deny the process of conflict. Our concern with substantive or realistic conflict serving a positive function in the group, along with an understanding of communication and group process, allows this startling observation—that conflict and deviance are normal and observable in group interaction patterns. That is, substantive realistic conflict and deviance are inevitably present in many phases of group interaction. Since they exist in nearly all groups and comprise a significant part of the group interaction, social conflict and deviance must be considered "normal."

Idea Testing in Decision Making

Some conventional wisdom maintains that since group decision making is a cooperative venture (which it certainly is), then arguments, disagreements, and conflicts over ideas should be avoided. But even if it were possible to avoid interpersonal disagreements, which is highly unlikely, such conventional wisdom is simply bad advice. Interaction during group decision making is a curious blend of persuasion, compromise, negotiation, argumentation, flexibility, and firmness of opinions. Issues are thrown into the hopper of group interaction and comprise the raw materials for the group's final consensus decisions.

During group interaction every idea, opinion, proposal, or suggestion contributed to the group is tested under fire. Involved members focus their critical abilities on these ideas and submit them to rigorous examination. During this process of critical discussion, some ideas are accepted; others are rejected; many are modified and combined with others. The eventual outcome of idea testing includes those decisions which achieve consensus. Because the group task is to achieve consensus on decisions, the critical exchange of opinions, ideas, and information is quite normal in the process of group interaction during decision making. A more detailed description of this process is included in the following chapter.

Coalition Formation

Within every social system of any size, subgroups form around some issue or idea. Subgroups typically form and maintain themselves because of some social conflict within the larger system. These groups within groups often command greater loyalty from their members than does the larger social system of which the subgroup is a part. Criminals in our society, for example, have a legendary code of conduct which the larger society apparently has been unable to break. "Honor among thieves" and the "code of silence" are familiar terms to describe this particular subgroup's norms. A small work group in a large organization also has greater influence on its members than the large organization. In a university, for example, students and faculty alike often perceive their closest identification with their affiliated department. The student generally considers himself a communication major, education major, physics major, or engineering major first and member of the larger university community second.

Subgroup formation is neither desirable nor undesirable to the larger social system. It is inevitable and should be fully expected as a normal occurrence. Too often subgroups, particularly those representing a minority, are ignored. The larger social system would do well to recognize their existence and take advantage of their apparent group strength.

Even a small group typically contains subgroups during the normal process of group decision making. Since the subgroup is usually temporary, a more appropriate term is "coalition." As such, a coalition refers to a temporary alliance, among two or more members of the group, oriented toward a difference of opinion regarding the means to achieve the group goal. Specifically a coalition unites certain group members who agree with noncoalition members on the nature and value of the group goal but disagree on how that goal can best be achieved. Such a coalition, then, involves social conflict and deviance over means but typically agreement on the goal itself.

Coalition formation emphasizes the importance of having a minimum of three members in the group. With only two members, social conflict is either destructive or unmanageable. Social conflict in a dyad (a two member group) exists without deviance. There is no minority, no prevailing opinion upon which to base a norm. Thus, dyadic conflict is resolved tvpically by one member dominating the other. And dominance-submission relationships thwart the group process of idea testing during decision making. Any consensus following conflict in a dyad is destined to be false or superficial consensus.

With at least three members, two-one coalitions are possible. In a four-member group several three-one and two-two combinations are possible coalitions. The five-member group is often viewed as the optimum size for small group decision making due to the numerous possibilities for coalition formation and management. But there is no hard and fast rule governing the number of members required in a small group as long as the minimum membership is three. As long as groupness can be achieved, no maximum limit is placed on the size of a small group.

Small group coalitions based on realistic and substantive conflict are generally temporary and revolve around a specific issue or group of issues. The normal process of achieving group consensus gradually merges the coalitions into the unitary whole of the group. That process of coalition formation and re-merging groupness is the subject of further discussion in Chapter 7.

The Leadership Paradox

Leadership is a most fascinating role in a small decision-making group. As a high-status member who is committed to the group, the leader is a strong conformist. Numerous research studies have illustrated the tendency of a leader to conform closely to group norms. The conformity of a leader has even found its way into the conventional wisdom of corny jokes. You are probably familiar with the story of the rotund little gentleman during the French Revolution who was observed huffing and puffing in the wake of a riotous mob. When asked why he was chasing after the mob, he replied innocently, "I have to follow them! I am their leader!"

The humor, if there is any, of this little story stems from the paradoxical nature of the leader's role as both conformist and deviate. A leader functions as an innovator who aids the group's progress toward their goal achievement. In times of crisis the leader must find new directions contrary to traditional norms in order to maintain the group and save it from impending disaster. If he doesn't innovate, the leader is soon deposed in favor of someone who can. Thus the leader gains and maintains his role by functioning both as a conformist and as a deviate.

Several explanations account for this self-contradictory behavior of the group leader. Hollander (1958) has suggested perhaps the most plausible explanation. Hollander describes gaining and maintaining leadership as an economic model whose central concept is "idiosyncrasy credits." In early stages of leader emergence, the leader conforms to the group norms and accumulates credits much like depositing money in a bank account. Later when the leader successfully exerts influence through innovative behavior, he is not regarded as a deviate because he has accumulated sufficient credits to allow him to exhibit idiosyncratic behavior. In a sense, he withdraws credits from his bank account and cashes them in when he innovates. According to Hollander, strict adherence to traditional group norms during periods of crisis is fatal to the leader's position and damaging to the group. Members perceive a leader who continues to conform in a stress situation as not knowing what to do and not helping the group achieve their goals.

Hollander's economic model of idiosyncrasy credits is a credible explanation for how a leader is able to deviate as well as conform. But the model should not be construed to imply that a leader innovates only during group crises. Indeed, a leader innovates through initiating themes and performing other leadership functions throughout group interaction. In fact, the leader must be recognized as an innovator before the crisis period so that the members expect innovative behavior from him and look to him for assistance.

If there were any doubts that deviant behavior was beneficial to a group, those doubts should now be dispelled. Maintaining the social organization of a group virtually demands deviant behavior. And the group demands deviant behavior not just from low-status members but from the highest-status member of all—the leader. Moreover, the leader's deviant behavior is not only beneficial, it is normal and to be expected.

THE PROCESS OF SOCIAL CONFLICT AND DEVIANCE

To summarize briefly, the LGD does not control its individual members' behaviors so much as it receives its organization and its very existence from individuals' behaviors. If behavioral standards and conformity to them develop through the process of group interaction, then behavior which deviates from those standards must also be integral to that same process. The periods in which deviant behavior occurs in the process and how the other group members respond to deviant behavior are extraordinarily important elements within the process of group interaction.

It is important to keep in mind that the process perspective inherently defines deviance and conflict instrumental to the group process as *behaviors* performed by members and not as roles occupied by one or more of the members. While role deviation may be present in a group, it has no significant impact on the pattern of group interaction. The process view, emphasizing the principle of interdependence, also stresses the interdependence of conformity and deviance and of cooperation and conflict in forming and maintaining groupness. As interdependent elements, they are viewed not as different processes but as different dimensions of a single process. And that process embodies all the communicative behaviors of all group members.

Flight Patterns

Several independent studies of small group interaction have discovered what appears to be a phenomenon common to many groups. When confronted with social conflict within group interaction, members typically run away from it, that is, take flight in their interaction patterns. Bennis and Shepard (1956), for example, discovered that a period of social conflict will typically be followed by a period of interaction in which members avoid discussing the task. Gouran and Baird (1972) also found that group members tend to change the theme under discussion soon after a period of social disagreement.

Why a group's interaction pattern exhibits flight from social conflict can be explained in several ways. One explanation assumes that conflict and deviance are unpleasant stimuli which group members wish to avoid. But this explanation is not very plausible in that it smacks of ignoring a problem and hoping it goes away. Sooner or later the group members must face the problem and resolve, manage, or control the conflict. Such a view also alleges that members invariably view social conflict as destructive.

Berg (1967) would probably explain flight patterns not as avoidance of anything but as merely a reflection of the short attention span of groups. A third explanation would describe flight patterns as reflecting the normal process by which groups progressively modify decisions on their way to achieving consensus. Neither of these views assumes that conflict is inherently destructive or constructive.

Whatever the explanation for apparent flight patterns in group interaction, it is obvious that disagreement spawns more disagreement, at least temporarily, in brief flurries of social conflict. It is also apparent that groups do not overtly attempt compromise as their initial response to social conflict. This observation is consistent with that made earlier—that groups often perceive compromise to be an unsatisfactory solution to group conflict. The group's first response to conflict among its members is apparently to fight it out in frequent, albeit brief, periods of interaction and then abruptly cease consideration of that proposal.

"Verbal Innovative Deviance"—A New Insight

Robert K. Merton (1957, p. 140) has presented a typology of deviant behavior which discriminates a form of deviance which is potentially beneficial and normal to the group process. His category of "innovative deviance" is perhaps the type of deviant behavior most common in the interaction patterns of small group decision making. According to Merton innovative deviance is behavior which reflects the deviating member's agreement with the group goal but disagreement with the majority view on the means for achieving that goal. Innovative deviance is thus differentiated from "rebellion," for example, which is behavioral deviance from the group goal as well as the means to achieve it.

Kristin B. Valentine (1972) utilizes Merton's concept of innovative deviance as the basis for a system of interaction analysis, the purpose of which is to observe more closely deviant behavior within the process of group interaction. Although her system has not yet been fully tested and the results are tentative, her discoveries demonstrate fruitful and enlightening progress in our understanding of normal deviant behavior and the group process.

Valentine classifies five varieties of verbal innovative deviance (VID) as well as noninnovative deviance (NID), which is generally classified as disruptive deviant behavior and not instrumental to group progress. Noninnovative deviance (NID) includes such examples of destructive conflict as "personal rejection," "task rejection," "irrelevant statements," and "negative commands." It must be emphasized that Valentine's investigations are not complete, and the results thus far are tentative and fragmentary. But even these preliminary results provide an insight into the process of deviant behavior heretofore only suspected in group interaction.

One startling discovery indicates that VID accounts for 20 percent of the total group interaction—a significant proportion indeed. On the other hand, the destructive conflict of NID accounts for only 1 percent. NID units of behavior are few and isolated, unlike VID units which appear in clusters, one following the other in the interaction sequence. Thus, VID behaviors stimulate increased group interaction and increased VID behavior. NID behaviors are apparently ignored by the group and do not foster additional deviant behavior.

The greatest proportion of deviant behavior occurs in the early and intermediate stages of group interaction, although periods of VID behaviors are present throughout nearly all interaction with the exception of the extremely late stages. During the period of interaction immediately preceding the group's final consensus, virtually no deviant behavior is present in the interaction sequences. This discovery apparently confirms the hypothesis that any temporary coalitions which have formed around substantive issues are merged together in a spirit of group unity as consensus is achieved. Another result consistent with this analysis reveals that most VID behaviors occur before the majority position is clearly established. That is, most VID behavior occurs before consensus and is apparently instrumental in forming that consensus. This discovery appears to affirm the belief stated earlier that conflict leads to consensus.

Valentine also discovered that VID behaviors are not sustained indefinitely. They tend to cluster in spurts of deviance, followed by periods of little deviance, which precede yet another spurt of deviant behavior. These "peaks" and "valleys" of deviant behavior suggest patterns of flight behavior exhibited by groups after a cluster of VID behaviors. But this discovery in no way suggests that the group attempts to avoid conflict. Rather, the group members may be able to withstand only so much conflict before they abruptly change the topic under discussion. But they invariably return to topics which precipitate additional VID behavior. This explanation of apparent flight patterns in the group interaction process will also be discussed further in the next chapter.

Many VID behaviors (nearly 40 percent of all VID behaviors) involve direct disagreement with the preceding assertion. This finding, too, is consistent with the notion that members test ideas under fire during group interaction. It also confirms the notion that group members apparently do not avoid disagreement. Certainly disagreement is not abnormal in the process of group interaction.

Perhaps the most startling discovery from Valentine's study involves the members who contribute deviant behaviors during group interaction. Amazingly enough, VID units are distributed nearly equally among all group members, except for those few low-participating members. This discovery is particularly amazing in that one of the groups contained a member who was perceived by his fellow group members as a deviate in the group and whose deviate role was confirmed through more subjective modes of group analysis. Yet that alleged deviate did not contribute significantly more deviant behaviors than any other member in his group, except for a single low-participating member. In fact, the alleged deviate performed fewer VID behaviors than another member in the group not perceived to be a deviate.

This last discovery emphasizes the fact that deviance, at least innovative deviance, must be defined in terms of behaviors performed by members and not as a role position or positions in the group's network of roles. Innovative deviance, as it affects the group process, is a function of behavior and not of an individual member's personality. Furthermore, innovative deviance must be considered normal to the process of group interaction, performed not by a few "oddball" members but by all committed group members. The potential importance of Valentine's fresh insight into deviant behavior in group decision making should not be underestimated.

SUMMARY

The right of dissent in our society is one of our most cherished privileges although conformity, inescapable and inevitable, is more often the rule. Conformity to behavioral standards of a social system implies not only uniformity of behavior but uniformity based on conflict among alternatives and avoidance of unpleasant social pressures. Pressures toward conformity in the small group are extraordinarily severe although a deviating member gains strength to resist such pressures when he has publicly committed himself to his deviant position or when another member agrees with his deviant position.

Many people in our society are ambivalent about social conflict and deviance and often view the social system functioning in a delicate balance of supportive and disruptive forces. Thus, conflict may be viewed as existing within the individual, between individuals, within the same social system, or between social systems. Social conflict is also classified as affective or substantive—emotional or intellectual.

When a perfect or ideal social system is assumed, social conflict appears as a failure of the social system and as inherently destructive. Others who adopt a functionalist approach perceive social conflict and deviance as often performing desirable, constructive, and even essential functions instrumental to the effective operation of the social system. If conflict is destructive, it must be resolved or controlled. On the other hand, constructive conflict must be understood and managed in order to achieve its social benefits. The multifaceted nature of social conflict and deviance dictates the emphasis on interpersonal, substantive conflict serving constructive functions for the small group.

Social conflict and deviance perform many functions beneficial to the group process. Conflict furthers group cohesiveness and increases productivity. Innovative deviant behavior is essential for progress as the group grows and changes through time. Groups manage deviant behavior through counteracting it with negative feedback loops or amplifying it through positive feedback cycles.

Realistically, social conflict and deviance are so common to the process of group development, they are considered normal within the group process. A decision-making group invokes social conflict as members test ideas in a critical exchange of information and opinions. Coalitions form temporarily around conflicting ideas before typically merging as the group achieves consensus. And the leader, paradoxically enough, normally conforms to and deviates from group norms in the process of gaining and maintaining his leadership status.

Verbal innovative deviance, an agreement on group goals but disagreement on means to achieve them, is suggested as an insight into the ongoing process of social conflict in group interaction patterns. Verbal innovative deviance appears to account for a significant proportion of group interaction and appears in clusters or spurts of deviant behavior with normal periods of group flight behavior. Normally only innovative deviant behaviors exert a significant impact on group interaction patterns and are generally distributed among all involved group members.

Chapter 7

The Decision-making Process

The process of decision making in a social setting is vitally important in a democratic society. Nearly every facet of our society's functioning—political, legislative, judicial, economic—functions through decisions made by groups. Laws are formulated by large groups of legislators. National executive decisions come from meetings of the President and his cabinet or small groups of advisers. The decisions of juries determine the fates of civil and criminal defendants in our courts. Negotiating teams decide the wages and benefits of millions of labor union members. The functioning of every business, educational, and political organization relies on decisions made by management teams. Group decisions ultimately determine what television programs we are able to view, what products are available to purchase, what new automobiles look like, what taxes we will pay, and so forth. Although we are often unaware of the pervasive influence of group decisions, the effects of those decisions on our lives are inescapable.

The past several decades have witnessed a growing concern over the allegedly clandestine nature of some decision-making groups in our society. The specter of a decision-making group in the proverbial smoke-filled back room is familiar to all of us. More often, the group making vital decisions is quite visible, but entrance into the group is highly restricted. Thus, the concern has concentrated on gaining a voice in the group decisions.

The reforms of the Democratic party in 1972 were based on giving more people a voice in the selection process of their party's candidates for political office. And the "student power" movement of the 1960s resulted in student representation on most university committees, faculty senates, and even boards of regents. Now that a voice in the decision-making process has been or is being secured by previously powerless minorities, the problem might appear to be solved. Unfortunately, nothing could be further from reality.

The sentiment of one newly named student member of a university's governing board aptly describes the persistent problem. He stated that he had worked long and hard for student representation on that board, but now that the students' voice could be heard he didn't know what to do about it. The simple fact is that membership in the decision-making group is necessary but not sufficient for effective decision making. A knowledge and understanding of the process of group decision making is absolutely essential for effective membership. Hundreds of business organizations seek assistance from professional consultants so that their management personnel can function effectively in decision-making groups. Being a member of a group is simply not enough. An understanding of how groups actually make decisions—the process of group decision making—is necessary for effective participation in group decision making.

The purpose of this chapter is to describe the process which characterizes group decision making. So that the reader doesn't expect more than is offered in this chapter, an unfortunate but true state of affairs must be emphasized. There is no "formula" which a group can learn and employ to ensure "good" decisions. Nor is there a convenient list of "dos" and "don'ts" which group members can memorize to improve their participation in group decision-making situations. All such lists (and there have been many) are universally unacceptable and doomed to failure when applied universally to all decision-making groups.

It is hoped that by understanding what knowledge of the group process is available, the group member will be more sensitive to and aware of what is occurring during group interaction. Such understanding and perceptiveness allow the group member to function at maximum effectiveness in a group situation. Awareness of the process without the use of "cure-all" principles of behavior, then, should be the goal of a prospective group member. But even awareness of the group process is no guarantee of group success, although the chances for group success are much greater. Such a view may be overly pessimistic, but it is probably realistic.

AN OVERVIEW OF KEY TERMS

Preliminary to the ensuing discussion of the group decision-making process is a full understanding of several key terms which will be used extensively in this chapter. All these terms are familiar and prompt immediate definitions. But in a sense, these terms are jargon. That is, each of these terms specifies a rather precise meaning, probably narrower than the meaning used in everyday conversation. It is for the sake of precision, then, that the following definitions are included.

The relationship between *decision making* and *problem solving* is not a source of universal agreement. Some view the two terms as virtually synonymous; others draw rather clear distinctions between them. Our concern is with all decision making which, for our purposes, includes some types of problem solving while excluding others. Recall the earlier distinction between tasks more appropriately performed by individuals and those uniquely adapted to the group process. The basis for that distinction also differentiates between two types of problem solving. One kind of problem possesses a "best" or "correct" solution which is determined by external and objective means. Such problems may be typified by a mathematical problem for which only one solution is acceptable, a logic puzzle governed by the invariable rules of induction and deduction, or a crossword puzzle. Certainly these problem-solving tasks are not within the province of group decision making.

On the other hand, some problems have no solution which is subject to external validation. The solutions to these problems can be discovered only through group acceptance—the willingness of the members to commit themselves to implementing the solution. Thus, the only possible check of the validity of the solution is whether it achieves group consensus. Such problems would include determining how to combat pollution or crime most effectively, problems of penal reform, the rising costs from inflation, and so forth. The value of such solutions may ultimately be determined by how well they work after they have been put into practice. But at the time of their achieving consensus in the group, only validation through group consensus determines the worth of these solutions.

Some decision-making tasks, of course, are not strictly within the scope of problems to be solved. Juries make decisions on questions of value and unverifiable facts. Voters make decisions on candidates for political office. These decisional situations do not stem directly from problems which require solving and include even such prosaic decisions as what clothing to wear tomorrow, what the theme for homecoming should be, what color to paint the house, and what brand of toothpaste to buy. Certainly decision making includes some types of problem solving and much more.

A *decision*, ultimately the outcome of group interaction, is inevitably a choice made by group members from among alternative proposals available to them. Rarely, if ever, does a group make a single decision in isolation. Although only one decision is sometimes apparent, such as a jury's decision of guilty or not guilty, many preliminary decisions are essential to that final decision and are made by the group on their way to achieving consensus on the final decision. The jury, for example, must decide which witness to believe, which piece of evidence is stronger, whether there is a reasonable doubt, and so forth. Group members, then, focus their attention on various proposals during their interaction and choose from among those alternative proposals which ones they will accept or reject. The sum of those proposals accepted constitutes the productivity of the group.

Although quantity of proposals initiated during group interaction is not a reliable measure of productivity, the fact remains that only those proposals which are initiated during interaction are available for final decision making. It is not yet clear whether more decision proposals yield higher quality decisions. Results of research efforts aimed at answering this question, particularly those efforts studying brainstorming techniques, are varied and conflicting. Common sense indicates that quantity of ideas proposed and quality of decisions achieving consensus are somehow related, but one must not neglect the factors of social conflict and intermember influence during interaction. As members discuss alternative proposals, they attempt to influence each other, directly and indirectly, to accept or reject a given proposal. The process of reciprocal influence during group interaction is one focus of this chapter.

A group reaches a decision as members achieve consensus on a proposal. The term *consensus* implies a variety of differing meanings. Some think of consensus as the will of the majority which proceeds from democratic voting procedures. Some believe unanimous agreement is necessary for consensus. Often consensus implies the absence of a formal vote but implicit agreement not necessarily verbalized by the group members. Obviously a consensus decision is one on which members agree, but agreement is again necessary but not a sufficient condition for consensus.

For our purposes consensus implies not only agreement but commitment to the decision reached. In fact, members may be committed to a decision to the extent that they work to put it into effect without ever fully agreeing with it. Zaleznik and Moment (1964, p. 142) clarify the nature of consensus as commitment:

> Our meaning of consensus lies in the degree of personal commitment the members feel toward the group decision after it is reached. This means, for example, that even though some members might disagree with the decision on principle, they will accept it and personally carry out their part. Their emotional commitment to the group is measured by willingness to put the plan decided on into effect, in their own personal behavior.

Simple agreement on a decision proposal, then, does not necessarily guarantee that the decision has achieved group consensus. In fact, group members who submit to pressures or external authority might express agreement without really accepting the proposal itself. In such instances the decision achieves false or superficial consensus, that is, agreement masquerading as consensus. The phenomenon of consensus without real agreement is not extraordinarily rare. For example, unsuccessful candidates for their party's nomination for political office often campaign strongly for the winning candidate. People may disagree on a new law or new tax passed by their elected representatives, but they generally obey those laws and pay those taxes.

The prime requisite for consensus, then, is not agreement with the decision, although agreement is highly common and even typical. The essential ingredient of consensus, however, is the extent of group loyalty shared by members. To the extent that the members are cohesive or have developed "groupness," the decisions reached by that group are most likely to achieve consensus as well as agreement. Thus, the rather cohesive group is more likely to be effective as a decision-making body.

The interdependence of the task and socioemotional dimensions of a group is again evident. As Zaleznik and Moment (1964, p. 155) point out, "Although this [consensus] may seem to be a purely task requisite, it is clearly a connecting link between task and social-emotional problems."

Consistent with the emphasis on communication and group process, the concern of this chapter is the *process* of group decision making. That is, this chapter is most concerned with questions of "how"—how groups achieve consensus on decisions over time; how members try to exert influence on each other during various periods of group interaction; how members' communicative behaviors occur in interstructured patterns during interaction. In short, the process perspective will emphasize how members interact during discussion of decision proposals and how certain proposals achieve consensus during group interaction.

PRESCRIPTIVE AND DESCRIPTIVE PROCESSES

There are two distinct though hackneyed approaches to the group process of decision making—each with limitations as well as advantages. The "prescriptive" approach attempts to illustrate how groups *should* make decisions. The "descriptive" approach attempts to document how groups *do* make decisions. As the name implies, the prescriptive method provides guidelines, an agenda, a road map to assist a group in achieving consensus. As its name implies, the descriptive method involves the observation of actual groups engaged in social decision making and seeks to describe the process which is common to all groups observed. While the prescriptive method is based on an "ideal" process, the crux of the descriptive method is the "reality" of observation.

Prescriptive approaches to group decision making rest on several inherent assumptions. First, prescriptive methods typically assume all members to be consistently rational. Prescriptive methods generally outline an agenda which provides the various steps a group goes through in making decisions. The various types of evidence are detailed along with methods of evaluating each type of evidence. The prescriptive method warns against emotional appeals or other nonrational aspects of group interaction, assuming that such techniques disrupt efficient group decision making. In other words, prescriptive methods often distinguish clearly between the task and socioemotional dimensions of the group process and assume the latter to be disruptive. Not only does this assumption deny the interdependence of the two group dimensions, but it delimits the primary advantage of group decision making over individual decision making—the socioemotional dimension.

A second assumption underlying prescriptive methods of group decision making is an attempt to improve the quality of the group's decision-making outcomes. Similar to a physician's prescription of medicine for an ill patient, prescriptive group methods assume that using the method will lead to a happy, healthy, and productive group. Although research efforts to discover the truth of this assumption are not in unanimous agreement, their results tend to cast doubt on the validity of this assumption. Many researchers, including Bayless (1967) and Pyke and Neely (1970), have discovered little significant difference in group productivity between groups using different methods of decision making. Assisting groups to achieve higher quality decisions is definitely a worthy goal. Apparently, however, present prescriptive methods have failed to achieve that goal.

Several assumptions also underlie the descriptive approach to group decision making. Probably most basic is the assumption that a "natural" process of group decision making exists. That is, groups develop their interdependent task and socioemotional dimensions in a normal, fairly consistent pattern leading to consensual validation of decisions. The process is assumed to be "natural" or normal because it occurs in all or nearly all effective or successful decision-making groups.

The natural process of group decision making, of course, is present to the extent that a group is free to develop its own task and social dimensions for itself without undue influence on the group imposed by some external source. In other words, the natural process occurs to the extent that the group is an LGD. Any external authority which inhibits the group's freedom to choose its own leader or establish its own norms results in a deviation from the natural process. In the absence of external constraints on the group, any significant deviation from the natural process may be considered a failure, to some extent, of that particular group. That group, then, may be considered to some extent unnatural or abnormal.

The perspective of communication and group process is best served by emphasizing the descriptive approach to the process of group decision making. And the descriptive approach will focus on observing the interaction patterns of group members—their interlocked communicative behaviors—as they occur and change over time as a group proceeds from the beginning of their task performance to consensus. So that this perspective may be understood in context, a brief survey of common prescriptive and descriptive methods will precede the descriptive model of group decision making employed in this book.

Prescriptive Models

Undoubtedly the most common prescriptive method used in group decision making is the "reflective thinking" model suggested by John Dewey (1910) over six decades ago. Although Dewey intended his model of reflective thinking to apply only to an individual's mental processes, his model has been widely employed as a guide to group decision making as well. Briefly summarized, Dewey's model includes the following six steps:

Step 1   A difficulty is felt or expressed.
Step 2   The nature of the problem is defined.
Step 3   The nature of the problem is analyzed.
Step 4   Possible solutions are suggested to solve the problem.
Step 5   The solutions are compared by testing each against selected criteria, and the best solution is selected.
Step 6   The best solution is implemented, that is, put into effect.

Dewey's model serves as a universal agenda to guide a group toward consensus in an orderly, step-by-step progression. The group is expected to discuss and complete each step before moving on to the next step in the sequence. Steps are intended to be followed in sequence without omitting any or reversing their order. Dewey's model also clearly applies to problem solving, assuming that decision making and problem solving are not significantly different. It is equally clear that Dewey's model assumes the superiority of rationality and omits consideration of a group's socioemotional dimension. But of course Dewey intended "reflective thinking" for individuals. When used to guide group decision making, the model does not allow for the socioemotional dimension.

A second prescriptive method which has gained popularity in the past decade is worthy of mention although not totally relevant to the process of decision making. Developed by the United States Navy the prescriptive method is known as "PERT," an acronym for Program Evaluation and Review Technique. PERT is not relevant to the process of decision making simply because it involves a detailed step-by-step method for implementing the decision after it has achieved consensus. PERT is a detailed method which embodies only one of the steps in Dewey's reflective thinking model—number six. Because it does not further any understanding of how groups achieve consensual validation of their decisions, the various steps of PERT are not included here. A concise explanation of the PERT method applied to implementing small group decisions is available elsewhere (Phillips, 1966).

Descriptive Models

The most familiar of all descriptive models of the group process is the three-phase model advanced by Bales (1950) and Bales and Strodtbeck (1951). These authors discovered that decision-making groups, the bulk of which were problem-solving groups, tend to discuss different kinds of problems dealing with their tasks at different periods in their group interaction. Their three phases may be briefly illustrated as follows:

Stage 1 Emphasis on problems of *orientation* (deciding what the situation is like).
Stage 2 Emphasis on problems of *evaluation* (deciding what attitudes should be taken toward the situation).
Stage 3 Emphasis on problems of *control* (deciding what to do about it).

Bales and Strodtbeck base their three phases of the group decision-making process on data compiled from using Bales's (1950) system of

Interaction Process Analysis (IPA). Figure 9 illustrates Bales's system of interaction analysis (see Appendix Two). The IPA classifies each communicative behavior performed by members during group interaction. The classes of behavior include twelve different categories—in reality, six bipolar pairs of categories. Each category in the pair is the antithesis of the other, for example, Agrees—Disagrees, Shows Solidarity—Shows Antagonism. The IPA also separates the group's task and socioemotional dimensions by labeling three pairs of categories in each area. And each bipolar pair of categories is assumed to deal with a particular kind of problem confronting the group. Each of the first three types of problems —orientation, evaluation, and control—is emphasized in order by each

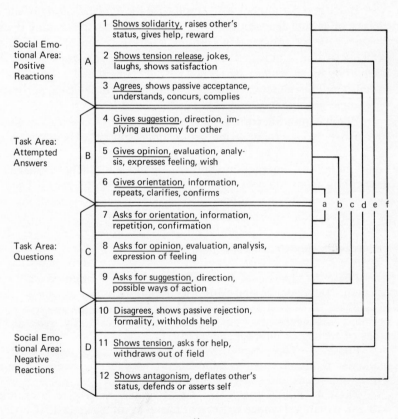

Key:

a Problems of orientation   d Problems of decision
b Problems of evaluation   e Problems of tension-management
c Problems of control   f Problems of integration

Figure 9   Bales's interaction process analysis.

decision-making group in three successive phases during their group interaction.

Bales and Strodtbeck's analysis of the group decision-making process indicates that members predominantly give and ask for orientation in the first phase, give and ask for opinions in the second phase, and give and ask for suggestions in the third phase. The authors also discovered that positive reactions and negative reactions also tend to increase progressively from one phase to the next. However, the third phase of *control* appears unique among the three in this respect. While increasing amounts of negative reactions are characteristic of the first part of the final phase, the latter stages of the control phase include predominantly positive reactions.

Bales and Strodtbeck also emphasize the cyclical nature of the three phases of group decision making. As a group completes one decision-making task by progressing through the three phases of orientation, evaluation, and control, the group tends to recycle back to the initial orientation phase as they perform each subsequent task. Thus, according to Bales and Strodtbeck, the three phases characterize each performance of a single group decision-making task.

Bennis and Shepard (1956 and 1961, pp. 753–755) developed a four-phase model to describe group development. Their observations were much more subjective and interpretative than the direct observational method of interaction analysis. Bennis and Shepard derived their description from the reactions of nonparticipant observers. Their findings, according to the authors, also reflect their interpretations over a five-year period of teaching classes in group dynamics. The following four phases of group development are labeled according to the level of work the group is able to accomplish:

Phase 1   One-Level Work. Personally need-oriented—not group-oriented. (Dependence and Authority Relations)
Phase 2   Two-Level Work. Maintaining the group task. Group-oriented and necessary—but routine. (Resolution-Catharsis and beginnings of feeling of interdependence)
Phase 3   Three-Level Work. Group-focused work with new methods of attack, goal establishment, idea-testing. (Interdependence with group focus and sense of direction)
Phase 4   Four-Level Work. Creative and integrative interpretation with immediate relevance to present problems of group task. (Consensual Validation and Maximum Productivity)

Several interesting observations emerge from Bennis and Shepard's model. For example, the model illustrates a group's progressive ability to do more sophisticated work. This ability is apparently gained in successively progressive stages as the group develops interdependence among its members. As the group begins its process of development, it is dependent upon some external authority responsible for the group task. In a T-group that authority is the trainer; in an organization he is the boss; in a classroom he is the instructor. The group can do two-level work only as they begin to reject the external source of authority. By the time they are able to do three-level work, they have completely rejected their dependence on the external authority.

Bennis and Shepard's model also maintains a clear separation between work and emotionality—the task and socioemotional dimensions. Although recognizing their close relationship, Bennis and Shepard emphasize the importance of achieving social interdependence as a prerequisite to task accomplishment. They feel that a group accomplishes the bulk of its task during the period of four-level work.

Bennis and Shepard also discuss the phenomenon of flight behavior—the group's tendency to escape from their task, often as a result of social conflict among members or with the external authority. Generally the group begins settling these conflicts during the resolution-catharsis period of two-level work and has them well in hand during the social interdependence of three-level work. Bennis and Shepard observe that running away from the task is an attempt by the group to avoid some unpleasant stimulus such as social conflict. The phenomenon of flight behavior will be discussed later in more detail.

Tuckman (1965) employed still another method for observing groups as he devised his four-phase model for group decision making. In fact, Tuckman himself did not observe any groups but synthesized the results of other published observations. Tuckman notes that groups simultaneously confront two kinds of problems in each phase of decision making. He labels these two problem types: (*a*) Group structure (how to get along) and (*b*) Task activity (how to proceed). Essentially these two types of problems are "social problems" and "task problems," thereby denying the inseparable interdependence of the two dimensions of group process. Tuckman characterizes his four phases and their corresponding social and task problems with a catchy rhythm of four rhyming words:

Phase 1 Forming   (a) Testing and Independence
                              (b) Attempting to identify the task
Phase 2 Storming   (a) Development of intragroup conflicts
                              (b) Emotional response to task demands
Phase 3 Norming   (a) Development of group cohesion
                              (b) Expression of opinions
Phase 4 Performing   (a) Functional role-relatedness
                              (b) Emergence of solutions

Tuckman's point of departure, like Bales and Strodtbeck's, is the type of problem under discussion at various stages in group interaction. Tuckman also clearly separates the members' communicative behavior into task and socioemotional areas. And, like Bennis and Shepard, Tuckman assumes that the group accomplishes the bulk of its productive output in the latter stages of the decision-making process.

Despite the different methods used to observe group behavior, these three descriptive models possess characteristics in common. Although the perspective of each observer is quite different, they agree on many elements of the decision-making small group. Quite naturally all three descriptions reflect a greater emphasis on the socioemotional dimension than on the task dimensions. But this emphasis should be expected since all the authors are psychologists or social psychologists whose primary interest is personality and social structure—not communication.

Consistent with the emphasis on the socioemotional dimension, all three models perceive a stable social structure as prerequisite to task productivity. Of course, this observation is possible only when one considers the two dimensions separate and even antagonistic to each other. Then, too, this observation denies the mutual influence of these dimensions on each other. The result of this separation is an emphasis on explaining *why* groups are capable of making decisions rather than *how* groups actually achieve consensual validation of decisions. The admitted emphasis of this book is on the "how" rather than the "why."

Although the three descriptive models do not completely agree on the nature of each phase, there seem to be four discernible phases of group decision making. Bales and Strodtbeck delineate only three phases, but they describe the control phase as including successive emphases on negative reactions and positive reactions in the early and latter portions of that final phase. Thus, four distinguishable phases seem to characterize group decision making.

Although the three descriptive models do not reflect identical characteristics of each phase, several phases include characteristics common to all three models. That is, the first stage of group decision making in all three models is a period of orientation—a period in which members adjust their individualities to group membership and accustom themselves to the task at hand. This orienting period generally involves a search process in which members search for ways to view their task with no particular focus or established opinion toward the task.

One of the middle phases in each of the models includes a period of social conflict among members, differences of opinion on task ideas and social norms. This similarity seems to confirm that social conflict and deviance are indeed a normal part of the group process. Moreover, social conflict and deviance are normal during only one period of group interaction. And that period of normal conflict is near the middle of the process and not near the beginning or the end of group task performance. Thus, the norm of social conflict and deviance characterizes a specific intermediate phase in the process of group interaction which ultimately leads to consensual validation of decisions.

A final stage of interaction in which members apparently accomplish most of their work on their task is common to all three models, although the exact nature of that final stage is not abundantly clear. Bales and Strodtbeck indicate the final stage is characterized by a maximum number of positive reactions. The other two models indicate that the group becomes capable of creative and effective task performance. But all three models agree that the group members achieve consensus and thereby validate their decisions during this final phase.

One final observation is appropriate concerning the descriptive approach to group decision making. Although two people can observe the same phenomenon and agree on many points of comparison, they also disagree fundamentally on what they have observed. The perspective of the observer significantly influences what he observes and concludes from his observations. I can recall my initial adolescent attempt to dive from the high board at my local swimming pool. When I looked up at the board from the water below, it didn't seem so high. But when I first looked down from the vantage point of standing on the board itself, it seemed astronomically high. One must remember that observation of reality is not reality. Observation is subject to the perspective of the observer and the tools which he uses to observe.

The descriptive model which comprises the remainder of this chapter agrees with some elements contained in the previous models and disagrees with some others. Discrepancies between observers should not be of significant concern when one understands the differences among observational perspectives. The process of communication is the perspective employed in the following model.

THE SPIRAL MODEL

Although the prescriptive and descriptive models described earlier are different in many significant respects, they are all "linear" models. Each model is based on a step-by-step progression toward the completion of task objectives. The steps in the linear model assume a given order. A group completes discussion of one set of problems before moving to the next. Each model assumes that solving one set of problems is prerequisite to solving the next set of problems. That is, the group is incapable of solving the second set of problems until they solve the first, and so on. Groups cannot or should not deal with problems out of sequence. Any step out of sequence would be considered a lack of group progress and an error of that group. The linear model outlines progress toward task accomplishment as a methodical progression along a straight line.

Thomas M. Scheidel and Laura Crowell (1964) discovered that group interaction aimed at developing ideas does not correspond to a linear model. Using a system of interaction analysis (see Appendix Two) as their observational scheme (Crowell and Scheidel, 1961), these authors describe the group process of idea development as a "spiral" model. One member introduces an idea, and other members respond with agreement or disagreement, extension or revision. The idea is the object of discussion, and it develops over time to reflect the group's viewpoint. When an idea is developed to the point that it is an object of agreement by all group members, the group anchors its position on that idea and introduces new preliminary ideas progressing from that anchor point of agreement. The spiral process, then, involves "reach-testing" forward from an anchored position of agreement. If the reach-tested idea is affirmed by the group, a new anchored position is established, and reach-testing proceeds from there. If the new idea is rejected, the group returns to its anchored position and reach-tests another new idea from that same anchor point.

The spiral process of anchoring and reach-testing is not linear in that the group constantly retraces its path of idea development. Groups develop new ideas not in linear sequence but cumulatively. One idea leads to another. One idea is progressively modified and remodified during the course of group interaction until the group achieves consensual validation of its final decisions. The spiral process is cumulative and progressive, reflecting continuous modification of ideas and backtracking to agreed-upon ideas as members reconfirm positions.

Several descriptive models indicated that the bulk of the group's task activity occurs in the final stages of interaction. The spiral model denies that allegation but explains the appearance that groups accomplish more work during the final stages. The spiral process is cumulative, and all ideas developed in the latter stages of interaction are the direct result of earlier agreements and anchored positions. But in the final stages, the group has acquired a vast background of many agreed-upon positions. Reach-testing in the final phase therefore proceeds from a broader base of agreement with increasingly diminishing need to backtrack to earlier anchor positions.

The springlike children's toy known as a "Slinky" illustrates this point. As you stretch the Slinky, you will notice that the spirals can be compressed at one end with relatively wide spaces between spirals at the other end and in the middle. But the spirals are all interconnected in a single continuous band of spring steel. In this way the spirals of reach-tested ideas are compressed during the final period as consensus decisions become increasingly obvious to the group members. But those decisions are possible only because of the previously anchored positions of agreement developed in earlier phases. The process is cumulative rather than linear.

The spiral model also accounts for the apparent inefficiency of group decision making regarding the use of time. Every beginning geometry student knows the shortest distance between two points on the same plane is a straight line. But group decision making apparently does not conform to a straight line of a linear model. Rather, the group process is more like a spiral of anchoring and reach-testing. But the spiral process is certainly not a disadvantage of group decision making. Anchoring and reach-testing ideas illustrate the group's superiority when performing decision-making tasks requiring high acceptance.

Other descriptive models depict the group decision-making process globally in terms of task and socioemotional dimensions. But the spiral model describes the group process in terms of the interaction patterns among members. The model which follows assumes the existence of the spiral process.

THE PROCESS OF DECISION EMERGENCE

Chapter 5 discussed the phenomenon of leader emergence—that groups do not "select" leaders so much as the leader and other roles "emerge" during group interaction. If the task and socioemotional dimensions of group process are truly interdependent, it seems reasonable that the decision-making process should be similar to the leadership process. Moreover, group decision making, like leadership, possesses no single "best" or correct answer to be discovered in a "Eureka!" or "Aha!" manner. It is reasonable to conclude that groups do not *make* decisions. Decisions *emerge* from group interaction.

If you were to observe a decision-making group as a participant or a nonparticipant attempting to determine the point at which the group makes its decision, you would find such a task extraordinarily difficult if not impossible. During some period of the group's interaction, the decision is probably apparent to you even though the group members continue their discussion.

The process of emergence is gradual and cumulative. A specific point in time at which decisions are made is not apt to be found. In fact, the emergence process presupposes that groups achieve consensus on their decisions *after* those decisions appear to have been made. The very final stage of interaction, then, fulfills the purpose of procuring members' public commitment, the essence of consensus, to decisions already reached.

Phases of Decision Emergence

Using interaction analysis (see Appendix Two) as the method for observing group decision making, B. Aubrey Fisher (1970a) discovered four phases in the process of group decision making. Unlike other observational schema, Fisher identified each alternative decision proposal suggested during group interaction and attempted to observe the process whereby preliminary ideas are transformed into consensus decisions. Thus, each member's communicative act functions on the decision proposal under discussion by expressing some opinion (favorable, unfavorable, or ambiguous) toward that proposal, providing evidence to support that opinion, modifying the proposal, clarifying it, and agreeing or disagreeing with another member's opinion. The group interaction is thus anchored to the subject matter of the group interaction—the decision proposals—and to members' attempts to influence the perceptions of other members toward those proposals.

The observed pattern of communicative behaviors—acts and interacts—indicates four rather distinct phases of group decision making, each characterized by a different pattern of interaction. Those phases are labeled Orientation, Conflict, Emergence, and Reinforcement.

Orientation Phase A group's early problems of socializing and excessive primary tension affect the interaction patterns in this early phase. Members clarify and agree most often in this phase. As each member is unaware of his social position initially and not sure of how to handle the task, he does not quickly or strongly assert himself or his opinions. Consequently he makes assertions tentatively in order to test the group, and he agrees with virtually everything. For example, a member states an ambiguous opinion toward the decision proposal, a second member agrees with that ambiguous opinion, which is followed in turn by another ambiguous opinion. Since members agree even with comments serving only to clarify points of information, agreeing with another member's comment seems to function in the Orientation phase not so much to reinforce other members' beliefs and opinions as to avoid disrupting the developing social climate.

Group members in the Orientation phase search tentatively for ideas and directions to aid their decision-making efforts. They are unaware of the direction the group will eventually take, so they don't commit themselves, favorably or unfavorably, to the newly introduced decision proposals. Rather, they express attitudes which are ambiguous toward proposals—attitudes which don't really take a stand one way or the other.

Many of the ambiguous opinions expressed in the first phase probably reflect favorable attitudes in the making. That is, since members assert opinions and arguments favoring the proposals with increasing intensity as the discussion progresses, those opinions must be in the preliminary stages of formation during this Orientation phase. As the issues become clarified and as the social climate becomes more conducive to the honest statement of one's true position, many members apparently change their ambiguous opinions to opinions favoring the decision proposals.

Characteristic of the Orientation phase, then, is getting acquainted, clarifying, and tentatively expressing attitudes. This stage is a period of forming opinions, not rocking the boat, and getting rid of social inhibitions—in short, the Orientation phase.

Conflict Phase The second phase of group decision making is characterized by dispute—ideational conflict over decision proposals. In the Orientation phase members only tentatively expressed their opinions, typically ambiguous. In the Conflict phase they appear to have made up their minds. Members are now aware of the direction the group is taking toward their decision-making task and of the relevant decision proposals which are emerging from the group deliberations. Thus, members typically express either a favorable or an unfavorable attitude toward those decision proposals. Gone is the tentativeness of ambiguity. Gone, too, is tentativeness due to social inhibitions.

Polarization of attitudes means disagreement and conflict. Expressing a favorable attitude is generally followed by another member's expressing his unfavorable attitude (and vice versa) in the Conflict phase. Members have different opinions and express them in argument with each other. Not only do members express less ambiguous attitudes, but they also express them more tenaciously. Members now provide data and evidence to substantiate their beliefs and engage in full-fledged debate with other members.

The interaction patterns of the Conflict phase reflect the formation of two coalitions formed from polarization of beliefs. That is, two coalitions are present in the Conflict phase—one favoring and one opposing those decision proposals which ultimately achieve group consensus. To illustrate, A and B favor the proposals and reinforce each other's favorable opinions; C and D oppose the proposals and reinforce each other's unfavorable opinions. Expressing an ambiguous attitude or the presence of a "mugwump" member is not normal in the Conflict phase. The norm is dissent, controversy, social conflict, and innovative deviance. In fact, the mugwump is the deviate in the Conflict phase in that he does not participate in the debate over ideas and opinions.

It is quite probable that the coalitions centered around leader contenders are the same coalitions formed by polarization of ideas during the Conflict phase. The interdependence of the task and socioemotional dimensions would seem to confirm that explanation.

Emergence Phase   Social conflict and dissent dissipate during the third phase. Members express fewer unfavorable opinions toward decision proposals. The coalition of individuals who had opposed those proposals which eventually achieve consensus also weakens in the third phase. The interaction patterns in the Emergence phase reflect significantly less positive reinforcement of each other's unfavorable attitudes. A few residues of overt social conflict remain in the Emergence phase, but they are not significant. Comments expressing unfavorable attitudes are not only not reinforced by subsequent agreement or more unfavorable attitudes from other members in the coalition, they are not expressed so tenaciously either. That is, opposing members typically assert unfavorable opinions without including supporting evidence or reason to substantiate them.

The hallmark of the Emergence phase is the recurrence of ambiguity. As in the Orientation phase, some members express opinions ambiguous toward the decision proposals and tend to reinforce them by responding with further expressions of attitudes ambiguous toward the proposals. Thus, ambiguity toward decision proposals is prominent in the Orientation phase, declines significantly in the Conflict phase, and rises again during the Emergence phase.

But while the proportionate number of comments expressing ambiguous opinions and interacts reflecting reinforcement of ambiguous comments does not differ significantly from the Orientation phase, the function performed by ambiguity in the interact patterns of the Emergence phase is significantly different. During Orientation members expressed opinions tentatively in the form of ambiguous attitudes toward the decision proposals. Some of these ambiguous comments were undoubtedly the initial expression of favorable or unfavorable opinions in rudimentary form of development. But group members have no reason to be tentative in the Emergence phase. They are certainly no longer searching for attitude direction. They plotted that direction in the Orientation phase and debated it during the Conflict phase. In the Emergence phase task direction is obviously no longer at issue. It is quite unreasonable to conclude that expressing an ambiguous opinion at this late point in the discussion reflects a tentative expression of a developing opinion.

The key to the function of ambiguity in the patterns of group interaction lies in associating the Emergence phase with the Conflict phase. Ambiguous communicative behavior functions in the third phase as a form of modified dissent. In the Conflict phase members either favored or disfavored the decision proposals. In the Emergence phase the bimodal distribution has shifted to favorable or ambiguous attitudes toward these same proposals. That is, the group member who expressed his opposition to decision proposals in the Conflict phase is in the process of changing his opinion from disfavor to favor through the mediating step of expressing ambiguous opinions.

Members expressing ambiguous opinions in the Emergence phase have already committed themselves to a stand of opposition in the Conflict phase and cannot be expected to change their opinions so abruptly. Thus, their dissent changes to assent *via* ambiguity. A dissenting member in the Conflict phase responded to another member's comment favoring the proposal with his opinion disfavoring that proposal. In the Emergence phase he responds in the same situation with an opinion ambiguous toward the proposal. He is still expressing his opposition to the proposal, but his opposition is dissipating as he modifies his own attitudes.

The two coalitions present in the Conflict phase also dissipate during the Emergence phase. The coalition of dissenting members opposing the decision proposals does not immediately disintegrate but turns to ambiguous comments as a final form of dissent. Just as the exact point in time at which a leader or a decision emerges cannot be pinpointed, neither can one determine the exact point in time of the death of the dissenting coalition. The dissipation of dissent and the dissipation of the coalition are gradual and mediated by ambiguity. In the absence of outright social conflict, decisions may appear to have been reached. But the expression of ambiguous opinions, while not totally unfavorable, is not yet favorable. As disfavor dissipates to ambiguity, however, favorable opinions toward the decision proposals increase concomitantly.

The third phase is probably the crucial stage in the group process of decision making. During this third phase the eventual outcome of group interaction becomes increasingly more apparent. Thus this third phase is called the Emergence phase.

Reinforcement Phase While group members tend to reach decisions during the Emergence phase, they achieve consensus on those decisions during the Reinforcement phase. Substantiating one's opinion toward the decision proposal is no longer necessary in this final phase. After all, the ideas were thoroughly tested during the Conflict phase, but members continue to provide evidence and reasons to support their opinions favoring the decision proposals, thus adding additional fuel to the fire of emerging consensus. Members constantly and consistently express opinions favorable to the proposals and positively reinforce each other's favorable opinions with expressions of agreement and additional social support. This overwhelming preponderance of interaction patterns which favor the decision proposals and positively reinforce those favorable opinions clearly identifies the final phase of group deliberations.

Dissent has all but vanished in the Reinforcement phase. The Reinforcement phase includes the fewest number of comments opposed to the decision proposals and virtually no interacts of social conflict—that is, a favorable comment followed or preceded by an unfavorable comment. Of course the Orientation phase contained few interacts of social conflict, too. But while the low level of conflict during orientation reflects a conscious avoidance of members toward conflict due to social inhibitions, the Reinforcement phase reflects unity of opinion among group members. The dissipation of dissent, both direct (unfavorable opinions) and modified (ambiguous opinions), is virtually complete in this final phase of group interaction.

Pervading this final phase in group decision making is a spirit of unity. All members seem to agree and strive to show that agreement through positively reinforcing each other. Their interaction patterns reflect virtually no tension as members are jovial, loud, boisterous, laughing, and verbally backslap each other. This is the phase of developing members' commitment to those decisions which were the object of conflict in the second phase and which emerged during the third phase. This is the Reinforcement phase.

Orientation, Conflict, Emergence, and Reinforcement are the four phases of decision emergence. They have been described above in terms of characteristic patterns of interaction. Where possible they have been associated with elements of the socioemotional dimension. The original purpose of the investigation which discovered these four phases was to observe verbal task behavior free from the confounding variables of the socioemotional dimension. That purpose, of course, was doomed to failure. The two dimensions are interdependent. Attempting to view only one dimension can only provide a perspective from which to view the interdependence of both.

The descriptions of the four phases are admittedly rather general and provide no examples of group interaction. In order to illustrate the phases more clearly and reveal the "flavor" of group decision making from the viewpoint of members' communicative behaviors, the Appendix includes "Anatomy of a Decision" (Appendix One). That section provides detailed examples of interaction patterns from an actual decision-making group. "Anatomy of a Decision" should clarify most questions raised in the preceding general description.

The Group Process of Modifying Decisions

The "spiral model" of idea development, described by Scheidel and Crowell (1964) and affirmed in the phases of decision emergence, reveals that group decision making is a process of cumulative development of consensus decisions. Groups achieve consensus on decisions through interaction patterns which modify, reject, accept, or combine previously introduced decision proposals. However, the specific nature of the interaction patterns which cumulatively modify decision proposals until they appear in consensus form is not evident in the discussion of either the spiral model or the phases of decision emergence.

Studying the interaction patterns of decision-making groups, Fisher (1970b) discerned a pattern of cumulative, step-by-step modification of decision proposals. That is, groups do not typically modify preliminary decision proposals by clear and direct amendments but in sudden jumps to different formulations of the same root proposal. Consistent with Berg's (1967) discovery of a group's rather brief attention span, Fisher found that groups apparently do not discuss each proposal for an extended period of time. Rather, a group member introduces a specific decision proposal, members discuss it for some length of time, drop it in favor of discussing another decision proposal, and reintroduce the first proposal later during the group deliberations.

Often groups reconsider the proposal in the same form. But on those not infrequent occasions when the initial formulation of a proposal is not precisely the one which eventually achieves consensus, members reintroduce the proposal in modified form. Sometimes a proposal is reintroduced several times, each with further modification. Thus, groups achieve consensus on decision proposals not in a consistent evolutionary pattern but, rather, in spurts of energy.

Following this pattern of decision modification, a member introduces a decision proposal which the members discuss briefly and then drop from consideration. Later a member reintroduces this same proposal in substitute form, and the group proceeds toward consensus in a cumulative and cyclical manner.

An example might illustrate this pattern of modification more clearly. A corporate management training group was engaged in making decisions regarding their management of a hypothetical corporation. One of their consensus decisions was to concentrate their sales and advertising campaigns for their mythical business in two market areas—one urban and one rural. Member B initially introduced this decision proposal in its rudimentary form—to withhold all attempts to sell their products until after the results of a market analysis were available. The following excerpt is from the group's interaction at that point:

> **B**   This is going to be our plan initially, to get this market analysis. I feel we should consider holding our market in inventory and not sell the first quarter until you find out where the market is.
> **A**   What would you do with the salesmen, then? Just let them sit around?
> **B**   Pay their salary. $8,000.
> **A**   But you're not getting any return on your money.
> **D**   You've got to put them out in the field.
> **C**   Put them out. It wouldn't cost us anything.
> **A**   All right. What should we do about advertising?

The group members did not respond favorably to B's proposal, and they quickly moved to another, as yet unrelated, proposal concerning advertising. Later, C reintroduces a substitute decision proposal regarding how to allocate the company's salesmen:

> **C**   As a matter of fact, if we were to take one area and blanket it with our salesmen and take another area for our market analysis, we might be able to calculate a second area based on the results of our sales.
> **A**   We might be able to. At least it's a better possibility than . . .
> **D**   It's an indicator.
> **C**   An indicator. You've got more information.
> **B**   We need to get a job description of the chairman.

The group members responded favorably to the substitute proposal. Yet they dropped the second proposal, too, before coming to a final decision and before exhausting their discussion of it.

The decision proposal to concentrate their salesmen in two market areas came closest to the form of a direct amendment to the decision proposal while it was being discussed:

> **C**   Our first shot at sales is really to obtain a market coverage.
> **B**   What do you mean by "market coverage"?
> **C**   I'm sorry. A market forecast.
> **B**   That's what we were saying. Get a forecast on each region and try to cover sales on each.

C But I don't think we can do that. I think we can blanket only one area.

B If you put two salesmen in each area, you use six salesmen. But I don't think you want to do that.

D No. We can't reallocate. If we put two in each one of those areas and reallocate one of them to the other area, then we cover it.

B You're covered if the first guy gets a sale.

A You've got to gamble a little bit, but I don't think you want to throw your whole sales staff into one area. I think we ought to distribute three and three. [By allocating the six salesmen "three and three," A proposes to distribute the six salesmen equally in two market areas. He appears to amend the earlier proposal to concentrate salesmen in a single area.]

C Three and three?

A Three and three. And then see what the results of our market analysis are. Based upon this knowledge, we can better reallocate.

D Where are we going to do our market analysis anyway?

Member A initiates a new decision proposal, largely by amending the proposal under discussion—to concentrate all six salesmen in one area—and introducing it in amended form—to distribute salesmen equally in two areas. But without exhaustively deliberating this proposal, the members quickly shift to another decision proposal regarding the area of market analysis.

Earlier the group had discussed the decision proposal of whether their company should advertise:

B How much for advertising?

C Mr. Marketing, would you recommend two pages of advertising for each of the areas we are going to cover?

D Yeah. I think that's the least we can do. If we are going to put salesmen in an area, we ought to support them.

B Remember, we haven't got much cost there.

C You can't make money unless you spend it.

B No. But we are just finding out where the market is right now. Why spend it for advertising?

C But what if the other people spend? We'll find out, of course, if we lose a sale to the competitors.

B Let's don't advertise.

C We ought to advertise something.

D I think we should have one page.

C One page, at least.

B But we don't have the money.

A How are we doing in formulating our long-range objectives?

Unlike the previous examples of decision proposals dropped after initiation and brief discussion, members responded to this proposal with a direct conflict of opinions. But without resolving the conflict, the group shifted to a totally different proposal—formulating their company's long-range objectives. The two decision proposals to concentrate their sales force in two areas and advertise in both areas were combined later in a further reformulation of the decision proposals:

A With the marketing advantage you have getting this information, you'd better spend as much as you can on advertising and sales in that place and ignore the rest.

B I don't know if we want to go into two areas or not. We aren't going to have enough to cover.

C I would suggest that we take a shot at two areas. If we hit area four, which is urban, and pick area two right above it, which is . . .

A strictly rural.

C If we hit area four and area two, we can draw conclusions and see if there really is a difference between the urban and rural markets.

Member C's addition of "urban" and "rural" to differentiate the two market areas is not so much a modification of the proposal as it is an advantage of concentrating advertising and salesmen in two areas. This point seemed to win over the obviously reluctant Member B. And this configuration was the decision proposal which eventually achieved group consensus.

Each of the reformulations of the initial decision proposal is introduced, discussed, and dropped several times. The excerpts included above illustrate only those moments in the group's interaction in which members initiated the proposal in a modified form and does not include other reintroductions of the same proposal. Thus, members modify decision proposals by leaps or jumps rather than continuously by direct amendment and prolonged discussion.

In short, reformulations or modifications of the initial decision proposal do not typically emerge from direct criticisms of the proposal while it is being discussed. Rather, group members appear to wrestle with the proposal, sometimes with conflict and sometimes without, and then put it aside temporarily until one of the members experiences an insight and suggests a reformulation that seems closer to what the group actually wants.

It seems clear that the process of decision modification reveals an interaction norm of a start-and-stop deliberation of decision proposals. Group members normally cease deliberations regarding a specific decision proposal and abruptly switch to another proposal. This norm is often frustrating to inexperienced group members. One classroom group's self-analysis reveals just such frustration:

> We would be talking about one subject and then all of a sudden in midstream change and start talking about something else. Our group has the trait of going around in circles.

This perceptive comment reflects the concern of a group who considered this "going around in circles" to indicate some failure in their group interaction. Unfortunately this group never realized during their interaction that they were behaving quite normally. Only their frustration was disruptive.

The tendency of a group to cease deliberations abruptly and switch to another topic is similar to the phenomenon of "flight behavior" discussed earlier. The term "flight" usually implies an attempt to avoid some unpleasant stimulus such as interpersonal conflict or extreme social tension. Yet groups exhibit interaction patterns characteristic of flight behavior whether there is dissenting social conflict or not. Each of the 163 decision proposals observed (Fisher, 1970b) was introduced, discussed, dropped, reintroduced, discussed, dropped again, and so forth, in essentially the same pattern. Rather than indicating that the group is "fleeing" from some unpleasant social problem, the spasmodic progression toward consensus seems to be an inherent and quite normal characteristic of interaction patterns during the process of group decision making.

The group norm of "flight" during decision making probably serves the purpose of managing tension as well as progressively modifying decision proposals. Because a group normally does not consider any decision proposal for an extended period of time, social tension does not easily or quickly rise to intolerable levels. Certainly participating in group interaction, continuously susceptible to social pressure, is by its very nature a highly intense experience. The pressures on each individual due simply to his group membership cannot be sustained indefinitely.

Some level of secondary tension is normal throughout group interaction. The spurts of task activity probably indicate the natural tendency of a group to manage its social tension by frequently conserving energy through abrupt transitions to different decision proposals. Thus, the spiral mode of the group decision-making process, though generally intended to describe the process of task performance, is highly interrelated with the group's social dimension as well.

Social Conflict and Decision Modification   Although the evidence is not conclusive, there is a justifiable basis for believing that the patterns of decision modification do reflect the influence of social conflict over decision proposals. That is, when members consistently respond to initiated proposals with a conflict of opinions, the successive reintroduction of those decision proposals follows a distinctive pattern. And when members experience little conflict of opinions toward initiated proposals, the successive reintroduction of those proposals corresponds to a different pattern.

The pattern of decision modification characterized by little social conflict dissent is generally a process of lowering the level of abstraction of the language phrasing the decision proposal. That is, each successive reintroduction of a substitute proposal is slightly more concrete than the previous one. The example of the corporate management training group corresponds to this essential pattern. Another example of this pattern of lowered abstraction appears in the interaction of a group of nursing experts planning a workshop-conference for educators in public health nursing.

Early in the nursing group's weeklong deliberations, the members discussed the present status of public health nurses and observed that public health nurses felt they were downgraded by the remainder of the nursing profession. The group then felt that the public health nurses attending the conference would be defensive and would resist new proposals. Later a member initiated a substitute proposal to begin the conference with "a nonthreatening something." After being discussed and dropped, the substitute proposal was reintroduced proposing "getting the conference feeling good and then change them." A later substitute proposal suggested that they begin the conference "on common ground." Eventually the proposal was reintroduced in the form which achieved consensus—"Begin the conference with a history of the contributions which public health has made to the field of nursing."

Each reformulated decision proposal follows from the previous one, and none elicited much dissent from the members. Furthermore, each succeeding decision proposal is more concrete or specific than the previous one. Thus, without social conflict group members modify decision proposals in an evolutionary and methodical process of lowering the level of abstraction of each proposal. This pattern might be illustrated in the following methodical sequence:

Statement of the problem—"Public health nurses feel their lack of status and will therefore be defensive and resistant to change."
Criteria for the solution—"Begin the conference with a nonthreatening something." "Get the conference feeling good and then change them."

Abstract statement of solution—"Start the conference on common ground."

Concrete statement of solution—"Begin the conference with a history of the contributions which public health has made to the field of nursing."

In the absence of social conflict or significant dissent, the lowering-of-abstraction pattern of decision modification seems to be painless, systematic, and eminently reasonable. But not all emergent decisions follow such a methodical route to consensus.

The presence of social conflict and dissent stimulates a different pattern of decision modification in which members introduce successive decision proposals at essentially the same level of abstraction. The same nursing group proceeded through the following reformulations of another initial proposal. The final reformulation achieved group consensus and was prerequisite to several other decisions to include specific programs in the conference:

1 "The public health nurse is engaged in treatment of pathology."
2 "Public health nurses should have more clinical work with patients."
3 "Public health nurses do perform tasks that require clinical nursing skills."
4 "Clinical skills are required for working with patients in the home as well as in the hospital."
5 "Public health nursing is a clinical nursing specialty."

This second pattern also reflects the characteristic start-and-stop cumulative development of a consensus decision. But unlike the lowering-of-abstraction pattern associated with minimal conflict and dissent, this pattern reflects substitute decision proposals which are virtually restatements of each other. Each proposal is essentially the equivalent level of abstraction of every other.

The lowering-of-abstraction pattern is methodical in that members express little disagreement on the credibility of each decision proposal. In the absence of social conflict group members apparently perceive their task as one of seeking or "discovery"—in this case, discovering what to include in the conference which would solve their problem and meet their established criteria.

The second pattern including social conflict seems to reflect a different task for the members. To some members of the nursing group, public health nursing was a form of community social work or civil service in a government sponsored clinic. To others, public health nursing was a clinical nursing specialty equivalent to, for example, psychiatric nursing. The issue produced disagreement and significant social tension among group members. Rather than perceiving a task of discovery, the task in the presence of significant social conflict is perceived to be "persuasion" or attitude change in order to secure intragroup agreement. While creativity is required to perform a task of discovery, persuasion is required to secure agreement.

Social conflict, then, does not affect the basic start-and-stop process of decision modification but apparently does result in a distinctive pattern of that decision modification. With little substantive conflict, members methodically reintroduce substitute proposals in a pattern which consistently lowers the level of abstraction of that proposal. With little interpersonal conflict, members perceive their task to be one of seeking or discovery. When a decision proposal precipitates social conflict among members, that proposal is typically reintroduced at essentially the same level of abstraction in successive equivalent restatements of the root proposal. In the presence of dissent, the group members perceive their task to be one of persuasion in order to secure agreement among all group members.

Jumping from proposal to proposal with little or no transition and without exhausting the discussion of a given decision proposal is characteristic of the process of group decision making. And the level of interpersonal conflict, along with the members' perception of the nature of their group task, influences the extent to which the process of decision modification is systematic in lowering the level of abstraction of the language in which the proposals are phrased.

SUMMARY

Decision making includes problem solving, which requires high acceptance of solution. Decision making also includes other types of decision making not clearly classified as problem solving. A decision is a choice among alternative proposals, the sum of which constitutes all or part of the group's task performance. Consensus signifies the commitment of members and their willingness to implement decisions reached by the group.

Prescriptive views of the group decision-making process attempt to illustrate how groups should make decisions and assume rationality of group members, an ideal process of decision making, and improved quality of group decisions. Doubt is cast on the credibility of those assumptions. The most commonly used perscriptive method of group decision making is Dewey's "reflective thinking" model.

Descriptive models of the group decision-making process attempt to illustrate how groups *do* solve problems and assume the presence of a natural or normal development of consensus decisions. Descriptive models differ on the basis of the perspective of the observer and the tools used to observe the group process. The most commonly used descriptive model is the three-phase model from Bales's IPA. Other descriptive models using different observational techniques reveal significant similarities with the three-phase model, but few models employ the perspective of group interaction patterns.

Unlike linear models of group decision making, a spiral process assumes a pattern of anchored group positions of agreement and reach-testing forward to develop new ideas. In this way group members refine, accept, reject, modify, and combine ideas progressively and cumulatively until the idea reflects the group consensus. The spiral process, normal to the group process, accounts for the apparent inefficiency of group decision making as well as the influence of the social dimension in achieving higher quality decisions.

The process of group decision making is compared with the process of leadership and role emergence so that decisions are not so much made by a group as they emerge from group interaction. This emergence of decisions is illustrated in the four-phase model of Orientation, Conflict, Emergence, and Reinforcement, each phase characterized by a distinctively different interaction pattern.

Group decisions achieve consensus in a spasmodic and cumulative modification of decision proposals in which proposals are introduced, discussed, dropped, and reintroduced in slightly modified form until the proposal appears in a form which achieves group consensus. Although this start-and-stop process of decision modification is typical of all introduced decision proposals, the presence of social conflict affects the pattern of reintroduced decision proposals and the members' perception of their group task. In every case, the spasmodic process of decision modification reflects the normal interaction patterns of group members and influences both the group's task and socioemotional dimensions.

Chapter 8

Communication
in the Small Group

Communication is probably the most talked about and least understood of all social phenomena. It is a term used freely in day-to-day conversations. It is the "solution" for virtually any social problem and nearly all international crises. It is the subject of literally hundreds of thousands of scholarly articles and books. No one can deny the immense popularity or importance of human communication.

Such a universal human endeavor as communication should not be so perplexing. But in truth, few people, scholars and laymen alike, agree on even the definition of the phenomenon. Estimates of the number of significantly different definitions or interpretations of communication range from sixteen to twenty-five, although the actual number may far exceed even the most liberal estimate. Many authorities, such as Dance (1970) and Martin and Andersen (1968), have expressed considerable concern over the confusion surrounding the various definitions.

But we should not totally despair over our apparent inability to agree on common boundaries, a common theory, or a common interpretation of communication. The very perplexity of the phenomenon makes it even more exciting. The feeling that he is exploring a new field, breaking new ground, spurs on the student of communication. The fact that so little is really known about communication is not as disappointing as it is intriguing.

The influence of communication in any social system is undeniably potent. Indeed, the basis for the system's entire organization and functioning is communication. If individual people are the bricks of a social system, then communication is the mortar. And mortar transforms numerous individual bricks into a unitary wall. Thus, communication transforms a collection of individuals into a group. Regardless how anyone approaches the study of group decision making, he must inevitably consider communication as a major portion of his study. For the purposes of this book, communication is *the* basis for our approach to studying group decision making.

THE NATURE OF COMMUNICATION

Our primary purpose, of course, is to analyze and describe decision making as it occurs in the context of a small group. And the perspective selected to accomplish this purpose is communication and the group process. While the purpose does not require a comprehensive treatise on human communication, some of its basic principles are essential to illustrate the underpinnings of this particular viewpoint of the group process. A few of those principles of communication have been discussed in earlier chapters. They will be summarized here along with additional clarification of how this book visualizes communication. The definitional confusion over the term demands the following brief discussion of the basic nature of human communication.

An earlier discussion described communication as inherent constraints placed upon the range of the communicator's choices. This basic principle should be intuitively obvious. Whenever two people communicate, each communicator inescapably accepts constraints on his own behavioral acts immediately upon entering into the communicative situation. Even the fundamental use of language is based upon constrained behaviors. English, as well as every other language, automatically imposes constraints embodied within that language on anyone who uses it. When we speak, we submit to the syntactical structure and semantic inferences inherent in the linguistic symbols of the language we use. Hence, the very symbols we use in the communicative act are in themselves constraints placed upon our behaviors.

As the act of communication progresses, each communicator behaves through speech and movement. And each subsequent behavior is constrained by the behaviors he and the other communicators performed earlier in the sequence of their communicative acts. Even the act of overtly attempting not to communicate is a behavior which constrains future behavior within the structure of the behavioral sequence.

For example, you may be standing in a line to pay fees, purchase some commodity, buy groceries, or whatever, and find yourself an unwilling member of a communicative situation. A total stranger may initiate conversation with you as you wait in line. If you ignore his attempts to engage you in conversation because you want to avoid communicating altogether, you still communicate with him through your behavior of silence. What you do later in the act of communication is unavoidably affected by your earlier act of silence. The other person may have typed you as rude and boorish, and your future communicative relationship with him will bear the impact of his initial impression. Perhaps you feel that he is overly aggressive by intruding on your passivity. Your future communicative relationship with him will also be affected by your initial impression of him. Whatever behavior is performed during the exchange of communicative behaviors, the pattern of behaviors constrains the pattern of future communicative behaviors. Whether you like it or not, a communicative system inevitably begins its process of development. Chapter 2 discussed this sequential pattern of behaviors as the functioning of a social system.

Communication, then, inherently involves the communicators in a patterned sequence of behaviors in which the behaviors of each communicator constrain and are constrained by the pattern of his own and the other's behaviors. This phenomenon of behavioral constraints may be called a process of reciprocal mutual influence of communicating individuals—in other words, interdependent behaviors among communicators. All people who engage in an act of communication, whether that act is a formal group meeting of coworkers or an informal conversation among acquaintances, are to some extent interdependent. And most importantly, they cannot avoid being interdependent. That is, the behaviors of communicating individuals inevitably develop some interdependent, sequential pattern during the act of communication.

If the social system inherent in a communicative act is allowed sufficient time to develop "groupness," the interdependence of those behaviors is more pronounced or in a more refined stage of development. Since communication inherently includes interdependent behaviors, any distinction between "communication" and "interaction" is either trivial or nonexistent. Therefore, the two terms are used interchangeably throughout this book.

Some authorities distinguish clearly between communication and interaction by restricting communication to the mere transmission and receiving of messages along some channel or medium. Elementary school children often study a unit called "communication," which typically involves the study of telephones, television, radio, telegrams, letter-writing, and so forth. The definitive characteristic of this view of communication is transmitting messages—moving an object through space from one point to another. The types of communication, then, become the different channels or media of transmission. Interpersonal communication becomes nothing more than a telephone hookup between people in which a source originates a message and sends it along some predetermined channel to a receiver. According to this highly restricted view, communication is only a channel linkage between people who transmit and receive messages to (or at) each other.

A channel linkage is essential for an act of communication to take place of course. A cannot communicate with B unless he is aware of B's presence and has some channel access with him. But the channel linkage is not the act of communication; it is simply a prerequisite condition for a communicative act to occur. Without a channel linkage an act of communication cannot occur. With a channel linkage an act of communication may or may not occur.

Viewing communication as merely transmitting and receiving messages can in no way account for effective or ineffective communication. Communicative effectiveness is wholly dependent upon the degree of behavioral interdependence developed by communicating individuals. Without considering interdependent behaviors, communicative effectiveness is a sterile and meaningless concept.

What, then, is a message? Certainly it is more than some object transmitted and received across space like electronic signals on a telephone line. And transmitting and receiving messages can be only a trivial portion of a communicative act. Messages are certainly behaviors performed by communicating individuals. As we have defined behavior, a message must be external to the individual and observable by other communicating individuals. An isolated message is also a sterile and meaningless concept related to communicative acts. But in the context of other messages—that is, in the pattern of behavioral sequences of communicating individuals over a period of time—the sequence of messages illustrates the interdependent relationship among communicators exhibited by their acts of communication. Communication is the process of developing and maintaining that interdependent relationship through behaviors.

Central to the foregoing discussion is viewing communication as a process. Communication as merely the transceiving of messages across space denies the *process* of communication and considers only the structure or spatial aspect of the communicative situation. Since a process embodies aspects of both space and time—structure and action—the spatial or structural view of communication is not so much false as it is incomplete. Therefore, the structural attributes of communication include only a portion of the entire communicative process. While the section of this chapter which considers communication only structurally may be misleading if viewed as the total act of communication, there are some structural ingredients of communication which reveal more vividly some aspects of the entire group process.

The major section of this chapter discusses the process attributes of group communication—the arrangement of communicative behaviors in both time and space. That section will discuss the sequence of behaviors in recurrent patterns, how those patterns change over time, and the eventual outcomes of the group's sequential patterns. In short, the process attributes of communication attempt to describe how and what people actually do in those sequential patterns of communicative behavior which reflect the social interaction during group decision making.

STRUCTURAL ATTRIBUTES

Thousands of studies viewing group communication as transmitting and receiving messages across space have appeared in scholarly journals over the past several decades. The following discussion does not attempt a comprehensive survey of those studies. Rather, specific areas of communicative structure have been selected since they are most helpful in furthering our understanding of the group process. Some structural aspects of communication have been omitted because they were considered of little importance to understanding the process of group decision making.

Networks

The most common structural approach to communication is the pattern of channel linkages among individual members of a group. Such patterns consider a group in terms of who can transmit and receive messages to and from each other while disregarding the content of the messages, how they are transmitted or received, and the sequence of the messages. Patterns of channel linkages are commonly known as communication networks.

In many groups the communication network exists prior to the formation of the group. Generally some outgroup authority establishes the network to be used by the newly formulated group. Groups within large organizations, for example, employ legitimate and formal networks established by legitimate authorities within that organization. Although informal networks may arise during the process of interaction among organizational members, the organization recognizes the formal network as the optimum network for that group's task performances. One often refers to the formal legitimate network of communication within an organization as "going through channels"—that is, utilizing those channel linkages formally recognized as the primary communication network of the organization. Going through channels, however, does not always include face-to-face confrontations with every communicating member of the formal network.

The LGD contains no formally established network indicating which members can or cannot communicate with each other. Nevertheless, as the process of group interaction continues, members use some linkages very frequently and others quite sparingly. Thus a network emerges during group interaction and reflects the developing social structure of that group. Figure 10 illustrates four common networks which may structure five-member groups. The all-channel network is really not a network at all. Since a network emerges during group interaction, the all-channel network implying relatively equal usage of every possible interpersonal channel linkage is the status of the communicative structure before a network has clearly emerged from the interaction.

Distinguishing between networks typically involves using concepts of "centrality" and "distance." The communicative distance from one member's position in the network to another is the sum of the communicative links required for a message to be sent and received along the shortest possible route. In a five-member group the maximum distance is four as illustrated by the distance between A and E in the chain network. The minimum distance, of course, is one—for example, the distance between A and E in the circle network.

The relative centrality of any member's position is the sum of distances between that position and all other positions in the network. The most central position in any network is the position with the lowest number representing relative centrality. For example, C's position in the wheel network needs only four communicative links to be able to communicate with every member in the group, while each of the other positions requires seven links to accomplish the same purpose. Therefore, C is the most central position in the wheel network. Figure 10 includes the relative centrality figure for each position in each of the four networks.

Many studies comparing communication networks have revealed

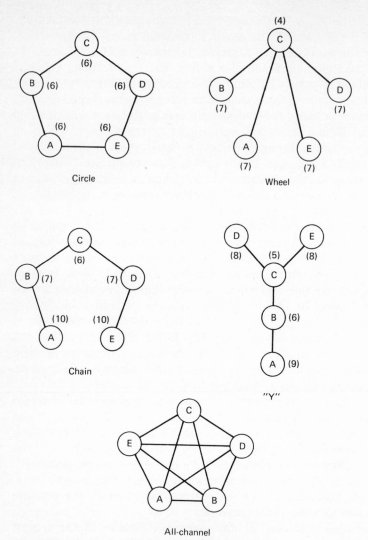

Figure 10   Common networks in five-member groups.

numerous differences between various networks using a variety of points of comparison. For example, in terms of speed and efficiency, centralized networks such as the wheel and the chain are superior to decentralized networks such as the circle (the least centralized). But this discovery is tempered by a further comparison in terms of accuracy of problem solving. For solving simple problems, centralized networks are much more accurate, but the decentralized networks are more accurate for solving complex problems.

Regarding the morale of group members, the members of decentralized networks experience greater satisfaction with their group experiences than do members of groups employing a centralized network. In short, centralized networks are considered superior networks in accomplishing tasks, at least simple tasks, although decentralized networks foster more cohesive groups and appear to have an advantage in performing more complex tasks.

Results from past comparisons of communication networks, however, may not be particularly significant to LGD decision making. In the first place, nearly all such comparisons have been performed in research laboratories under rigidly controlled conditions. The laboratory context itself is no reason to dismiss comparison results as insignificant. But one of the typical laboratory controls has unfortunately been the severe restriction of time allowed for group interaction. A few studies which allowed more time for group interaction, such as that performed by Cohen, Bennis, and Wolkon (1961), revealed that the differences between groups using different network patterns diminished significantly over time. (Network research has also typically restricted other aspects of communication such as sending only written messages without face-to-face confrontation. But the restriction of time may be a more significant restriction of the group process.)

A group needs time to develop any satisfactory organization. As soon as the group members accustom themselves to the network they are using, the particular pattern or network they employ should be of little consequence. The success of centralized networks in the task dimension of the group process should increase the cohesiveness of group members over time. Time is absolutely essential for the natural interdependence of the two dimensions of group process to assert itself. And, too, the social success of decentralized networks should also allow members to strive harder in the task dimension and thereby increase their speed and efficiency of task performance. Whatever the reason, the differences among networks as to speed, efficiency, accuracy, organizational stability, and group morale appear to diminish to the point of insignificance over time.

The importance of time has been emphasized earlier but is still worthy of mention. When a group does not have sufficient time to establish their social organization, the members begin to compensate. Under severe time restrictions, members compensate by short-circuiting the group process. One shortcut method used by groups in the absence of a clear social organization is to substitute the simple majority vote for the consensual process to validate decisions (Hall and Watson, 1970). Group members functioning under severe time pressure simply don't have sufficient time to proceed through all the steps of decision modification in order to achieve consensus on their decisions. Therefore, they resort to shortcuts to decision making such as simple majority votes. The inevitable result, of course, is false or superficial consensus. Members allegedly perform their tasks and make their decisions, but they do not commit themselves to carrying them out. Decisions may be "made" but they have not achieved consensus.

The purely structural view of communication networks does contribute to the understanding of group process in some respects. Centrality is a concept which has been consistently related to leadership and status. The most central position in an emergent network is most apt to be the position occupied by the emergent leader. The various levels of centrality generally reflect the status levels of the group's hierarchy.

Figure 10 illustrates two status levels (levels of centrality) in the wheel network. The relative centrality of C is four, and the relative centrality of all other positions is seven. Three status levels are reflected in the chain network. C is the apparent leader with a relative centrality of six, B and D are the second status level with relative centralities of seven, and A and E are the third status level with centrality figures of ten. The "Y" network illustrates four status levels, a rather uncommon status hierarchy to emerge in a five-member group. Only the circle network has a single status level and illustrates another extremely improbable network to emerge in a decision-making group.

The network which finally emerges from extensive group interaction is not the only network employed by the group during the process of their decision making. A group may employ one network at one stage of the process and shift to a different network later on as their group enters a new phase of the process. In this respect, centrality does not necessarily reflect leadership or even high status during the intermediate stages of the group process.

The verbally active "problem member," for example, may at some point during interaction be the recipient of influence from every other member verbally attempting to modify his problem behavior. During this period of group interaction the network would probably reflect the deviate in position C in the wheel network—a highly central position. This network reflecting a problem member in a central position is undoubtedly temporary. If the problem member or extreme deviate does not modify his behavior, other group members will eventually ignore him as a contributing group member and literally exclude him from their interaction. Such action virtually expels the extreme deviate from the network and from effective group membership. Centrality, then, is linked to leadership and status in the network which finally emerges from group interaction. But network centrality during intermediate stages in the process of group decision making may also indicate an extreme deviate under group pressure to conform.

Another stage of network development involves the coalitions or subgroups formed during various phases in the group decisional process. The network used at that time generally reflects the existence of coalitions. To illustrate, the "Y" network might reflect the presence of two coalitions, one composed of three members (C, D, and E) and the other composed of two members (A and B). We might hypothesize further that the three-two coalitions have formed around two leader contenders. The two most central positions, B and C, would then reflect the two contenders representing each of the two coalitions.

Discussing network structures of group communication would not be complete without mentioning the limited number of networks included in the discussion above. Obviously there are more possible network combinations than the four (omitting the all-channel network) included in Figure 10. But other combinations are simply variations of these basic models. For example, the wheel and chain networks can be combined by adding to the wheel network two additional channel linkages between A and B and between D and E. The same network can be formed from the chain network by adding channel links between A and C and between A and E. This wheel-chain network is then a network variation formed by combining channel linkages included in two of the basic network models.

Further variations should be obvious. The important point is that emergent network structures can be observed in a small group and that these structures provide insight into various aspects of the group process of decision making.

A final point to remember concerning network structures involves the nature of a process. Interaction patterns change through time as the group moves from one phase to another in the decisional process. Network structures also change. Structural change should reflect processual changes so that the developing network structure can be viewed as an emergent process changing over time and culminating in the final emergent network characterizing the group's status hierarchy. Thus, action (time) attributes are added to the otherwise purely structural (space) attributes of the network.

Those discoveries based upon comparing the different purely structural attributes of the various networks can probably be dismissed as rather trivial and irrelevant to developing a richer understanding of the process of group decision making.

Channel Capacity

A field of study known as "information theory" also approaches communication from a structural perspective. While highly specialized and restrictive as a comprehensive view of human communication, information theory has provided some fresh insights into the process of human communication. One of those insights is "channel capacity" and, simply speaking, refers to the maximum number of information items a human can effectively handle.

According to one authority on information theory, George A. Miller (1956), the number of information items which an individual can identify and deal with effectively is incredibly small. Miller indicates the maximum limit (or channel capacity) is probably seven, plus or minus two. While information theorists vary slightly in their estimates of a human's channel capacity, from fewer than seven to more, all agree that man's capacity to process information is highly limited and generally very small.

Information theory has also discovered that the human individual can increase his channel capacity significantly by combining items of information into larger classes of items. That is, you can combine several items of information into a larger class of items and identify that class as a single unit. For example, rather than process items, "747," "Chevrolet," "Pontiac," "DC9," "Ford," you can combine the five individual items into two representative classes—"automobiles" and "airplanes." Thus, you increase your channel capacity by treating groups of items as individual items.

In the jargon of information theory, a single item of information is known as a "bit." A class of information items formed by combining several "bits" has been labeled (Don't laugh!) a "chunk." The point is that an individual can learn with experience to increase his channel capacity by reclassifying and grouping unitary items of information.

If a single individual can increase his channel capacity with experience, it seems logical that a group of individuals should be able to increase their channel capacity, also. Lanzetta and Roby (1957) discovered the existence of that very phenomenon. Over a period of time a group learns to increase the amount of information it can effectively handle. Apparently during the process of group interaction members develop the ability to process an increasingly larger number of information items. According to the precepts of information theory, the group members effectively increase their channel capacity through a normal process of grouping and classifying different information items into "chunks," thereby remaining within their channel capacity but effectively handling a greater quantity of information "bits."

The group process of decision modification illustrates an apparent increase in channel capacity integral to the group process. Group members introduce numerous decision proposals, many of which are continually reintroduced for further discussion. Rather than modifying those proposals directly and increasing geometrically the number of information items group members would have to identify, the members reformulate old proposals when they are reintroduced. If group members modified each proposal through direct amendment, they would be required to deal with each original proposal and each amendment separately. A reformulated proposal, however, is a single item which ·replaces the former proposal and does not increase the number of information items to discuss. Moreover, a reformulated proposal may combine several earlier proposals into a single proposal which actually reduces the number of information items discussed by group members. The group process of decision modification, then, allows the group members to increase the amount of information they can effectively identify and discuss during group interaction.

Some evidence has indicated that the quality of group decisions increases in proportion to the number of ideas members generate during group interaction. This may be true, but there is certainly a point of diminishing returns as the number of contributed ideas approaches the limits of the group's channel capacity. The group's limitations on the amount of information it can identify may explain why some research studies indicate no significant increase in the quality of final group decisions when members did generate more ideas. The structural attribute of channel capacity is, like network structures, also related to the process (both structure and action) of group decision making.

Social Structure

The social structure of roles and status levels also affects communication among members of the small group. Group members communicate with each other in different patterns and networks dependent to some extent on the status levels of their group's social structure.

Collins and Guetzkow (1964, pp. 170–177) have adequately documented that the social structure in a group does affect the structural aspects of its communication. Leaders and other high-status individuals, for example, are high participators during group interaction, both as initiators and as respondents of messages. Low-status members communicate a disproportionate amount of their time with high-status members, thus affirming that network centrality is linked with leadership and status. The usual explanation for this structural phenomenon indicates the individual's desire to aspire to higher status. When the individual finds that he cannot rise to high status through his own achievements, he substitutes for actual status a vicarious membership in a higher status by communicating upward in the status hierarchy.

During the process of leader and status emergence, however, the structural patterns of communication change over time. During early stages of the emergent process, contenders appear to communicate most often with their lieutenants and not with each other. Such a communicative structure is consistent with the assumption that coalitions form around leader contenders. The communication network also reflects those coalitions. After a group completes its process of leader emergence, however, the leader tends to initiate and receive messages to and from all group members and assume a central position in the network.

Certainly the status of the group member affects the messages he initiates and receives. *Who* says it is as important to perceiving the relative importance of the message as *what* is said. Status endows a message with value. In the study of persuasion and attitude change the "ethos" or credibility of the communicator appears to be a significant factor in how people attend and react to persuasive messages. Thus, the communication structure in a small group affects and is affected by the social structure of the group members. Communication structure and social structure exert a mutual and reciprocal influence on each other and may therefore be considered interdependent.

Barriers and Breakdowns—A Fallacy

Too often instances of ineffective communication are dismissed as the result of communication barriers or breakdowns. This mechanistic rationalization of communicative failures has enjoyed widespread popularity in everyday usage and even in group communication research (Black, 1955). It is not necessary to dwell on this common misconception of the communicative process. Smith (1970), among others, has already illustrated the fallacy in the reasoning allegedly justifying the existence of barriers and breakdowns in communication.

Briefly a communication barrier or breakdown is a purely structural attribute of communication assuming that messages travel through space from one person (a source) to another person (a receiver). Thus, communication is not so much a process as a linear flow of messages across space. A "barrier" is a "dam" which blocks the flow of messages so that the receiver cannot receive an initiated message. A "breakdown" assumes that the connecting link between communicating individuals ceases to exist—in the same sense as a broken telephone line. In any case, barriers and breakdowns consider a linear flow of messages across space as the central feature of communication.

The basic analogy of communication barriers and breakdowns is the machine in which a barrier (for example, a clogged fuel line) or a breakdown (for example, a broken fuel line) could certainly be said to exist. If human communication were so mechanistic, it would certainly be much less complex than it is. Fortunately human beings and their social systems do not correspond accurately to the mechanistic analogy.

The assumption of linearity is contrary to the principle of interdependence. Communicators don't send and receive isolated messages; they engage in a process—the development and maintenance of an interpersonal relationship. And that relationship is defined by the recurrent, sequential patterns of messages in the context of the entire interaction. Communication as an interaction process denies the possibility of its being partially blocked or breaking down. Can an interpersonal relationship be blocked or break down? In group communication that interpersonal relationship is groupness, inextricably interdependent with the process of group communication. As long as any vestige of groupness exists, communication continues to exist. A barrier or breakdown assumes an absence of communication, but it ignores the more important problem of ineffective communication.

Furthermore, earlier discussions have demonstrated the normalcy of social conflict and deviance. If the linear flow of messages is central to group communication, social conflict and deviance must by definition be inherently disruptive. That is, conflict would lead to closed channels and communication barriers or breakdowns. That social conflict disrupts the free flow of messages is blatantly false for much if not most social conflict and deviance.

Occasionally members of an unsuccessful group do believe that social conflict is harmful and disruptive. Because of their belief the members overtly avoid conflict until their tension level and suppressed hostility become so extreme that communication barriers and breakdowns do seem to exist. Such a group illustrates a classic example of the self-fulfilling prophecy in action. If group members believe that conflict is disruptive and harmful, they tend to behave as if it were and eventually succeed in actually disrupting effective group communication and harming the group process.

Too many common misconceptions about communication and the group process prevail in our society. One step in improving the effectiveness of communication is for all members to discard their misconceptions about groups and about communication. Truly, understanding communication and the group process includes not misunderstanding it.

PROCESS ATTRIBUTES

Several structural attributes of group communication have proved fruitful in understanding more about the group process. In most cases, though, the structural perspective serves to reinforce principles gained from other perspectives. Most importantly, initially perceiving communication as a process allows for the discovery of new principles of group communication not otherwise available. The following section attempts to do just that—to seek new understanding, as well as to reaffirm other knowledge.

Feedback Sequences

Chapter 7 included a brief discussion of feedback as a mechanism developed within a social system enabling the system to regulate its own behavior and functions. To summarize briefly, feedback is a sequence of events in a cyclical pattern so that each event stimulates each subsequent event in the sequence in a chain-reaction effect. Eventually that chain reaction exerts influence on the original event in the cycle.

There are two types of feedback loops—positive and negative. Negative feedback is a mutually causal sequence which counteracts or neutralizes some initial deviation from the steady state. Positive feedback sequences amplify the initial deviation and stimulate further deviation.

In the context of communication and the group process, feedback may be considered a double interact, that is, a sequence of three contiguous acts. Scheidel and Crowell (1966) also defined a feedback sequence in small group interaction as a double interact. A says something to B. B responds with his own message, which in turn is followed predictably by A's subsequent comment. The key to this definition of feedback is the word "predictably." Every double interact in group interaction certainly does not serve the function of feedback—to regulate the system. But those double interacts which groups use so frequently that one can predict the next comment in the sequence identify the feedback sequences which serve to regulate the system of group interaction. Thus, the double interact sequences which recur during group interaction with predictable frequency are the feedback sequences of the system.

Knowing how group members interact in each of the four phases of decision emergence should allow for the identification of those feedback loops which characterize group decision making in each phase of decision making. As a group begins interaction during its initial Orientation phase, the group members have developed no predetermined attitudes toward the topic. In other words, they have not had time to develop their ideas and do not know the direction that their interaction will take. Any departure from this initial position of neutrality must be considered a deviation.

During the Orientation phase, no feedback loops exerting any significant effect have been established. Members remain unsure of their direction and do not deviate significantly from this position. Therefore, there is no real need for feedback, and no loops are developed in the interaction patterns.

During the Conflict phase two attitudinal positions deviating in opposite directions from the members' initial uncertainty are discernible in the interaction patterns. One coalition of members deviates in the direction which favors decision proposals which have been introduced. The second deviating coalition disfavors those same decision proposals. The second phase is labeled the Conflict phase because the interaction during this phase reflects the diametrically opposed ideational positions of those two coalitions. And the interaction patterns reveal both positive and negative feedback loops. Members within each coalition interact with each other and reinforce each other's ideas providing positive feedback for each other. And interaction between members of the two opposing coalitions reflects negative reinforcement in the form of negative feedback sequences.

Within the coalition of members favoring the decision proposals, the interaction patterns reflect positive feedback sequences amplifying deviation in the direction of favoring those proposals. For example, one member expresses a favorable attitude toward a decision proposal, and a second member agrees. His expression of agreement is followed by another comment favoring the proposal followed by still another favorable comment.

Members of the coalition opposed to the decision proposals also interact with each other. Their interaction patterns reflect positive feedback sequences amplifying their deviation against accepting the proposals. One member initiates a comment unfavorable to the decision proposal followed by a comment agreeing with that unfavorable opinion which, in turn, is followed by another unfavorable comment. Thus the two lines of deviation—favoring and disfavoring those decision proposals which eventually achieve group consensus—are amplified through positive feedback loops within the interaction patterns among members of each ideational coalition.

The interaction between coalitions reflects negative feedback sequences during the Conflict phase. One member initiates a comment favoring the decision proposal. Another member expresses an opinion unfavorable to the proposal followed by another comment favoring the proposal and another comment disfavoring the proposal, and so forth. The two directions of deviation cannot counteract each other during this phase, which is another way of saying that the negative feedback loops during the Conflict phase are not stronger than the positive feedback loops. And positive feedback loops appear to be of nearly equal strength in amplifying each of the two opposed lines of deviation.

During the Conflict phase of group decision making, the group is relatively unstable. The interaction patterns demonstrate that the system cannot effectively manage deviation. And deviation in opposite directions does not reflect stability of the system. The group-system apparently functions out of control. But this lack of systemic control is temporary since it occurs only during this second phase of decision emergence.

As the group moves to the Emergence phase of decision making, the members strengthen their positive feedback sequences, amplifying the deviation favoring those decision proposals which will eventually achieve consensus. The coalition disfavoring those decision proposals dissipates and returns to their initial state of no deviation. That is, members of the coalition opposed to the decision proposals no longer express unfavorable opinions but, as in Orientation, contribute ambiguous comments which express neither favorable nor unfavorable opinions toward the decision proposals. The negative feedback loops between members of the two coalitions are revised to counteract only the deviation away from the direction of the consensus decisions. Thus, negative feedback sequences during the Emergence phase substitute ambiguous comments (similar to the members' initial position of uncertainty) for the comments expressing an unfavorable opinion toward the proposals.

At this point in the group decision-making process, only one direction of deviation remains—deviation in the direction favoring those proposals which eventually achieve group consensus. The only negative feedback loop appearing to counteract that deviation includes ambiguous statements within those double interacts. At this point in the process of group interaction, the direction of group consensus becomes progressively clear to group members.

Two kinds of statements tend toward closure of an interaction sequence—silent responses and oblique or ambiguous statements. This truism can be illustrated by that same hypothetical example of standing in line among strangers. If one of your fellow line-standers attempts to initiate interaction with you, you may choose to extinguish further interaction with either of two kinds of communicative responses. By remaining silent, you force the other person into a negative feedback sequence. He is a deviate in that he initiated the interaction, thus deviating from the original state—simple awareness of each other's presence.

You may also choose to respond with an ambiguous or oblique statement. For example, in response to a ritualistic query of your identity and state of your health, you may reply, "I'm just standing here minding my own business." Another ambiguous reply to the ritualistic, "Nice weather we're having, isn't it?" could be, "Is it? I hadn't noticed." In either case, the ambiguous comment, like the silent response, is a denial of willingness to communicate and generally leads to closure of that interaction sequence. Thus, the ambiguous statements in the negative feedback loops during the Emergence phase mark those interaction sequences for extinction.

In the Reinforcement phase the negative feedback loops including ambiguous comments have virtually disappeared. The positive feedback loops amplifying the favorable opinions regarding decision proposals increase in strength to maximum. Those positive feedback loops continue to amplify favorable opinions toward the consensus decisions throughout the final phase, which prompts the phase to be called the Reinforcement phase. Continued positive feedback during the final phase heightens the commitment of group members by consistently and repeatedly amplifying their deviation which favors those decision proposals.

In summary, opinions favoring decision proposals are amplified with steadily increasing strength throughout the group interaction patterns. These positive feedback loops become progressively stronger as the group moves through the Conflict, Emergence, and Reinforcement phases. Opinions which were unfavorable toward the decision proposals are amplified through positive feedback sequences only during the Conflict phase. During this second phase of group decision making the group is temporarily unstable and out of control. The group regains stability during the Emergence phase as the unfavorable opinions succumb to negative feedback loops. Group stability increases to a maximum during the Reinforcement phase as the positive feedback loops amplifying favorable opinions become the group norm and the group's final product.

In this manner groups utilize positive feedback in their interaction sequences to regulate their progress toward consensus decisions. Because of the nature of deviation and positive feedback, group progress inherently includes a temporary period in which the group-system is unstable and briefly out of control. But during the Reinforcement phase progress toward consensus is no longer a deviation but integral to the group's functioning and behavior as a system. The group then returns to a steady state as the group members establish consensus.

Decision Proposals

Groups involved in the process of decision making focus their efforts on discussing ideas proposed by group members. These ideas comprise the subject matter of group interaction and serve as the basis for those decisions which achieve group consensus. Because each idea initiated during group discussion is potentially a decision which will achieve consensus, each contributed idea is called a decision proposal. During the process of group interaction, the members introduce and reintroduce these proposals in the pattern of decision modification discussed in Chapter 7.

Fisher's (1970a) study of decision emergence identified a total of 163 different decision proposals introduced during the interaction of the ten groups included in the study. Comparing these proposals with the decisions which ultimately achieved consensus in each group, Fisher found that not all decision proposals introduced are consistent with or even relevant to the consensus decisions. The bulk of the decision proposals, 121 of 163, were proposals instrumental to those consensus decisions, but 30 decision proposals were anti-instrumental to consensus in that accepting them would have denied the consensus decisions. Therefore, group members rejected anti-instrumental decisions as a necessary step toward achieving consensus. The remaining twelve proposals were irrelevant to consensus decisions, and members dedicated only a minute portion of their interaction to discussing them. And members rarely reintroduced irrelevant proposals during subsequent group interaction and never reformulated them in a pattern of decision modification.

It is intuitively obvious that group members initiate most decision proposals in the early stages of group interaction. If crucial social conflict over proposals occurs in the second phase, the members must have developed their opinions based on ideas which were first introduced before or during the Conflict phase. Fisher's study of decision emergences confirms that group members initially introduce the bulk of decision proposals during the Orientation and Conflict phases—100 or 77.6 percent of the total. Hence, they have discussed most decision proposals before the Emergence phase during which consensus decisions are actually reached. Members initiated twenty-six or 20.2 percent of their proposals in the Emergence phase, nearly all of which were reformulations of earlier proposals. Apparently, then, the process of modifying decisions through reformulations and combinations of decision proposals continues during the third phase.

The bulk of the decision-making performance of groups most

certainly does not occur in the final stage of group interaction as some descriptive models have suggested. In fact, most proposed decisions are introduced and discussed in the first two phases of group interaction. Although the process of decision modification apparently continues through the Emergence phase with additional reformulations of proposals previously introduced, the final phase of group interaction (the Reinforcement phase) includes little if any actual task performance. Consensus decisions are reached during the Emergence phase and achieve consensus in the form of heightened members' commitment during the Reinforcement phase.

Processing of Information

At this point we already know a great deal about how group members handle information during their group interaction. The interaction sequences which identify each of the four phases of decision emergence describe what members do with information at their disposal. The earlier section on feedback sequences and initiation-reformulation of decision proposals also describes group interaction in terms of how members process those facts and opinions introduced into the group discussion. The discussion of process attributes of group communication would be incomplete, however, if it did not include a few additional principles concerning how members of a social system handle information—specifically information directly associated with making decisions.

In the first place, according to Grunig (1969), members of decision-making groups tend to seek new and additional information in order to assist their efforts in performing decision-making tasks. That members seek information, however, does not imply that they utilize that information in the most rational and efficient manner. In fact, Pruitt (1961) and Lucas and Jaffee (1969) found that decision-making groups often, perhaps typically, do not use new information very rationally.

One might realistically assume that all items of information available to the group are not consistent with each other. Accepting one item of information necessarily involves rejecting other information items which disagree. Nearly every jury must decide which witness to believe when the plaintiff's and defendant's witnesses contradict each other's testimony. For example, one defense psychiatrist might testify that the defendant did not realize the difference between right and wrong and was legally insane. A psychiatrist called by the plaintiff might testify that the defendant was legally sane. The jury must then exercise its judgment as to which item of information, that is, which witness's testimony, is most acceptable or credible.

The process of group interaction during group decision making includes many such judgments. Often group members make those judgments on nonrational bases. A common basis for judgment compares the new information with the previously established position of the group. If the item of information is in conflict with the group's already established position, the members tend to reject the new information out of hand. At such times the members consider the information irrelevant or of inferior quality, whether it is or not. Thus, group members sometimes treat information nonrationally. Occasionally they will be irrational and reject obviously relevant information on the grounds that it is irrelevant. In either case, members reject the information first. They then search for a basis for rejecting it, after the fact, to rationalize the judgment they have already made.

The nonrational approach to information processing in group decision making emphasizes the importance of timing. The point in time at which an information item is introduced is sometimes more important than the quality of the information itself. Certainly if the information is introduced after the group has already established an ideational position, the quality of that information will have little impact on the process of group decision making.

It is vitally important that members submit information important to a comprehensive discussion of the proposals relatively early in the group interaction. Information takes on its greatest significance in the Conflict phase during which members cannot so easily dismiss it on nonrational bases. During the Conflict phase members utilize the information to support their own positions or to review critically the positions of others in opposition to their own. In the Conflict phase the critical testing of ideas is at a maximum level and requires a generous amount of information. After this period of social conflict and idea testing, new information tends to lose its impact (Holder and Ehling, 1967).

SUMMARY

Communication commands the respect and popularity of laymen and social scientists alike. Nevertheless, the present level of understanding communicative phenomena is deplorably low. Communication is viewed as a pattern of behaviors in which the acts of each communicator constrain and are constrained by the pattern of his own and other's behaviors. All people who engage in communication develop to some degree an interdependent relationship embodying both structural and action attributes of a process. This interdependent relationship is the process of communication.

Viewed structurally, group communication has been perceived as a network—the pattern of channels linking members of the group. Networks are distinguished by relative centrality and distance between network positions. The most central position has been linked with leaders and with deviates under extreme social pressure to conform. During the process of group decision making, several networks generally emerge from the interactive patterns reflecting coalition formation and leader emergence at various stages in the group process.

Channel capacity, the structural restraints limiting the amount of information which can be processed effectively, illustrates a potential reason underlying the group process of decision modification. Social structure also influences the structural characteristics of group communication. But barriers and breakdowns of communication are considered as untenable concepts inconsistent with communication as a process.

Process attributes of communication include feedback sequences of double interacts which illustrate how and why decisions emerge during group interaction. The positive and negative feedback loops indicate the progress of a group from its early orientation period to its achieving consensus among members on final decisions. Other process attributes include the pattern of initiating and reformulating decision proposals and processing information regarding them. The process of group decision making occurs throughout the four phases of decision emergence with the bulk of the actual task performance occurring in the early and middle stages of group interaction.

Chapter 9

Effectiveness of Group Communication

Even a brief survey of the other chapters will reveal that the present chapter is by no means the longest in the book. But the brevity of the present chapter should not be construed as an indication of the simplicity of increasing the effectiveness of group communication. In fact, quite the opposite is true. The average person spends probably more time communicating than any other human activity. One would normally think that if practice makes perfect, the years of communicative experience would make any adult human a highly effective communicator. Would that that were true! To the contrary, people probably perform no human activity more ineffectively than simply communicating with each other.

Developing effective communication within a group is no mean chore. There are no sure-fire principles of effective communication, no magical formulas for maximizing cohesiveness or productivity. There are no models to follow, no lists of things to do and things not to do in order to be an effective group member. All such lists of prescriptive "good advice" do little more than give the participant the impression that he is doing a good job without actually increasing his effectiveness or that of the group. If the truth were admitted, this entire book serves the purpose of this chapter. Knowledge and understanding of communication and the group process do more to increase one's communicative effectiveness than all the prescriptive advice now available.

Improving the effectiveness of group communication is not achieved through direct methods but indirectly through increased understanding. Personal health provides a figurative comparison of the principle of indirect methods for increasing communicative effectiveness. Health is essentially a process of living normally from day to day. Certainly health should not be defined as taking medicines when you get sick. If you know and understand the biological processes of the body, you will be guided as to what activities to perform, what foods to eat, what clothing to wear, what situations to avoid, and so forth. Such activity becomes part of your normal routine of living and is more effective than attempting to abide by some prescriptive advice allegedly leading to eternal health.

In the same way, knowledge and understanding of communication and the group process provide a frame of reference which guides the effective member's activity as a group member. He analyzes what behaviors are appropriate to maximize group effectiveness and adjusts his behavior accordingly. In short, the healthy person is not the one who devours patent medicines and pops daily vitamin pills in order to achieve health. But he is effective nonetheless. The effective group member knows there are no shortcuts to effective communication other than serving a lengthy apprenticeship of learning and experience.

SOME COMMON MISCONCEPTIONS

Dozens of textbooks and pulp paperbacks expound the "ten easy steps" to just about everything, including effective communication. There are numerous "cures" suggested for ailing groups and tried-and-true "vitamin supplements" to achieve successful communication. Many of these lists of principles or "dos and don'ts" are reasonable and often quite true. But such lists are typically so general as to defy any practical application in any specific group situation. Even well-meaning lists are quite unsatisfactory.

Many lists of principles, however, are patently deceptive and based on gross misconceptions about communication and the group process. It is unfair to talk about both kinds of "good advice" as being similar, but the results accrued from using either type of list to guide one's communicative behavior range from none to insignificant. Consequently all such lists are rejected as unsatisfactory. A full understanding of communication and the group process, however, requires knowledge and avoiding misconceptions. Hence, the following discussion includes a few of the popular but nonetheless misleading misconceptions about group communication.

Rationality

One popular approach used in the training of participants for effective group communication has included the principles of argumentation. Many textbooks of this type include sections on the various types of reasoning and procedures for testing the validity of arguments. Chapters illustrate the various kinds of evidence used to support assertions, such as statistics, examples, analogies, testimony, including the various tests of quality and quantity of evidence. Such training is, of course, highly valuable and may be helpful indirectly to the prospective member of a decision-making group. Certainly training in argumentation serves to develop one's ability to think critically, and critical thinking ability is an asset to idea testing—an integral part of the group's decisional process. But courses in mathematical logic also develop critical thinking abilities. Such training is simply not central to group decision making and detracts from the primary purpose of understanding communication and the group process.

The basis for most prescriptive advice for discussants, including training in principles of argumentation, is the pervasive assumption of rationality. And that assumption rests on two faulty premises. The first premise asserts that that which is rational is best. On the face of it, such an assertion seems eminently reasonable. But the assertion is not necessarily true. If we believed that the best decision making proceeds on purely rational grounds, juries would not exist. Defendants would be tried before only a judge who is trained in the law and in the doctrine of rationality. But extenuating circumstances often surround an alleged crime and require the presence of juries and nonrational means of decision making. We often speak respectfully of the "spirit" as well as the "letter" of the law.

If rationality were always the most desirable basis for making decisions, no religion or code of ethics or any moral value would be desirable. Such principles or values exist only through nonrational belief—a belief based not on reason but on faith. The philosophy of logical positivism assumed the supremacy of rationality and proved highly unsatisfactory for most people. After all, there isn't any rational basis for the confusion of people with the same names such as Jim Smith. It would be more rational for each member of our society to be known by only an identifying and unduplicated number. (When you stop to think about it, we seem to be getting closer to that point all the time!) Democracies and representative forms of government would be replaced with benevolent despots. We would no longer have "hunches," and progress would virtually cease if rationality were considered the sole basis for decision making. Certainly this first premise cannot be long sustained.

A second premise assumes that humans normally behave rationally. That is, reason typically guides human actions. Such an assumption is patently absurd. Instances of highly normal but nonrational behavior are just too numerous to include but a very few. Take the case of the necktie. There is no contemporary reason for wearing a necktie, but men do it nevertheless. Women's skirts and nylon hosiery are equally unreasonable. The desire to conform to social norms of personal appearance is certainly nonrational. Today we shudder at the unreasonable personal-appearance norms of past cultures. We are appalled at the former Chinese custom of binding young girls' feet so that they would remain small in adulthood—so small the women could not even walk by themselves. We consider as totally unreasonable the customs of some "primitive" tribes to elongate earlobes and pierce noses to conform to their norms of personal beauty. Some future generation will probably laugh at our contemporary neckties, eye makeup, false eyelashes, long hair, and bouffant hairdos. And who can consider war, riots, hatred, poverty, pollution, prejudice, and vandalism rational? Certainly much, if not most, human behavior is not rational. Sometimes it appears even irrational.

Chapter 8 indicated that even the process of information processing during group decision making is nonrational at times. Members of small groups, like members of all social systems, do not always behave in conformity to the laws or principles of reason. This does not imply that humans necessarily behave in conflict with laws of rationality, but it does imply that one does not always have sound reasons for his behaviors. When a person behaves on the basis of faith, he is not necessarily *ir*rational, but he is inherently *non*rational.

Proponents of rationality often admit that human behavior is not always rational, but it should be. After all, they say, what harm can training in argumentation do to prospective group participants? The answer is deceptively simple. Training in argumentation obviously benefits the individual. The ability to think critically is potentially valuable for any individual. The greater problem is the assumption of rationality underlying such training as requisite to effective group participation.

If rationality imposes demands on the group beyond the capabilities of its individual members, the members become frustrated, tensions rise uncontrollably, and the natural group process is disrupted. Relying too heavily on rationality disregards the socioemotional dimension of the group process while exalting the task dimension and thereby denies the inherent interdependence of the two dimensions. Such an assumption also assumes the existence of a "best" decision—that is, the most "rational" one.

Perhaps most importantly, empirical evidence indicates that the natural group process tends to persist even in the presence of such assumptions. Groups whose members have been trained in the methods of argumentation typically behave normally, that is, nonrationally, anyway.

Agendas and Forms of Analysis

Some readers of this book will be disappointed not to find a model agenda which systematically guides the group members to consensus decisions. The agenda is generally used as a "road map" to follow in order to improve efficiency and quality of group decision making. The typical model agenda is an adaptation or a variation of Dewey's reflective thinking model for problem solving.

In addition to the objections raised concerning the assumption of rationality and the corresponding deemphasis of the socioemotional dimension of group development, relying on agendas or models to guide group interaction is unsatisfactory for other reasons. The desire to improve efficiency of group decision making may be misplaced. We should probably admit that groups are inefficient as decision-making mechanisms, but the reasons for that apparent inefficiency are precisely the same reasons why group decisions are of higher quality compared to decisions made by individuals when the decision-making task is adapted to group decision making. Social testing of ideas and reinforcing group decisions make group decision making slow. But the result of group slowness is more effective implementation of group decisions.

Probably the greatest reason to dismiss the use of agendas as a misconception of the group process is that they just don't work. Carl Larson (1969) found that groups instructed in some forms of analysis developed group products which were superior in some respects to those of uninstructed groups. However, the groups Larson observed were allowed to interact over a very brief period of time, highly insufficient to develop much "groupness." This severe restriction of time quite obviously short-circuited the natural group process and required the members to utilize shortcut methods to arrive at decisions within the specified time. (Shortcuts to decision making in response to time pressure were discussed in Chapter 8.)

Maier and Thurber (1969), on the other hand, discovered that when members are allowed sufficient time to establish groups, "forces" within the group effectively counteracted the influence of outgroup sources, which would include the use of an agenda. Thus, when the natural group process is allowed to run its full course, the influence of an agenda or prescribed form of analysis is minimal and superseded by the information-processing norms developed within the group.

Interestingly enough, Larson compared several different forms of analysis and found that Dewey's reflective thinking model did not significantly affect the group product. On the other hand, Sharp and Milliken (1964) found that groups whose members had been trained to think reflectively did achieve superior outcomes. The results of using this particular model, then, appear to be ambivalent. Whether Dewey's model has a significant impact on group decisions remains questionable. But both of these studies observed only groups who were not allowed sufficient time to establish themselves as a group. The influence of the natural group process would probably counteract the influence of any outgroup agenda, regardless of its particular form.

Other more general comparisons of groups, such as Lanzetta and Roby (1960), have demonstrated that prior prescriptive training of one type or another does not exert a significant impact on group effectiveness. But Hall and Williams (1970) compared groups whose members differed on the extent of their understanding of the group process and the general functioning of group decision making. Those groups whose members possessed knowledge of group dynamics were observed to be most effective. Members' understanding and experience in communication and the group process may be an indirect method of improving group effectiveness, but it does seem to work. The more direct method of using model agendas or prescribed forms of analysis to keep group members "on the track" cannot make that same claim.

SUGGESTED GENERAL PRINCIPLES

The cardinal principle underlying effective group communication involves experience. There is no substitute for the experience of being an active participant in the process of group decision making. The more experiences and the greater variety of group experiences will lead inevitably to more effective group participation. Understanding the process is a vital prerequisite to effective participation in group decision making, but the experience of participating is equally essential. Reading books on how to play chess will not make you an expert chess player. Neither does reading a book on group communication make you an effective group participant.

The adage of "practice makes perfect" should be amended to include practice based on understanding. A group member who is naïve about the nature of communication and the group process is able to increase his effectiveness as a participant only up to a certain point regardless of how many group experiences he may have had or will have. Understanding communication and the group process heightens the value of the experience of being a group member. Conversely, group experience heightens one's understanding of communication and the group process. Each mutually and reciprocally influences the other in the classic relationship of interdependence. The principles which follow are admittedly general but are intended to illustrate that interdependence instead of providing a convenient list of things to do and things to avoid doing.

Active Verbal Participation

It should be intuitively obvious that effective group decision making is highly correlated with the active verbal participation of the members. In other words, the effective participant actively participates verbally during group interaction. Typical of much past small group research, authorities have empirically discovered the obvious (Bass, 1949; Bass et al., 1953). They have "discovered" that members who do not communicate are not effective communicators!

Earlier discussions of group cohesiveness indicated that active participation is not essential for members to experience satisfaction with their group; only the freedom to participate is' necessary for group satisfaction. But if group decision making is to be more effective, nearly all members must actively participate in the interaction process. And the interaction process inherently involves verbal and oral participation.

The silent member does little to benefit the process of group decision making. Moreover, contributing only infrequently to the group's interaction does not significantly benefit the individual member. A benchwarmer on a football team does not contribute much to the team's success nor to the development of his own abilities. Spectating is not playing. One learns to play the game by playing it. While the bench warmer may have little choice in whether he gets to play, the group member is silent solely of his own volition.

Active verbal participation does not imply equal participation of all members. Obviously equal participation is not only abnormal and impossible, it is also not even desirable. The contributions of some members are more valuable than those of others. The more capable members should participate more. Abilities and expertise vary among the members. Each member should seek during group interaction to participate actively but not necessarily equally with every other member.

This first principle also does not imply that any member should attempt to monopolize the discussion or control the group interaction. You will recall from the model of leader emergence that excessive verbalization results in the elimination of leader contenders during the second stage of leader emergence. Active participation implies frequent contributions but not necessarily lengthy ones. The knowledgeable and verbally active member contributes brief comments but does so without inhibition. The first general principle for increasing one's communicative effectiveness in group decision making may seem overly obvious but is nonetheless essential. The effective communicator has something to say, and he says it.

Communicative Skill

There exists an old and hackneyed controversy among authorities in rhetoric and public address. The controversy dates back to ancient Greece, centuries before Christ, and is occasionally heard even today. It concerns the relative importance of "content" and "delivery" in the effectiveness of communication. Which is more important for effective communication—what is said or how it is said? Most authorities today consider the controversy irrelevant and trivial. Increased knowledge concerning the process of communication has revealed that the content-versus-delivery controversy is naïve and highly incomplete. Not only is the content of a message inseparable from its delivery, but the communicative process includes additional and highly significant elements which the controversy ignores.

First of all, the value of an expressed idea is determined in part by the manner in which it is presented. A skillful presentation affects the perceived importance of the message. Only the most naïve student of human communication would argue that an idea has intrinsic worth apart from its use in the communicative situation and its expression within the sequence of communicative acts. The evidence that communicative skill does affect the message content is virtually indisputable. For example, one of the dimensions of leader behavior in group decision making discovered by Russell (1970) was communicative skill.

Specific characteristics of communicative skill are rather unclear. Certainly the skillful communicator is fluent, articulate, and above all dynamic in the conversational situation. Communicative skill also involves a knowledge and understanding of the communication process and the ability to be flexible, adapting to the demands of the social system and the situation. Without such knowledge and adaptive ability, the communicator is not perceived to be so fluent and articulate as much as he is perceived to be merely glib. The stereotyped used-car salesman, for example, is considered glib and smooth, but these are negative characteristics, while skill is generally considered a positive attribute.

Learning communicative skills is not at all similar to learning the skill of hitting a baseball or playing a trumpet. These kinds of motor skills are based on mastering techniques and performing those techniques as an individual. Communication, however, never occurs in isolation but always in a social system with the interconnected communicative behaviors of other persons. And there are no magical or even nonmagical techniques of communicative skill, no list of principles to memorize. The ability to analyze the other person and the situation and to be perceived as articulate and dynamic requires a thorough knowledge of the communicative process and a great deal of hard work. Certainly experience and practice in many and varied communicative situations are essential for developing communicative skills. And that experience always occurs in the presence of other people—the complex social system.

Sensitivity to Group Process

Because of the nature of a process, the importance of timing cannot be emphasized too much. Increasing one's communicative effectiveness is more than knowing what behaviors to perform or even how to perform them well. The most important principle of effective communication in group decision making is knowing when to communicate what.

Being sensitive to the group process enables the group member to judge fairly accurately in which phase the group is interacting. Sensitivity to the process allows the member to perceive roles and decisions as they emerge probably before other members of the group are aware and undoubtedly before the emergence process is completed. If the group member also possesses a modicum of communicative skills, he is capable of adjusting his communicative behavior so that he behaves appropriately in each specific phase in the process of group decision making.

Sensitivity to the group process also allows the member to pinpoint the causes of social problems and devise strategies to solve those problems. When a group is in trouble and is not functioning effectively as a group, the members generally recognize the existence of some problem. But knowing that the group is in trouble and knowing what to do about it are two separate elements. The knowledgeable and sensitive group member becomes something of a consultant—an expert in the group process. He is able to discern the cause of his group's difficulties which might, for example, be a problem member. His sensitivity to group process does not lead him to reject the member. Rather, he seeks to discover the cause of the problem member's dissatisfaction with the group and to do something to alleviate that dissatisfaction.

Even sensitivity and expert knowledge do not, however, enable any member to manipulate other group members at will. Sensitivity to the group process will not necessarily allow the member to be the group leader. To the contrary, the process-sensitive member is not interested necessarily in becoming leader, but he is interested in encouraging the group process to function smoothly. He may or may not be leader, but he always behaves in the best interests of the group and their performance of their decision-making task. As such, he will probably be a leader contender and certainly a high-status member. But there are no known techniques, principles, abilities, or behaviors which give anyone license to manipulate members of an LGD.

Commitment to the Group

Quite clearly the effective communicator in a decision-making group is a member who is deeply committed to the group and its task. In fact, active verbal participation is highly correlated with commitment. That is, committed members tend to assume a very active verbal role in the group interaction. And in true interdependent fashion, very active participants generally possess a deep level of group commitment. If you feel strongly about something, you want to talk about it. Conversely, if you talk about something actively, you come to feel strongly about it.

One point must be emphasized. Effective communication in the group and low commitment of members are totally incompatible. If you feel you are not committed to your group, you are a liability in the process of group decision making. You have but one recourse in such an untenable situation. If you are unable to perceive value in your group membership or in the group task, then quit! You will undoubtedly think you are better off without the group, but don't be deceived. The group is infinitely better off without you! Without experiencing commitment to the group and the task, you cannot be an effective group member. Without your commitment as a member, the effectiveness of the group is severely curtailed.

Attitude toward Group Slowness

The member who understands the group process does not despair over the apparent inefficiency of the group's efforts. Particularly in the early stages of group interaction, the group mechanism seems excruciatingly slow. It is only normal to be somewhat frustrated and anxious. The inexperienced member will be distressed and eager to "get the show on the road." The effective member may be frustrated, but he is not overly anxious. He exercises patience and observes the process getting underway.

There is a sound rationale for not being overly eager for the group to increase its efficiency. What appears to be inefficiency at a snail's pace actually reflects one of the advantages of the group process of decision making. While the group sputters and spurts in pursuit of consensus, members are allowed time to develop new ideas and reformulate earlier proposals. Too often time is at a premium, particularly if a group operates under pressure of a time deadline. Nevertheless, the importance of "mulling time" must not be underestimated. It is a crucial step in creative and high-quality decision making. And it is an integral part of the group-decision making process.

The apparent inefficiency of the group process is also advantageous for the management of social tension in the group. Demanding greater efficiency of the group through placing tight controls on departures from the topic and requiring prolonged discussion of specific proposals probably creates more severe social problems which naturally affect the group's task efforts. The interaction process allows members some opportunities for venting their tensions and reducing the rate of their tension buildup through features inherent in the process—abrupt changes of topics and brief spurts of intensive interaction, particularly during the Conflict phase.

The process of modifying decision proposals through spurts of energized interaction and reformulating proposals is apparently inherent in the process of decision making in every social system. Thus the group process inherently includes devices to manage tension—devices which are effective in the long run, even though they appear to the shortsighted and naïve member to be symptoms of gross inefficiency. The effective member is patient because he knows the process works.

Confronting Problems

Occasionally groups demonstrate inefficiency in their decision making which is not normal. The sensitive member who understands communication and group functioning is able to distinguish between inefficiency which is normal and inefficiency which stems from avoiding social problems. Sometimes group members spend the bulk of their interaction time on topics and proposals which are superficial to the real issues the group should be facing in order to accomplish their decision-making task. Groups are often warned about a "hidden agenda," problems which inhibit group process but are not openly discussed during group interaction. A hidden agenda may involve conflict over identity of group goals or conflict over superficial issues during which members avoid revealing the true bases for their expressed differences of opinion. Whatever the nature of the specific hidden agenda, the result is the same—failure to solve problems restricting group progress by avoiding discussion of them.

No problem can be solved by avoiding it. When the problem is sufficiently potent that it affects the effective functioning of the group, it must be recognized and openly considered. The sensitive group member increases the effectiveness of group communication by recognizing those problems and bringing them into an open and frank discussion. Tom's group, discussed in Chapter 4, illustrates dramatically the effective results of confronting problems in this manner. Directly considering problems through interaction strips away personal facades and releases suppressed frustrations of members. The ensuing interaction is often quite painful for the group members and raises the group's social tension to intolerable levels. But this uncomfortable condition is usually temporary. More importantly, it is essential for effective group functioning.

The best advice for group members is to confront social problems as soon as they are recognized. If the group is to survive as an effective mechanism for decision making, the members must confront their own problems by themselves and solve them for themselves. No one but the group members is able to assist them. Often just talking about problems by discussing them thoroughly in overt interaction is sufficient. Once recognized for what they are, problems turn out to be less significant than they seemed in their suppressed state. In any case, the group develops into a much more effective system after confronting their problems, whether their confrontation is successful or unsuccessful.

Several earlier chapters have suggested that compromise as a technique to further group decision making is generally unsatisfactory. This point demands some clarification. Compromise is often a highly effective solution to resolve differences among group members, particularly when interpersonal differences are absolutely irreconcilable and when all members are highly committed to their group membership. Too often, however, group members turn to compromise solutions before they have thoroughly discussed the issues and problems leading to interpersonal differences. Compromise becomes, then, a normal technique for resolving differences among group members, regardless of the variations among groups and particular instances of interpersonal differences.

When the compromise reflects a middle ground whose mutual

acceptance by all parties is an honest acceptance, the compromise is an excellent solution for the resolution of conflict. Too often, though, the compromise solution demands that each side "give in" until the compromise is reached—the average between two extreme positions. Mutual appeasement satisfies no one and more often reflects the group's continuing to avoid the real problem by not "fighting it out." A good rule of thumb regarding the use of compromise is to consider it only as a last resort—certainly not until after the group has thoroughly discussed the original problem in its entirety.

Formula Answers

The talented Steve Allen once remarked that you can use just one simple sentence in virtually any conversation and gain typically excellent results. That sentence is, "Well, you know the old saying!" This comment is universal and explains everything while contributing nothing. Allen emphasizes the point that a cliché or adage of conventional wisdom is available for any and every issue. Strangely enough, the cliché often commands immediate and universal acceptance even though for every cliché there is usually another which contradicts it. If you believe that "Two heads are better than one," do you also believe that "Too many cooks spoil the broth?" "Absence makes the heart grow fonder," but then, "Out of sight, out of mind." While it is certainly true that "Haste makes waste," everyone knows that "A stitch in time saves nine." Tidbits of conventional wisdom are more often perceived to be true rather than actually being true in the sense that they reflect reality.

Some group decisions are similar to clichés in that they oversimplify at the expense of realism. Groups discussing problems confronting the society, such as poverty, crime, or discrimination, often agree that such problems are caused by the ingrained attitudes of the society's members. The group members then decide that changing the attitudes of society with a program of education will eradicate the cause and solve the problem. The solution is true, of course, but it is unmistakably naïve, simplistic, and totally unrealistic. How will education change society's attitudes? Who will administer this educational program? How will they do it? Are they able to do it? Is such a program possible? How long will it take? What about the influence of peer groups and opinion leaders in the society?

In short, the formula answer does not really solve anything. It only gives the appearance of having solved it. I am reminded of my former high school football coach just before we played the conference championship team. When asked how we were going to beat them, he replied simply and without the slightest trace of a smile, "Score more points!" That answer solves the problem of how to win the game, all right. But its formula was not adequately detailed to be put into effect. (We lost the game, too.)

Groups formed in a classroom situation and discussing a policy problem have a penchant for devising formula answers. But classroom groups engaging in policy discussions are not typical of most decision-making groups in this respect. Classroom groups discussing such remote problems do little more than participate in intellectual exercises. After all, no classroom group has the power to legalize abortion or marijuana or abolish censorship laws or affect the national economy. They engage in interaction as a classroom exercise and often discuss problems remote from their own capabilities as a realistic group. The real-life group, however, cannot afford shortcuts to realistic wisdom. Groups in the "real world" generally have the responsibility for implementing the decisions they make. They can then observe the success or failure of their consensus decisions in actual practice. Nor does their job end with the conclusion of an academic term. The formula answer is potentially a much more prevalent problem for the classroom group than for most decision-making groups in the society.

Creativity

Although there is obviously a point of diminishing returns, the greater the volume of ideas and decision proposals which members contribute during group interaction the higher the quality of consensus decisions. Chapter 5 discussed how leaders initiate a large number of themes during group interaction. Each of these discoveries illustrates that one ingredient of communicative effectiveness is creativity. As a participant in group decision making, then, you would be well advised to increase your creativity. Let the mind go. Give imagination a free rein. No relevant idea should be considered too wild or far-fetched. The best advice for developing creativity is not to stifle the formation of ideas.

Certainly groups do not accept all ideas which members contribute during group interaction. In fact, the more ideas that members contribute, the more ideas the group will reject. Indeed, the period of idea testing during group interaction, particularly during the Conflict phase, involves the rejection of many decision proposals. But this is the period during which members should be encouraged to contribute new ideas, too.

The member who does not fully comprehend the nature of group process will probably consider the group's rejection of his ideas, an extension of his self, a rejection of his own value as a group member.

Consequently he tends to inhibit his creative impulse, which leads to his contributing fewer ideas. Brainstorming techniques, recognizing this human tendency, do not allow brainstorming members to respond critically to any contributed idea despite its apparent irrelevance. The effective group member, on the other hand, knows in advance that the other group members will reject many of his ideas, but that knowledge does not inhibit his creativity. He continues to introduce new and different proposals for group consideration. He probably suffers psychologically from the group's rejection of his ideas, too, but his creativity does not suffer as a result.

Actually the slowness of the group process and the inherent start-and-stop process of modifying decisions encourage creativity from group members. Each member has the time and the opportunity to mull over his own ideas and the ideas of others and exercise his own potential for developing new insights. Experts in creativity consider the incubation period essential to the creative process.

The process of group decision making again suggests the importance of timing. New and different proposals benefit the group efforts most during Orientation and Conflict phases. During these early stages of group interaction, the creativity of members in devising new and different ideas should be at a maximum. During the Emergence phase members should confine their creativity to reformulating and combining previously discussed proposals. Creativity in any form is definitely not an asset but a liability to the group process during the Reinforcement phase of group decision making.

Criticism

A highly normal and understandable human tendency of inexperienced group members is to avoid criticism of and conflict with other members. Normally no one wants to run the risk of hurting another person's feelings. Inexperienced group members tend to avoid criticism for fear of harming the developing feeling of groupness. All of us have been taught from childhood that courtesy and tact are inherently superior to rudeness and boorishness. So we examine an atrocious painting on our neighbor's wall and call it "interesting." We may suffer through a boring party, but we will invariably tell the host and hostess as we leave that we had a great time. Certainly effective group decision making does not require that we rid ourselves of good manners and respect for others during group decision making.

Group decision making in some respects is a unique social situation. What we would consider courtesy and tact in one situation is tantamount to ineffectiveness and avoidance of social problems during group decision making. The fear of hurting the feelings of others and suppressing realistic opinions characterize members of a group with rather low cohesiveness. Criticism and conflict are typical norms of a highly cohesive group. In fact, group decision making may not be so unique after all. For instance, we rarely if ever have arguments with acquaintances, but we argue vehemently and say whatever we feel with our very close friends. Knowing that you can be honest with each other is knowing you are in the company of good friends.

The amount of criticism is irrelevant to the group process but the timing of criticism is again all important. Criticism in the wrong place at the wrong time is as harmful to group process as no criticism at all. Let yourself go in exercising all your critical faculties during the Conflict phase. Otherwise you should probably control your critical impulses and use them sparingly.

Basic to the principle of criticism during group decision making is the avoidance of neutrality. It is absolutely impossible to remain neutral and be an effective participant during group interaction. High-status members are invariably dynamic contributors who take stands and defend them. And other members consider those stands to be helpful to the group's performance of its task. A "mugwump" is destined to be a low contributor and an ineffective group member. Group interaction virtually compels members to speak out on issues and assume an argumentative stance. ("Anatomy of a Decision" in Appendix One illustrates how language choices of individual comments often force members into taking a stand during the Conflict phase of group decision making.) A neutral member is usually perceived to be wishy-washy and is generally peripheral to the action of group decision making.

One vital ingredient of group decision making and one of its principal advantages over individual decision making is the process of testing ideas. Such idea testing among multiple sources of criticism results in higher quality decisions when high social acceptance is a key criterion of decisional quality. This process of socially testing ideas is the principle behind the "free and open marketplace of ideas" in which criticism is absolutely essential. During idea testing the group norm should encourage as much criticism as possible, both in amount and diversity of that criticism. The effective group member is not necessarily tactless, but he is highly critical of others' ideas as well as his own.

Honesty

Underlying several of the principles above is the keystone of honesty. That is, say what you believe, and believe what you say. Candidness is an essential characteristic of group communication. Without being overly dramatic or absolutely devoid of tact, the effective communicator honestly strives to benefit the group's efforts. Certainly honesty is not always the best policy. Earlier discussions have illustrated that courtesy is sometimes best served by harmless distortions of the truth. But some distortions may not be so harmless in the long run. Conscious and consistent submission of your true feelings creates hidden agendas which can only disrupt the effective functioning of the entire group. Again the member's judgment based on a sensitive understanding of the nature of communication and the group process is essential for effective group communication.

One of the superordinate goals of the many types of training groups is the development of intrapersonal and interpersonal honesty. Such groups attempt to strip away individual facades and the inhibitions of personality defense mechanisms in order to achieve the group's goal to develop greater sensitivity to and for other people. The process of group decision making is most effective when that same goal is applied to honest expressions of opinions and attitudes. Idea testing is most effective when it reflects the realistic criticism that comes from true differences of opinion. Thus decision-making groups and training groups are both committed to the principle of honesty. While training groups emphasize revelation of the member's "inner self," decision-making groups seek honesty directed toward those decision proposals under group consideration.

POSTSCRIPT

This chapter has intended to demonstrate the hopelessness of developing cardinal rules or techniques to increase communicative effectiveness among members of decision-making groups. The process viewpoint with its inherent emphases on structure and action demands that effectively communicating members be flexible and adaptable. Timing—perceiving what behavior is most appropriate at a particular point in time during the group process—and the ability to perform the appropriate communicative behaviors demand a thorough understanding of how communication and the group process function.

Experience of group membership and understanding of the group process are inseparable dimensions of effective group communication. The general principles of communicative effectiveness included in this chapter are derived from one's experience and understanding rather than leading to them. You can't learn to swim without first getting wet. But neither does floundering in the water teach you how to swim effectively. The flailing movements motivated by a desire for survival may keep you afloat, but they are no substitute for effective swimming. Similarly, anyone can be a member of a small group and actually participate in a decision-making task, but that experience does not make anyone an effective contributor to the group discussion. Only a working understanding of communication and the group process, coupled with the experience of group membership, enables the member to be effective. Thus the entire book actually serves the intended purpose of this chapter.

SUMMARY

Increasing the effectiveness of group communication is possible only through the indirect method of improved performance guided by knowledge, understanding, and experience of communication and the group process. Some lists of principles prove disappointing because they rely on misconceptions of communication and the group process. Such common misconceptions include an assumption of rationality and a linear decision-making process embodied in prescribed agendas and forms of analysis.

Several general principles which may guide but do not guarantee effective communicative behavior in group decision making require that you: (1) be verbally active, (2) develop communicative skills, (3) be sensitive to the group process, (4) commit yourself to the group, (5) avoid despair over apparent slowness, (6) confront social problems, (7) avoid formula answers, (8) be critical, (9) be creative, and (10) be honest. All principles assume and are based on the interdependent relationship between understanding communication and group process and experiencing group membership.

Chapter 10

Epilogue: Some Final Considerations

It is a sad but inescapable fact that every book on any subject is inevitably incomplete. This book is certainly no exception. Literally thousands of relevant research studies and viewpoints have been excluded from these pages. The problem of omission is compounded further because the present book embraces two extremely broad fields—human communication and small groups. Neither field by itself has received comprehensive treatment in the previous chapters.

Earlier chapters have emphasized the importance of choosing a perspective and its pervasive influence in one's observation and subsequent understanding. The perspective of this book, communication and group process, has severely restricted the range of material which can be considered relevant to the study of group decision making. Furthermore, the emphasis on decision making restricts that perspective even further by excluding some groups whose purposes are not oriented toward performing decision-making tasks.

This book, like many others, is committed to a rather narrow focus and does not attempt to cover the waterfront of group communication. This final chapter attempts to illuminate that focus and thereby explain, at least in part, the process of selecting and omitting otherwise relevant materials and including others. The chapter also includes some apparently random observations which are intended to round out the understanding of communication and the group process. The result is a potpourri of ideas and concepts which provide the rationale for understanding and applying the perspective of group decision making employed in earlier chapters.

THE "NATURAL" GROUP PROCESS

A major assumption underlying the present perspective of group decision making is that a "natural" process of group development and task performance exists in nearly every group. The process is called "natural" not only because of its pervasive presence but because it continues to exist even though members may be unaware of its existence or its influence.

That members need not be aware of the group process is important to understanding a "natural" process because it embodies a fundamental assumption underlying all sciences—physical, social, or behavioral. The "scientific" approach assumes some order in the universe—that events occur and people behave according to some set of "rules." Whether those rules are known is quite irrelevant to the fact of their existence. For example, physical laws of the universe need not be known as a prerequisite to their existence. The earth revolves around the sun and will continue to do so whether we are aware of it or not. Man existed on this planet for thousands of centuries before becoming aware of even that simple fact of physical science.

It takes time to develop observational tools which will uncover even the most fundamental of scientific laws. Although the study of human behavior is incredibly immature, there is indisputable evidence that humans regulate their behavior to conform to laws not unlike, in principle, the physical laws governing the universe. But because the laws which govern behavior are not as apparent as laws which regulate the motion of a pendulum, for example, many people often find it difficult to believe that such laws do exist. The tools for observing human behavior are as yet simply too rudimentary and too unsophisticated to provide the precision to prove to everyone's satisfaction that natural laws of human behavior do indeed exist.

Although a "natural" process does regulate the behavior of all groups, many variations from that process occur as conditions internal and external to the group vary. Of course, our physical laws also vary in different situations though we don't often think about it. Everyone knows that water boils at 212 degrees Fahrenheit, but the boiling temperature of water varies according to the elevation. Anyone who has ever waited for water to boil on a camp stove in the mountains at 11,000 feet above sea level knows the effect of elevation on this "law" of 212 degrees. Try following the "normal" baking instructions on the package of cake mix if you live in the mountains. Few people will come back for more of that cake.

The "natural" group process described in previous chapters assumes the existence of a "normal" LGD. But many groups are not normal LGDs, and they exhibit variations from the natural group process. If the "natural" process describes a group which develops from a primitive state, the extent to which the group varies from a primitive state at the beginning of its decision-making efforts determines the extent to which their group development varies from the natural process. Each of these variations among groups produces variations in the group process but in no way does a variation deny the existence of the natural process inherent in group decision making.

Legitimacy

Earlier chapters have discussed the impact of legitimacy on the natural group process. The present discussion need not dwell on this fact. In an established social organization the status hierarchy, role system, and leadership—the entire social structure—are often prescribed by the organization itself. Many organizations also prescribe norms and procedures as well. The worker on the assembly line, for example, has a prescribed function to fulfill, and he is not expected to deviate from the organization's prescribed procedures for performing that function. The university student, too, must fulfill prescribed requirements such as a minimum number of credits, minimum GPA, and specific required courses in order to earn a degree. The armed forces also prescribe procedures for performing every function, no matter how trivial, required of a soldier. According to another old cliché, "There is a right way, a wrong way, and the Army way."

The legitimate status hierarchy, norms, roles, and procedures constitute the "formal" structure of a social organization. Obviously these legitimate forms are not subject to deviation or change through the natural group process. On the other hand, neither do they prohibit the natural process from developing a companion social structure. In virtually every social organization a nonlegitimate structure develops over a period of time consistent with the natural process. A status hierarchy, a role network, a set of procedures evolve into the "informal" structure of the organization. The inevitable development of an informal structure persists despite efforts of formalized legitimate authorities to inhibit its growth. But the wise legitimate leader recognizes both structures and attempts to function in both.

The formal structure sanctioned by legitimacy and the non-sanctioned informal structure are not always consistent with each other. Occasionally the informal structure prohibits efficient functioning of the social organization when instructions and procedures designated by formal authorities are not followed. It has long been known that when the formal structure of a social organization clashes with the informal structure, the informal structure often demonstrates greater potency (Coch and French, 1948).

Legitimacy certainly inhibits the development of the natural group process, but it does not prohibit its development. Rather, legitimacy prescribes one structure while the natural process allows the evolution of another structure which may or may not conform to the formal structure. But the formal structure may also thwart the natural process to the point of virtual extinction.

When the formal structure possesses sufficient power to quell any sign of a developing informal structure and when the persons in formal positions of authority choose to use that power, the informal structure has little opportunity for successful development. On a large scale, the totalitarian rulers of the Roman Caesars, Nazi Germany under Hitler, and Stalinist Russia ruthlessly purged even the slightest indication of an informal social structure in conflict with the formal authorities. Herman Melville also illustrated the formidable use of unrestricted power possessed by a ship's captain in *Moby Dick*.

Perhaps the most common example of a legitimate structure thwarting the natural group process in group decision making is that of the status-dominated discussion. When the legitimately sanctioned leader of a decision-making group exerts his power by "pulling rank" on his subordinate fellow members, the "group" consists only of a leader and his "yes men." In such instances the sole function of the group members is to wait for the leader to express his opinion and then agree with it.

The status-dominated group discussion thwarts the natural group process and actually degenerates into an individual making decisions. Group members do not develop ideas through a critical exchange of opinions and information. Members are not free to develop and express their own opinions. The spiral process of decision emergence and decision modification is not present. Consequently the status-dominated group typically develops a false or superficial consensus. Members experience no natural compulsion to work toward successful implementation of the group decision since they had no real voice in actually making those decisions. Hence, status-dominated discussion forfeits a significant advantage and value of group decision making. In fact, the status-dominated group discussion is not group decision making at all but an instance of individual decision making masquerading in the guise of a group effort.

Legitimacy probably results in the greatest variation from the natural group process but rarely prohibits its development. When legitimate structures exert a significant impact on group members, the natural process undoubtedly requires more time to develop. And the extent of power at the disposal of formal authorities and their willingness to use that power restrict the extent and range of the informal structure developed through the natural process. For most social organizations in our society, those persons in positions of legitimate authority generally recognize the informal structures within their organization and their significance in affecting members' behavior. Realizing that informal structures will evolve anyway, they then take advantage of them by attempting to function in an authoritative role in both formal and informal systems.

Types of Groups

The primary concern throughout this book has involved group decision making. The "natural" process has consistently been described in terms of group decision making. But many other groups exist in our society, though not for the purpose of performing decision-making tasks. The question persists as to how relevant the "natural" process of group decision making is to groups whose purposes do not include decision making. As usual, the answer to such a question depends on the type of group being compared with group decision making.

The purpose of a therapy group is certainly different from that of decision making. Even the role structure is markedly different. One of the members, the group therapist, is not even a group member in terms of the purpose served by the group. Members are typically suffering from some form of mental illness and engage in abnormal or antisocial behavior. In fact, a therapy group has no real group purpose at all. The group is only a means, a context, for the cure and treatment of the illness of each individual member. If any group is significantly different from group decision making, it is the therapy group.

Talland (1955), as well as Smith et al. (1962), discovered that the interaction patterns exhibited by members of a therapy group are markedly different from those of group decision making. There is probably little reason to doubt the validity of their conclusions. While a decision-making group attempts to manage its social tension and achieve a steady state of controllable tension (in Bales's terms, to maintain equilibrium), the therapy group strives to achieve an unsteady state. The therapist attempts to "unsettle" the patient and place him in a state of disequilibrium so that his illness is more susceptible to treatment. In other words, the process of group therapy appears to be quite different from the process of group decision making.

Although there are some ingredients of small groups which would characterize both decision-making and therapeutic group purposes, for example, cohesiveness and social conflict, the processes of the two types of groups are undoubtedly significantly different. The most valid conclusion, then, is that the natural process of group decision making probably has little relevance to the process of group therapy.

One would normally think that a family group would have little in common with group decision making. But Pollay (1969) and Tallman (1970) have discovered the process of group decision making useful as an insight into the family group. Certainly the family interacts frequently enough to develop characteristic interaction patterns. And families obviously make numerous decisions as a group—decisions ranging from which color to paint the house to whether to purchase a new automobile to what time the children in the family are required to go to bed.

Research is presently underway to discover those interaction patterns which characterize the family group. Such knowledge, when it is gained, would certainly be a boon to family counselors. At any rate, there is apparently reason to believe that a "natural" process based on patterns of interaction does characterize the family group, although the nature of the process may differ slightly from that of group decision making. But the natural process of group decision making may be more relevant to the family group than some would normally think.

One type of group, the training group, has achieved so much popularity in recent years that it must be mentioned here. Many authorities seem to believe that a training group, whether it is sensitivity training, group encounter, creativity workshop, or another variety of group training, is significantly different in process, purpose, scope, and structure from a task-oriented group with a decision-making purpose. The differences between the two types of groups may be much less significant, however, than many think. Pyke and Neely (1970) indicate the process and results of both kinds of groups are really quite similar. Schein and

Bennis (1965, pp. 102–104) go so far as to advocate that the training group be assigned a realistic decision-making task in order to promote the reality of the group situation.

When the pattern of interaction among training-group members focuses on decision making as Schein and Bennis suggest, there can be little difference between training groups and decision-making groups. Tuckman (1965) has also demonstrated a striking similarity in the process of group development for training groups and for decision-making groups. Although the present volume has not dealt specifically with groups whose goals emphasize the interpersonal growth of members, the natural process of group decision making is apparently highly relevant to the interaction patterns exhibited by training groups.

Although it depends on the type of group, the variation from the natural process observed in group decision making is often insignificant. Except for the therapy group whose process is apparently quite dissimilar, the natural process of group decision making is highly relevant to the interaction patterns of other types of groups with nondecision-making purposes.

Idiosyncratic Group Structures

It is intuitively obvious that the structural characteristics of groups vary widely. Some groups may be composed of all women, all men, or a heterogeneous mixture of men and women. Groups also vary widely in other structural characteristics such as age of members, political beliefs, personality traits, physical attributes, experience, perceptual acuity, and so forth. Thousands of studies have attempted to discover the effect, if any, of different group structures on the functioning of the group process. The results of those studies are as varied as the structures themselves.

The most significant impact of a group's structural characteristics apparently affects the outputs of the group process and not the process itself. That is, different combinations of structural factors often lead to different group decisions. On a common-sense level, one would expect that the decision made by a group of Northern liberals on the merits of school busing to achieve integration would differ significantly from the decision on the same topic made by a group of Southern conservatives. And a group of women liberationists would not view the *Playboy* philosophy in the same way that a group of male chauvinists would. Certainly some differences in selected structural characteristics of groups will affect group productivity both in terms of the nature of the decisions and the decisional quality.

On the other hand, there is little reason to believe that structural characteristics in a particular group exert significant influence on the process of decision making itself. While the level of sophistication and personal biases of individual members and their comments may vary from one group to another, the *pattern* of interaction among group members remains essentially the same regardless of the structure of the particular group.

A few pieces of evidence have indicated that certain structural characteristics such as sex (Gouran, 1969) and personality traits (Bass et al., 1953) of members may affect the functioning of the group process, but the bulk of evidence seems to point to the opposite conclusion. Kent and McGrath (1969), for example, found that compared to task characteristics, structural characteristics of a group exert only an insignificant impact on the group process. And Fisher (1970a) discovered the phases of decision emergence in a variety of groups discussing a variety of decision-making topics. These groups reflected great disparity of group structures including variation in the number of members, their ages, sex, socioeconomic status, expertise, intelligence, educational achievement, and many others too numerous to mention. While differences in structural characteristics among groups may affect the nature and quality of decisions reached by that group—the group outcomes—idiosyncratic group structures apparently exert minimal influence on the natural process of group decision making itself.

THE "GROUP MIND"

The "group mind" has been discussed earlier as a concept that has been largely rejected by contemporary authorities on small groups and is rarely used today. Floyd H. Allport (1927), among many others, long ago laid to rest the belief that a group can feel and think as an entity separate from the feeling and thinking of its individual members. While the controversy over the existence of a group mind is now ancient history, many of the principles embodied in the concept of a group mind are commonly accepted today. [Gordon W. Allport (1968, pp. 43–56) has thoroughly traced the issues of the old controversy and the problems associated with the "group mind" for those readers who are intrigued with the concept and wish to explore it further.]

It is an indisputable fact that the group does possess an identity of its own. The boundaries of group membership are clear. Members and nonmembers can be easily separated and identified with amazing regularity. Members recognize the identity of the group when they refer to it in the first person as a single entity, for example, "our group," or "we."

Obviously no group exists apart from its individual members.

Indeed, the group exists only because members belong to it. The social structure of the group is totally dependent on the interpersonal bonds developed between individual group members, one with another. Only individual people can behave, and the collective patterns of interaction which characterize group process are abstracted from the total sequential behaviors performed by individuals. The group does not exist as any mystical force apart from the existence of its individual members. The group exists as a whole entity directly because of its individual members.

On the other hand, the group as a social system is more than the simple sum of its individual members and their behaviors. Consistent with the principle of "wholeness," to be discussed later, a group is "more than the sum of its parts" and cannot be adequately analyzed simply by listing its individual components, that is, members. In analogical terms, the human body is more than the total value of the elements which comprise it. Years ago the Mills Brothers recorded a song indicating that although the body was only "ninety-eight cents worth of elements," the dollar value of the chemical properties of the body do not assess the true worth of a living human being. With inflation over the years, a human body now is probably closer to a $5.00 value for the elements which compose it, but this value is still meaningless in attempting to account for the value of human life. Simply stated, life is more than the sum of its chemical components. The artist's statue is much more than a simple block of marble. The specific arrangement of the components of the human body or the statue renders it much more valuable than the sum of the components taken separately. The same principle is true of a group—it is more than merely the total of its individual members.

One common perspective views the small group by emphasizing the properties of each individual member. Thus, a group would have no properties of its own but would be defined solely in terms of the properties of its individual members—their beliefs, opinions, expectations, motives, attitudes, perceptions. The communication process perspective employed throughout the preceding chapters employs quite a different viewpoint. Conversely, our perspective views individual members from the viewpoint of the group. In this respect the individual and all the properties of his personality are essentially insignificant. Only that segment of the individual who is the group member is relevant to the group. Who the individual is and what he does outside the group do not concern the group unless these facts affect the natural group process.

The group is an abstraction of the characteristic behaviors performed by those individual human beings who comprise the group membership. The group exists because of the interdependence of its members and the reciprocal influence which members exert on each other through their communicative acts. The group is not the members but the interdependent relationships among members—the arrangement of the components and not the components themselves. A leader is not an individual person. In fact, it is not a phenomenon which even exists outside the group. The leader is a characteristic of a particular group which typically identifies one of its members who has developed, with the other members, a reciprocal relationship of leadership-followership.

A group most certainly exists both because of and in spite of the individual human beings who are its members. The group assumes its identity from its individual members, and the members assume their identities from the existence of the group. To term the identity of the social system a "group mind" is a distortion of the commonly accepted existence of a "group."

GROUP FAILURE

Our earlier discussions of the group process have consistently assumed that the process of group decision making invariably leads to successful task performance. That is, the groups discussed in earlier chapters all successfully performed their decision-making tasks and always achieved consensus on their decisions. But as Bossman (1968) has demonstrated, the value of the group process lies not in making the decisions but in the commitment of the members to work toward effective implementation of decisions once they are made. Therefore, the value of the natural group process is the effective implementation of decisions and not assuring that the group always achieves consensus on decisions. Group decisions do not easily fail when they are implemented.

Some groups do not successfully achieve consensus on their decisions. Some groups conclude their decision-making efforts with superficial or false consensus. But false consensus is not so much a failure of the group to make decisions as a short circuit of the group process. Sometimes, though, groups cannot agree on consensus decisions even superficially. A "hung jury" is not uncommon in our courtrooms. Nor are other nonjudicial groups who meet for hours without ever achieving consensus decisions.

What happens to groups that fail to perform their decision-making tasks? Do they give up? Do they disband? A group that consistently fails to make consensus decisions and that suffers through a prolonged string of failures will probably cease to function as a group eventually. Group members cannot endure indefinitely such consistent and prolonged instances of failure. Even a professional baseball team that loses year after year cannot sustain such consistent failure indefinitely. They change manager, trade for new players, or move to a new city. In short, they disintegrate the group and form a new group with massive structural and environmental changes. A decision-making group cannot so easily change the structure of its group. Consistent and prolonged failures may eventually lead to dissolution of the group. But these instances of group self-destruction are extremely rare.

Groups rarely disintegrate due to consistent failures to reach consensus decisions because groups rarely experience such a consistent lack of success in such frustrating proportions. The typical reaction of group members in the aftermath of group failure is that they persist. Streufert (1969) discovered that groups continue to persist when faced with failure on past decisions. After previous decisions have failed, group members persist in making decisions consistent with those past decisions. When that does not work, they resort to trial-and-error methods for finding new decisions. But a group does not easily give up out of frustration over consistent failures. In fact, a group with a history of past failures rarely even seeks assistance or new information from sources outside the group. They prefer to sink or swim on their own. Thus, in the case of group failure the members continue to function as a group until they succeed.

A primary characteristic of group decision making, then, is stick-to-itiveness. While an individual may experience intolerable frustration rather quickly, a group is able to continue its efforts and even increase its efforts after initial failure. One useful technique employed by groups to achieve success is self-analysis. Smith and Knight (1959) indicate that the group that seeks to analyze its own group process may increase productivity in certain situations. But an understanding of the group process, however, would tell us that self-analysis benefits the group most if their productivity were being hampered due to the members' tendency to avoid some serious social problem. In that case, analyzing the process of their decision-making efforts might reveal that problem and encourage the members to confront their problem in a conscientious attempt to solve it. In instances of groups whose failure is attributable to other reasons, group self-analysis may be enlightening but will not necessarily lead to increased productivity.

What happens in instances of group failure to achieve consensus on decisions? Typically group members persist and often achieve success later. The interdependence of group members apparently provides the process of group decision making with another advantage over decision making performed by an individual acting alone. Groups are more persistent and less susceptible to task failure.

THE THEORETICAL PERSPECTIVE

By now, it is blatantly obvious that we could have employed many perspectives to view small group decision making. Not all perspectives lead to the same conclusions, and no single perspective has achieved anything approaching universal popularity. Stated in other terms, there is presently no unified theory of small groups, nor is there any unified theory of communication. The need for theory is commonly known and has been advocated by many authorities too numerous to mention. Anyone, then, who purports to describe and analyze small group communication must necessarily select that perspective which he finds most useful and advantageous.

Selecting a single unifying theoretical perspective of small group communication necessitates omitting many others. And a great many partial theories and models and descriptions of small groups and communication have been necessarily ignored in previous chapters. For example, the theoretical perspective selected has virtually ignored Kurt Lewin's (1951) field theory of small groups, Robert F. Bales's (1953) equilibrium model, George C. Homans's (1950,1961) external and internal "systems," Peter M. Blau's (1960) social integration model, and Thibaut and Kelley's (1959) social exchange model. While earlier chapters have alluded to certain aspects of some of these perspectives, they have essentially ignored the basic precepts of those perspectives and consistently emphasized another perspective of the process of group decision making.

The theoretical perspective employed throughout this book is taken from general system theory, more specifically, modern system theory. While many fields of endeavor, ranging from biology to computer science, have employed versions of systems theory, the particular systems approach used has been specifically adapted to communication and group decision making. More specific discussions of the theoretical underpinnings of systems theory applied to group communication appear elsewhere (Fisher, 1971; Fisher and Hawes, 1971), but a few basic principles of this theoretical perspective should explain in part the basis for our present discussion of the group decision-making process.

Wholeness

Perhaps the most basic of all systemic principles is that of "wholeness"—that every component of the system affects and is affected by every other component and that a change in one component inherently effects changes in all other components. Every system, including a small group, possesses some degree of wholeness. Analyzing each component part of the system individually destroys the essence of the system. For instance, analyzing the personality traits of each individual is inconsistent with the principle of wholeness which would neglect a comprehensive analysis of individuals in favor of a comprehensive analysis of the group as a single entity.

The principle of nonsummativity—"the whole is greater than the sum of its parts"—is integral to the principle of wholeness. To analyze components individually denies the interdependence of those components. A particular act or message by itself is virtually meaningless. No act or message possesses any intrinsic meaning in isolation. It takes on meaning and significance only in the pattern of acts and interacts in the social system. If it rains today, there is no particular meaning or significance in that event of raining. But if we had earlier planned a picnic in the city park, the rain-event takes on meaning in that system's context. If the farmer's crops have been suffering from a drought, the rain possesses a different significance and meaning in that system's context. The isolated behavior of the individual member is quite unimportant by itself. It is the pattern of behaviors which comprise the system and provide its identity as a systemic whole.

But the sequential pattern does not possess intrinsic meaning or significance, either. That sequence must be "punctuated"—that is, organized—in order to have any meaning. Punctuating the sequence in different ways will lead to different meanings. Every language is punctuated or organized into words, phrases, clauses, sentences, and paragraphs. Changing the punctuation rules changes the meaning.

For example, the phrase "TOTI EMUL ESTO" leads one to wonder about the translation of this unfamiliar but obviously Latin phrase. If the letters were punctuated differently in order to form different words, however, the phrase is transformed into nonsensical English—"TO TIE MULES TO." If Pavlov's dog had been able to speak, he might have said, "See how I have this dumb human trained! Every time I feel hungry I just salivate. Then he rings the bell and gives me food." But Pavlov himself, the "dumb human," punctuated the sequence of events quite differently so that old Fido was the one who was conditioned.

The organization of interaction sequences is particularly vital when considering those sequences which serve as feedback loops. Since a feedback loop is a self-reflexive cycle of events, there can be no beginning or end. A circle can have no beginning or end. Therefore, any designation of a beginning or end—that is, the punctuation of the sequence—is purely arbitrary.

Take the case of negative feedback loops occurring in the Conflict phase of group decision making. The feedback loops are precisely the same, but members of each coalition organize the sequence differently so that each coalition interprets the sequence as negative feedback of its own expressed opinions. Thus, a sequence of acts favorable and unfavorable to the decision proposals—"f,u, f,u, f, u, f, etc."—is punctuated differently by members of each coalition. The coalition favoring the decision proposals punctuates the sequence as "f–u, f–u, f–u, etc." But the coalition opposed to the decision proposals punctuates the feedback loop diametrically opposed to the previous organization—"u–f, u–f, u–f, etc." In each case, the coalition punctuates the identical sequence of acts differently so that the sequence is interpreted as negative feedback.

Another question arises concerning the function of feedback during the process of group decision making. An earlier chapter described the changing feedback loops as the group progressed from one phase to another until the group achieved consensus on decisions. Does the feedback loop change and thereby cause the group to achieve consensus? Or does the group approach consensus and thereby cause the feedback loop to change? In other words, which comes first—the chicken or the egg, feedback or decisions?

Such a question is naïve and essentially irrelevant. The principle of wholeness emphasizes the interdependence of mutually causal, reciprocal relationships among interaction sequences. Unilateral causal relationships contradict this principle. If causation is mutual, there is neither a precise cause nor effect. Neither precedes the other; they occur simultaneously. A leader does not lead followers any more than followers follow leaders. The relationship is reciprocal and interdependent. The causal relationship binding them is mutual. To discover which causes the other—feedback or consensus—is to designate an arbitrary distinction of beginning and end so that a unitary cause would precede its effect. But the principle of "wholeness" contradicts the existence of one-way, cause-effect relationships in a system. Organizing or punctuating the sequence of events is always arbitrary.

Redundancy and Constraint

The system perspective of communication and group process has consistently emphasized the patterns of interaction which serve to characterize the group. The interaction pattern, of course, is a pattern because it occurs over and over again in identifiable sequences. And the group members change their characteristic patterns of interaction sequences from one phase of group interaction to another. To ask why members

typically communicate in certain repeated patterns and consistently
repeat those patterns during their period of interaction is to engage in idle
speculation of one-way causality again. The existence of the pattern is its
own cause; it stands by itself.

If group interaction were not patterned, the sequence of events
would be random. That is, no act would follow or precede any other with
greater probability than any other interact. In short, the interaction would
reflect no predictable organization and would therefore have no meaning
or significance. Likewise, no group would exist, either. Interaction would
consist solely of non sequiturs. However, as certain acts follow other acts
more and more often—that is, as interacts and double interacts tend to be
repeated and occur with greater frequency—the sequence of interaction
becomes less random and hence more predictable. Therefore, redundancy
leads to predictability, and a pattern emerges.

Take the case of discovering a pattern of falling rocks. If we observe
that one rock falls, we have little basis for predicting anything about the
tendency of rocks to fall. But as more and more rocks are observed to fall,
a pattern of falling rocks has emerged. We are thus able to predict that
rocks generally fall.

To say that redundancy of interaction sequences leads to predictable patterns of group interaction is to say that group members choose to
constrain their behavioral choices by performing acts in patterns which
are not random. Given a certain antecedent act during group interaction,
the responding member willingly, though not necessarily at a high level of
awareness, restricts his choices of behaviors to those appropriate to that
phase of the group process. If it rains at the designated time for the picnic,
the choice of where to eat is constrained to some sheltered area. The
process of group interaction is similar, although the members are often
not as aware of the constraints placed on their choice of responding
behaviors.

The evidence of behavioral constraints is not so overtly obvious as
rain falling from the heavens. Nevertheless, members learn to communicate in redundant sequences or patterns that are mutually recognizable as
having meaning and significance for other group members appropriate to
each particular period of group interaction. If members exercised total
free choice and did not behave according to any rules or patterns of
behavior, their behavior would be random and therefore meaningless. If
interaction occurs in redundant patterns, however, members have necessarily constrained their range of behavioral choices.

Thus patterns of interaction, redundancy of certain sequences of
acts, and constrained behaviors are all aspects of the same phenomenon.
Group members organize their behaviors into patterned sequences of
behavior during the course of group interaction. Why members choose to

conform to apparent rules governing their behavior is an idle question. That they do is sufficient explanation as well as justification of the group process. Searching for some ethereal initial cause for any phenomenon is irrelevant to understanding the operation of the system. Causes are inevitably mutual and reciprocal in a system, and the search for any basic cause is inevitably doomed to failure. ✓

Peter McHugh (1968) illustrates how human beings consistently and inevitably organize meaning during social interaction by seeking out behavioral "rules" in the patterns of interaction. Without meaningful patterns of interaction, communication is simply impossible. The existence of the pattern is in itself evidence that interaction patterns and progressive changes in patterns characterize and serve to organize the social system of group decision making.

A POSTSCRIPT

The study of communication and the group process is certainly perplexing, confusing, and highly frustrating. At the same time, it is exciting and eminently worthy of the time and effort spent in its pursuit. After all, what aspect of human life is more worthy of understanding than how people achieve mutual understanding, how people form interpersonal ties, how people cooperate and compete in social interaction—in short, how people communicate with each other. It has been said that the human being spends more of his waking time in the activity of human communication than any other endeavor. Certainly the quest for greater understanding of human communication is vitally important.

The formal study of communication and the group process is still very young. Compared to what remains to be discovered, the present state of our knowledge is infinitesimally small. Nevertheless, we have now a broad basis for understanding and that understanding comprises the basis for the present volume. A spirit of progress toward increased understanding of group communication is highly contagious. And progress has been so rapid even within the last ten years that virtually any book becomes obsolete by the time it sees print. This book should be no exception.

"But I," you say, "am not concerned with devoting my life to the study of group communication. I am only interested in the subject as a practicing group member. I want to know how I can be more effective and productive as a member of a decision-making small group." The response to this question is deceptively simple. The practitioner and the researcher of group decision making share one trait in common. They are both students of group communication.

Effective performance in small group decision making is absolutely dependent on being aware of the nature of human communication and the group process. The greater the member's understanding of communication and the group process, the more sensitive the member is toward both his own behavior and the behavior of others. The greater the member's sensitivity to communication and the group process, the more effective he is as a participating member of a decision-making group. His sensitivity directs his behavior to communicate appropriately and effectively in the group process. He knows he cannot easily manipulate other members, but he also knows he can discern problems confronting the group and aid in devising strategies for the group to solve them. And he is not burdened with the disadvantage of naïvely trusting the clichés of conventional wisdom concerning group decision making.

One cliché seems appropriate as a postscript to this book. "The more you know, the more you know that you don't know." You have now completed one small step toward understanding group communication. For many people that first step is addictive.

Appendix One

Anatomy of a Decision

Chapter 7 includes a description of the four phases involved in the process of group decision making. Those phases—Orientation, Conflict, Emergence, and Reinforcement—may appear confusing in the abstract description of the model in Chapter 7. That description of the basic model of decision emergence did not include specific comments made by specific members during actual group interaction. As a result, the model may need a more concrete description. The following pages attempt to capture the "flavor" of group discussion. This section describes the actual communicative exchanges of specific group members as the group progresses through the four phases of decision making.

"Anatomy of a Decision" illustrates through actual group interactive sequences, taken from audiotaped transcripts of group interaction, what the four phases of decision emergence "look like" in actual group discussion. You should probably refer to the general model of decision emergence in Chapter 7 during and after your reading of this section.

THE SITUATION This six-member jury is deliberating over a verdict after observing a mock trial. The dramatized trial involved a civil suit seeking damages for alleged injuries suffered in an auto-pedestrian accident. The plaintiff, Alfred Derby, is the pedestrian who brought the suit. The defendant, Roger Adams, was the driver of the automobile which struck Derby. The jury group ultimately decided in favor of the defendant, Adams, and did not award damages in any amount to the plaintiff, Derby. Instrumental to this final verdict, the jury achieved consensus on a key decision that the plaintiff was negligent and therefore contributed to the accident. The opening excerpt of group interaction occurs during the first five minutes of the jury's deliberations. The ellipsis (. . .) signifies a pause in the interaction and does not imply omitted materials.

A First of all, we decide whether it's a case of liability or negligence.
D Yeah . . . negligence.
A It's the same thing. In other words, you all feel that Roger Adams alone was negligent without the contributory negligence of Derby—or was it Derby's fault as much as Adams's fault—or was it either's fault—or was it just plain accident.
C Guilty or not guilty.
A It's not just those two choices, though. We've got three choices.
D What else can there be, though? I mean . . .
A It's not a criminal action like whether he robbed a store. It's just whether he is negligent, both of them are negligent, or whether . . .
D Yeah, I see. But there are still only two verdicts. Do we give the plaintiff any money or not.
A First of all, how many people here feel that just Roger Adams alone was negligent and that Alfred Derby, the person who was hit, in no way contributed to this negligence and therefore should receive compensation?

Typical of a group's Orientation phase are the members' attempts to accustom themselves to the topic and to the procedure. In this case the group must accustom themselves to the procedure of the law and the legal directions they received from the judge.

In the excerpt above, members proceed to discover what choices of final decisions are available to them. Essentially they are asking themselves, "What precisely is the task we are expected to accomplish?" With this fundamental step out of the way, the members proceed to probe each other's attitudes. Member A's final comment requests a preliminary survey of the first impressions of group members. How difficult will it be to achieve agreement? This first excerpt, then, typifies the early efforts of members to acclimate themselves—first to the procedures, and then to each other.

Member B responds to Member A's request for his initial opinion and stimulates responses which are typical of the Orientation phase. As Member B provides argument for his opinions, A and C seem to experience discomfort. They respond by invoking procedural rules formulated on the spur of the moment in order to keep B in check. In essence, they are telling B to withhold his evidence and reasons until later, at which time the group will thresh things out. For the present A and C don't want to "rock the boat."

A more typical manner of expressing a member's initial attitude during the Orientation phase is the following comment of A:

A   I feel that . . . I don't know about you guys, but it could have been me. I'm a reckless driver, and I can picture myself in a hurry to school. And there were a lot of mistakes brought out in the testimony . . . on both sides. First of all, I have always thought that the banker's lot is the one next to Administration.

A is attempting to advance his opinion which includes supporting reasons. But his specific opinion is not totally clear from this comment. His manner of presenting his attitude is tentative and ambiguous. He even seems to apologize for attempting to express an opinion. He includes self-deprecation lest his attitude appear too forceful to the other members. He tempers his attitude by condemning "both sides" for having mistakes in their testimony. He concludes by citing an innocuous error of fact—the location of a parking lot—which is calculated to offend no one annd which he even attributes to his own misunderstanding. He delivers this comment with considerable hesitancy, with numerous pauses, and with trepidation. Such ambiguity is characteristic of nearly all substantive comments during the Orientation.

Another excerpt of the group interaction demonstrates a series of ambiguous responses which follow the initiation of a decision proposal of questionable relevance to their forthcoming decision:

A   I'm a little bit confused about this whole thing. I don't know if we can assume that what the attorneys said is true or not.

C   Not in summation you can't—unless it was brought out in testimony.

D   That one in the gray suit based his mostly on emotion, and if we were to go by that alone without regarding anything . . . I mean emotion is fine but . . .

A   You're right. A lot of it was based on emotion. I realize that, but still I don't know whether we should accept it or . . .

C   That was his job. We can't blame him for . . .

A   I guess not, but . . .

A originates this decision proposal by claiming he is confused and is seeking clarification. He does not appear to be looking for any argument. Only C expresses a definite attitude or opinion toward this proposal concerning the credibility of the attorneys. A and D respond to the proposal with ambiguous reluctance. Members continue to participate hesitantly. Note the number of unfinished sentences and phrases left dangling. Two members, A and D, appear to favor the decision proposal, but they are carefully tolerant of other members' opinions. A twice agrees with the attitude which he apparently disfavors, but he qualifies his agreement with a hint of disagreement—for example, "you're right . . . I realize that, but . . ." and "I guess not, but . . ." Including the qualifier "but" and implying both a favorable and unfavorable opinion toward the proposal typify ambiguous attitudes toward nearly all decision proposals during the Orientation phase.

The individual member may have an opinion, but he feels inhibited in actually expressing it. He is neither sure of his own status in the group, nor does he know the social consequences of taking too strong a stand on any issue. Consequently he "tests" his ideas, his opinions, and the opinions of the other members first. Just as one "tests" the temperature of the water in the pool before taking the big plunge, the group member during the Orientation phase "tests" the group before risking his "self." He sends up trial balloons and takes a reading of the group climate before committing himself.

Following the transition to the Conflict phase, the members have completed developing their opinions. The period of testing the group atmosphere is over, and the general trend of idea development seems to be clear. Opinions and ideas in the Orientation phase existed in their formative states. During the Conflict phase, the process of formulation is complete. At this point the group members proceed to "choose up sides" and engage in verbal battle over substantive issues. The following excerpt is typical of the interaction during the second phase of group decision making—the Conflict phase:

A The thing to decide is was Roger Adams in a hurry. And did he act in such a manner that a reasonable, adult, mature person would.
C You have to consider him a reasonable, prudent person. He was waved on by another person who was going to make the turn, irregardless [sic] of whether he was in a hurry or not.
A I would say that if he is reasonable, he wouldn't take another person's word for it.
C Oh, come on now! There is only one car on the street.
A I certainly wouldn't do it.
C Do you consider yourself reasonable?
A I'm not reasonable. I'll admit it, too. But what does that have to do with it? I wouldn't want to use myself as an example. That doesn't say that he wasn't reasonable.
B Then we're not going to get any place. You have to give some criteria. You can't just say he wasn't reasonable and let it go at that.

The tentativeness of expressed opinions, characteristic of interaction during the Orientation phase, is certainly absent during interaction of the Conflict phase. Member A's comment, which initiates the decision proposal concerning the possible negligence of the defendant, does not indicate his opinion toward the decision proposal. It is clearly a comment expressing an ambiguous opinion toward the proposal. But the tone of this ambiguous comment is clearly different from the tone of the typical ambiguous comment of the Orientation phase. At this point A does not hesitate, verbally or ideationally. He self-assuredly asserts, "The thing to decide is . . ."

Tolerance for any dissenting opinion is not apparent in the language choices of any of these comments. The this-is-my-opinion-but-I-could-be-wrong comment which was characteristic of the Orientation phase becomes a this-is-my-opinion-and-it-is-correct comment in the Conflict phase. C also asserts, "You *have* to consider him . . .," and B asserts, "You *have* to give some criteria. You *can't* just say. . . ." These stylistic characteristics of the communicative acts implicitly compel the responding group members into a for-against choice. Neutral opinions are no longer acceptable. The language used during the interaction of the Conflict phase virtually forces the members to express definite opinions. Essentially stylistic features of the interaction itself force members into conflict over ideas.

Member A is now clearly identified as a spokesman for the plaintiff while B and C appear to be spokesmen for the defendant. The next excerpt from group interaction involves a discussion of the same decision proposal and illustrates more vividly the ideational division of the group members:

C   Most people, I think, would make sure that the other side was clear for him to go. I think it would be reasonably prudent to take a glance over there to make sure that the guy was still signaling you on.

A   I don't think you can trust another person. It's a fact that . . . I don't know if you've ever traveled on the highway behind a semi-trailer . . . You're following, and semi-trailers don't usually go as fast as you would like or necessarily the speed limit. You're back of the semi-trailer. You keep swinging out to see if you can pass. You see the driver wave his arm out like this. That's illegal. You can't use this as evidence in court that it was safe to pass the truck.

C   We can't consider that. We judge on the testimony we heard in court today and yesterday.

D   That's kind of irrelevant.

A   But the truck driver said it was safe to pass just like this guy in court said.

D   It is the custom on the highway, illegal or not, for big trucks to be courteous enough to flick on and off their lights when it's safe for the guy behind him to pass.

A   How long has it been since you have traveled on the highway?

D   Last fall.

A   Well, most of them don't do it anymore. Besides, if this guy was a reasonable man, he would have wanted to find out for himself. Not just take another guy's word for it.

C   We shouldn't take in anything that we didn't hear in court.

A   But this pertains to what we heard in the courtroom. If he was a reasonable man, he wouldn't have taken this driver's word for it that he should go.

C   How many people agree with you on that statement? I don't for one.

D   I don't.

B   I would take the driver's word for it.

A   No, you wouldn't!

C   A reasonable person would.

The dissident A is fighting a losing battle to have the group consider his analogy regarding highway driving. His antagonists continue to be B and C. These three members engage in a heated verbal exchange over this issue.

During the Conflict phase group members know which members are on which side in the conflict over ideas and feel fewer inhibitions regarding the necessity for social facilitation. Disagreement is not only definite, it is vehement.

Comments such as "Oh, come on now!" and "No, you wouldn't!" are quite common during the Conflict phase. In fact, some comments are virtual insults and certainly not intended to win close friends. The question, "Do you consider yourself reasonable?" may be insulting; but C's final comment in the excerpt above, "A reasonable person would," is more than insulting. In the context of this interaction that comment is tantamount to character assassination.

At this point A appears to be the sole member of the group who favors the plaintiff's side in the civil case. Member D, not very active in earlier interaction during Orientation, sides against A on this issue. But D's comments don't appear to be as vehement as B's and C's opposition. Note that D tones down his charge of irrelevance by saying, "That's kind of irrelevant," while C flatly asserted, "We can't consider that." Later D dispassionately appeals to A's reason about "custom," and disregards the issue of its legality. In fact, D continues to discuss the issue as though it were relevant.

Eventually D disagreed with A on this issue, but his disagreement is clearly not equivalent in tone, language, or manner to the disagreement of B and C. The next excerpt from the Conflict phase casts more light on the role D plays in this second phase of decision emergence.

A Do you think our Roger Adams testified truthfully on the stand?
D I think he fudged a bit.
A I do, too. That was my opinion. I realize that these are fixed situations, but let's pretend that it isn't. I mean, I think that he was trying to get himself out of a bad situation . . . as any normal person would, I suppose.
C But the three witnesses for the defense—they all collaborated [sic] his testimony perfectly.
A Which ones?
C All three for the defense.
B The guy that waved him on, the girl . . .
D That is not strictly true, because the girl was a little off.
A One person said that he stopped for one or two seconds and then shot out. Another one said he was there for half a minute. They didn't collaborate [sic] on that.
E But one of them was watching him, and the other one was driving his own car and getting ready to go. They collaborated [sic] on the things that were important, though.
A I can't see how you can say that. They didn't collaborate [sic] at all. Time was just one of the factors they didn't agree on.

Member A seems to have procured a lieutenant in D. Both are now identified with the plaintiff, while B and C continue to favor the defendant. One of the two most infrequent contributors to the group interaction, member E, identifies himself with the defendant in the excerpt above. Hence, two coalitions appear to be developing in this second phase of the group decision-making process. A and

D comprise one coalition which favors the plaintiff. B, C, and probably E are members of the other coalition, which favors the defendant. Only Member F remains clearly outside either coalition.

This jury is composed of six members. The sixth member, F, is still to be heard from in the excerpts taken from the group interaction. While he has contributed to the group interaction sparingly, his participation during the Conflict phase is virtually nonexistent.

One can probably speculate that F's withdrawal from group participation results from a feeling of discomfort brought on by the vehement substantive conflict over ideas during this phase. F is undoubtedly aware of his low status in the group, which may or may not be of his own volition. Whether from apathy toward the group purpose or from an abiding fear of social conflict, F has chosen to withdraw from group interaction rather than take a stand and join one of the coalitions involved in social conflict over ideas.

In terms of the developing status hierarchy in the emergent group setting, leader contenders are clearly emerging during this Conflict phase. Member A is the most vehement spokesman for the "plaintiff's coalition." Member C, or possibly Member B, seems to represent the strongest leader contender from the "defendant's coalition." The conflict over substantive issues is undoubtedly relevant to the contention over the leadership roles, too. But member A, the leader contender from the coalition opposed to the decision which ultimately achieves group consensus, will not remain in active contention for leadership much longer. As a member who has committed himself to a position opposing the consensus decision, his bid for leadership is doomed.

Following the transition to the Emergence phase, the substantive conflict among members begins to dissipate as illustrated in a later excerpt taken from the group interaction:

A Let me ask one more question. Do you think Derby (the plaintiff) was in the crosswalk?
D I don't think so.
C No, I don't. I don't think that has too much to do with it, though.
D I agree.
C I know there are some statutes about the crosswalk, but I mean the fact that he was in . . . I don't know. That might be kind of important.
D He was on the roadway is really the issue.
C I don't think it really happened exactly the way the defendant described it. I think he embellished it a little toward his side. I think it happened close enough to it, though.
F As far as that goes, Derby may have his own story, too. I mean each would be looking out for himself. That's only natural.
D Of course you are going to get this in any situation.
F That's just it. Both of them. You can't use the two prime subjects. You have to try and go on the witnesses. Of course they are witnesses, too, and you have to consider them. And they are important, too, but. . . .

A has initiated another proposal for consideration, but his statement initiating the proposal expresses an ambiguous opinion toward it. He uses simple and straightforward language without argument. The communicative acts in response to his proposal emphasize the irrelevance of his proposal rather than attempting to deny its factual nature. During the Conflict phase, the responses to such a proposal would have been an intense denial and consequently additional substantive conflict. In the Emergence phase, though, the conflict over issues is muted.

In the second phase, members hammered out the issues and proposals they felt were important to getting their task accomplished. But their response to a new issue in the Emergence phase is to dismiss it as irrelevant rather than to engage in additional conflict.

The level of social tension seems to be appreciably lower during the Emergence phase. Member C is now much more tolerant of A's opinions and feelings as illustrated in the last excerpt. He even admits to the possibility that the issue raised by member A "might be kind of important." He even goes so far as to admit that the defendant "embellished" his testimony, an admission he would never have made in the Conflict phase.

The emerging decision becomes progressively clearer during the Emergence phase, and all members seem to sense the direction the group has taken. Even F joins the interaction "jumping on the bandwagon" to offer his opinion in support of the defendant. When the other members don't wholeheartedly welcome his offer to join their side, F begins to flounder in his comments and becomes extremely ambiguous and vague in his comments. His final comment is a classic example of ambiguity. At any rate, the decision becomes increasingly evident, and even F knows it.

The overt conflict over substantive issues characterizing the Conflict phase moderates during the Emergence phase. Both A and D ameliorate their dissent of the decision proposals favoring the defendant. For example, while A vehemently and tenaciously expressed his dissenting view during the Conflict phase, he expresses only ambiguous opinions without much tenacity at all during the Emergence phase. The following excerpt clearly illustrates this change in A's verbal behavior.

A I just wondered. Maybe this isn't really relevant, but I never really understood exactly where the point of impact was. Not in relation to the car, but in relation to the street. How far out from the curb he was. It appeared from the drawing and three or four witnesses that it was in the lane closest to the curb that Derby stepped off of. If this is the case, Adams made an illegal left turn. Of course, I might be mistaken.

C Yeah. Right.

B I think it was right in the middle.

C Was it in the middle?

D It was probably about twenty feet off. That might be closest to this curb.

E He said he was about eleven feet off the curb, but he also put him closer to the middle.

A If it was closer to the curb than it was to the intersection, it wasn't an illegal left turn. But it might have been eleven feet this way, and that would have been an illegal turn.

D Eleven feet puts it right about the middle. No illegal left turn.

C Remember he's turning, so he's got to come a little bit into the other lane on the turn.

D Well, not necessarily.

C It's pretty hard not to, with at least his front bumper.

B It's pretty close, but he was probably all right on his turn. If he was out eleven feet, he was right there in the middle.

D In that case he was only. . . . He's not negligent.

A This is irrelevant, then.

C I don't think it's possible to hit him in the middle. I don't think that it is physically possible.

A No. He did make a wrong turn, but he wasn't completely out of his lane from where he should have been.

C He was probably wrong in not watching exactly as he was turning. But I don't think it was too far away to be reasonable.

Another "last-ditch" effort by A to advocate the plaintiff's side in the discussion! Did the defendant make an illegal left turn? But A fails to raise many doubts concerning what is becoming increasingly apparent as the consensus decision. But the strength and tenacity of A's argumentativeness has dissipated. He initiates his proposal with reluctant ambiguity. Note his apologetic phrases which appear throughout his contributions—"I just wondered. Maybe this isn't really relevant," "It appeared . . .," "If this is the case . . .," and the final "Of course, I might be mistaken."

During the ensuing discussion, A contributes another ambiguous argument which indicates only the possibility—not even the probability—that the defendant was negligent in making an illegal left turn. Compared to his self-assured stance in the Conflict phase, A has moderated his attitude considerably. He does not express certainty about any opinion he expresses in the Emergence phase. He qualifies nearly everything with ambiguous language, such as "if" and "might." He resigns himself to losing the fight over this issue. In fact, he doesn't try very hard to win it. He offers his resigned statement of capitulation, "This is irrelevant, then," even before the other members have completely rejected it. In fact, C again expresses amazing tolerance for A's proposal and once more appears to give A's proposal serious consideration before he rejects it. A has evidently succumbed to the apparent consensus decision. C apparently knows it and is softening the blow somewhat. C is definitely the leading contender for group leader, and he is willing to accept A as a high-status member whose opinions are worthy of consideration.

The two coalitions of the Conflict phase also appear to dissipate during the Emergence phase. While members of opposing coalitions responded to their "opponents" with open hostility and even contempt in the Conflict phase, they now respond with active rational consideration. The prime example of this change is illustrated by C's comments. He preferred to insult A during the Conflict phase as a response to A's position favoring the plaintiff. But during the Emergence phase C actively considers A's proposal, admits to its potential significance and credibility, and then rejects it.

Again the basis for rejecting proposals favoring the plaintiff's case is irrelevance. While members argued against proposals during the Conflict phase on the basis of their truth or falsity, the basic issue on which members typically evaluate proposals in the Emergence phase seems to be relevance.

In the Reinforcement phase decisions have completed the process of emergence. Interaction during this final phase of the group process confirms decisions already made and develops the members' commitment or consensus toward those decisions. The following excerpt appears very early in the Reinforcement phase:

E Everybody saw the car coming.
B Besides that, he said his lights were on.
C His turn signal was on. It was obvious that he was coming. That would make it all the more easier [sic] to see the car coming.
D Practically everybody saw that car coming. His lights turning.
E That guy that was on the sidewalk. . . . He saw all this traffic, and he also saw Adams coming. That's why he didn't go. Why did Derby go? He has to be at some fault.
C I feel sorry for him, and I'd like to help him out, but I just don't think I can.
D I agree.
B You can't base it on an emotion . . .
D Of course not.
C I don't think we should take into any account what they told us at the beginning, either—about Adams being a drunkard and that.
B No. Don't even mention that.
F No. Don't worry about it.
C No.

Members B, C, D, and E all express agreement with the decision proposal that Derby, the defendant, was guilty of contributory negligence. They not only agree with each other, but they provide superfluous evidence to support their agreement. Interaction consistently includes statement after statement expressing agreement with the one before it. Member C initiates a "straw-man" proposal contrary to their decision already made. But he immediately expressed an unfavorable opinion toward it. Members B and F immediately concur, and they drop the proposal immediately.

The major dissenter, A, is conspicuously absent from the previous interaction. But his former lieutenant, D, has certainly joined the other coalition. Even F is growing bolder and bolder with his comments now that absolutely no doubt remains regarding the decision made by the group. As the group's interaction draws to a close, A leaves no doubt as to his completely modified position.

A I guess I'd have to say that it was both their faults.

C I say it is both their faults.

A Evidently it probably is.

B Derby really never should have stepped off the curb.

D Right.

E And there he was out eleven feet already, and he was trying to avoid another oncoming car. That's just plain stupid.

F When you step off the curb, you know you are taking chances. You have to stay on your toes.

A Well, he obviously didn't see him turn. But he should have.

F He was right in front of him. He should have seen him turn.

D Right. He must have been looking some place else.

A I think Derby stepped off the curb, started walking and was halfway through the first lane when this guy started to make his turn. It doesn't take long for all this to happen. Only a few seconds.

C The plaintiff was making some kind of inference that Adams was going excessively fast across the turn. I don't think that's really possible.

D No.

B How fast can you take a turn without crashing into the corner or something?

D Yeah. When you're accelerating, you still aren't going more than nine or ten miles per hour.

C The average turn is about six miles per hour, maybe a little faster, but that isn't excessively fast.

B It varies if he was trying to beat this other car.

C But he couldn't have been going even fifteen miles around a turn.

D If you do, you're pulling out like a sports car.

C If you have good cornering, you'll probably make it. If you don't, you might not.

A We agree unanimously right now that it is both their faults.

(A chorus of "Yeah!")

A It was both their faults. There is nothing more to do then.

E I would say that it was mutual negligence—more Derby's (plaintiff) fault.

F I say it is all Derby's fault.

A You say all Derby's fault?

F Yes.

A I think it is more Adams's fault. But both are still negligent.

C Okay. Then it's unanimous.

F I say that Derby was completely at fault. He shouldn't even be suing.

C You mean that Adams should be suing?

F Right.

A There are two possibilities on this sheet. Let me read them both. "Number one. We, the jury, find in favor of the plaintiff and against the defendant and assess damages to the sum of . . . ." In other words, we think it was Adams's fault, and Derby should pay.

C Throw that one out.

A Okay. We'll throw that one out. "Number two. We, the jury, find in favor of the defendant and against . . ." In other words, if they think it is more Derby's fault.

D No. Just the plaintiff.

C In favor of the defendant legally means it isn't the plaintiff. It doesn't mean that the defendant can claim damages. It just means that the suit has been dropped.

B We find in favor of the defendant.

C Yes.

A That's how we do it then.

B Write "contributory negligence."

D We are all decided.

C Unanimous decision. No dissenters.

Throughout these final moments of group interaction is a pervading spirit of harmony and unity. All members agree, and everyone knows that all members agree. But they continue to discuss the decision while verbally slapping each other on the back even to the point of initiating another "straw man" decision proposal. Three of the members join in verbally demolishing the plaintiff's argument concerning Adams's excessive speed.

Meanwhile, A firmly commits himself to the position that Derby is also at fault. His language still includes traces of reluctance. But his language of agreement is completely understandable, given his earlier attitude of vehement opposition during the Conflict phase. He closes his comments in the language of willing reluctance with such statements as "I guess I'd have to say . . ." and "Evidently it probably is." Nevertheless, he is firmly committed to the consensus decision.

The nonparticipant in the Conflict phase, F, is caught up in the spirit of consensus, and he overreacts to the obvious consensus decision. He goes so far as to assess 100 percent negligence to the plaintiff. Not even members B and C want to go this far. They don't pay too much attention to F's Johnny-come-lately enthusiasm. They have made their decision, and they have reinforced it.

To avoid any doubts and probably in deference to A's rationale for making the decision unanimous, B suggests that the group explain to the court that the basis for their decision was "contributory negligence." The addition of their rationale is superfluous, but they do it anyway. The final comments allude to the written record which they return to officials of the mock court confirming their consensus decision.

The process of group decision making thus progresses through four phases of interaction—Orientation, Conflict, Emergence, and Reinforcement. The decisional process, closely allied with characteristics of the social dimension reflecting the interdependent relationship of the two dimensions, is a cumulative and cyclical process. Group members anchor their interaction to tentative decision proposals leading to and culminating in consensus on final group decisions.

Excerpts from an actual group's interaction reflect the "flavor" of the discussion and the importance of stylistic features of the language and changes in individual members' attitudes as groups progress toward consensus. Although the four phases seem to be clearly separate in the excerpted interaction from each of the four phases, the transitions between phases are in reality quite gradual and not nearly as dramatic as they appear in selected excerpts. This, then, is the process of group decision making in action.

Appendix Two

Analysis of Small Group Interaction

The phenomenon of human communication is extremely complex. If there were ever any doubts as to the truth of that statement, they should be dispelled by now. Perhaps because of its highly complex nature, human communication has intrigued social scholars for centuries, dating back to Aristotle and beyond. Undoubtedly because of its complexity, communication yet evades our attempts to grasp a complete understanding of it. Simply stated, human communication is extraordinarily difficult either to analyze or describe.

One commonly overlooked barrier to understanding communication is the tendency to conceive of communication as someone doing something to someone else. The syntactical structure inherent in our English language (subject—verb—object) encourages this unfortunate view of human communication. From our first reading of sentences, such as, "The boy hits the ball," we have been encouraged to view communication as some action being perpetrated by someone on someone else. We commonly describe acts of communication in subject-verb-object language—a person persuades, informs, entertains, comforts, convinces, cajoles, dominates, leads, follows, etc., another person. The common tendency to view communication as the transmission and reception of messages also encourages a one-way linear view of action transmitted by a "source" who affects a "receiver" of that action.

This linear view of communication, highlighted perhaps by the structure of our English language, does not easily correspond to the view of communication as a process—an interdependent relationship developed among communicating people who willingly engage in a system of interstructured behaviors. The linear view of communication is also inconsistent with the view of leadership described in Chapter 5 which equated leadership with followership—again as an interdependent relationship between people's behaviors. The problem of viewing acts of human communication free from the restrictions of transmitting and receiving action is a difficult one to solve.

This section overviews some methods commonly used for the observation of human communication in the context of a small group. This overview serves as a preliminary step toward understanding why the method of interaction analysis is probably a superior method to observe communication and small groups as an interactive process. Central to the model of decision emergence discussed in Chapter 7 and "Anatomy of a Decision" is a specific observational system of interaction analysis. A general description of that system is also included as an example of how interaction analysis may be applied to the observation and analysis of communication and group process in ongoing decision-making groups.

COMMON OBSERVATIONAL METHODS

The number of different methods used to observe small group communication staggers the imagination. Nearly every method employed in the broad spectrum of social and behavioral sciences has, at one time or another, been applied to group communication. This section attempts to review only a few of these methods and does not describe any single method comprehensively. It should soon be obvious that these methods, widely used and certainly valuable for certain purposes, provide only a limited insight into communication and group process, which naturally is our primary interest.

Self-Reports

Undoubtedly the most simple (and often overlooked for that reason) method to discover what people think or feel is to ask them. The Gallup and Roper polls of public opinion, along with the almost infamous Nielsen ratings of television programs, reflect specifically this method of social observation. Small group members often complete self-reports in the form of oral interviews or written questionnaires. The diary, another self-report from group members, has been mentioned in several chapters. Members of classroom groups are often asked to record in such a diary their impressions and reactions immediately following each group meeting. Usually the diary does not require specific answers to specific questions but asks only what the member thinks has happened to the group and to his own role in that group during that specific meeting.

Member diaries are valuable as an observational method in that members frequently record in their diaries those feelings and thoughts which they might not wish to express during actual interaction with fellow group members. People are generally more willing to confide in the impersonal diary those thoughts which might otherwise escape observation. They tend to be much more frank in their diaries than in actual communication with other people, particularly in a newly formed group. Self-reports thus provide valuable additional information to the observer of group interaction. This information is particularly valuable in order to gain insight into the group's social dimension.

Despite the obvious value of the self-reporting method of observing small groups, there are problems inherent in the method itself. In many respects, the least knowledgeable source of information on any specific person is that person himself. He is often unaware of how he behaves, what he does, and particularly what he is thinking or feeling. Many behaviors are performed from habit or at least without willful concentration. If it is true that people act in accordance with behavioral "rules" and that they need not be aware of those rules governing their behavior, then people are not necessarily aware of what they do or why they do it.

It is also extremely difficult to put thoughts and feelings into words. We just don't have the appropriate language or ability to express a feeling. Most of us find it difficult even to put our sensations into words. Try, for example, to describe the taste of an avocado or an artichoke to someone who has never tasted one. Describe the smell of some exotic cologne or perfume to someone who has never experienced that aroma. An insurmountable problem, and one that has been encountered personally, is to describe the sensation of sub-zero cold to a person who has never left the Hawaiian Islands. Our literature of song and novels is replete with attempts to put into words the common emotion of love. Such attempts have proved futile in addition to being amazingly contradictory. We simply don't have the language to express many of our feelings, emotions, and sensations—even those which we are aware of having experienced.

Furthermore, self-reports often distort the truth. All of us have naturally developed defense mechanisms which serve to protect our ego, our personality. When the truth is harmful to our image of self or when reporting reality would embarrass us, we typically distort our perception of our true feelings, behaviors, or motives. Perceptual distortion is not necessarily conscious prevarication. In fact, we often believe the distortion to be the truth and are not even aware of having distorted anything. Under any circumstances, self-reports from group members are to be suspect. Relying on such an unreliable method as the principal means for observing group communication could easily lead to inaccurate as well as incomplete information.

The members' degree of involvement in their group and their group task may also stimulate distorted self-reports. The overly involved member tends to idealize the group and evaluate the group's behavior higher than he probably should. Conversely, the member with an extremely low level of commitment to the group tends to judge the group lower than he probably should. An example might clarify this. Students routinely filling out questionnaires designed to evaluate their university classroom experience once demonstrated the effects of involvement, both high and low, on their self-reports. Responding to an item asking students to evaluate the written examinations required in the class, one student rated the exams at the maximum, "very good." Another student in the same class rated the exams at the minimum, "very poor." The response of neither the highly involved nor the lowly involved student reflected reality. In fact, most students didn't respond to that item on the questionnaire because that particular class did not include any examinations!

Finally, self-reports from group members should be suspect because they inherently rely on the individual's memory. Rather than observe individuals during group interaction, self-reports ask for responses from group members after the fact. The human memory is quite fallible with incomplete and distorted information typically present. You may be familiar with the classroom exercise which involves one person telling a story to a second person who in turn relays that message to a third person who tells it to a fourth person and so forth. After the second or third transmission, the story bears little resemblance to its original form. The human memory is simply imperfect. It forgets and distorts information as a normal occurrence.

Group Outcomes

Perhaps the method most commonly used for observing group decision making is measuring the outcome of group discussion—the quantity or quality of decisions reached by the group members. This procedure typically involves determining the structural attributes of the group as it begins its task efforts and observing the results which accrue from their efforts, allegedly as a result of the particular combination of structural attributes. For example, a five-man group and a five-woman group may be given the same decision-making task. The decisions reached by those two groups would then be observed and compared. Any difference in the decisions reached by the two groups would be attributed to the group's predominant structural characteristic of difference—the sex of its members.

Concentrating on the outcome from group discussion also possesses serious and inherent shortcomings. For example, the quantity of decisions which a group makes is typically irrelevant. Often a group has only one decision to make, such as guilty or not guilty. But the quality of decisions is also difficult to measure when there is no objective method outside the group interaction available to validate the group decision. When a group decision-making task is involved, there is no externally valid decision; the sole criterion of quality is the extent to which the decision achieves group consensus. How, then, can the quality of a group decision-making task be reliably measured? No adequate answer to this question is currently available.

Because of the insurmountable difficulty involved in measuring the quality of group decisions, observers of group decision making often observe groups performing tasks more suited to individual decision making. Such tasks have a single "best" or "correct" answer, and their quality is objectively evident. But groups performing tasks intended for expert individuals are doing little more than playing pseudo-intellectual games. Such tasks severely restrict the group process and encourage expert individual members to dominate other group members. At the very least, no advantage is gained from observing groups who perform tasks unsuitable to the social context. But such observations unfortunately occur routinely.

Observing the group from the perspective of their outputs also assumes that structural conditions at the time of group formation determine what outcomes the group will eventually achieve. That is, a structural characteristic (for example, all males) or combination of structural characteristics causes the group to arrive at their decisions. Such an assumption absolutely denies the inherent interdependence of the members, their behaviors, the group dimensions, and so forth—interdependent relationships inherent in the nature of a process. In fact, the assumption that group structure determines group action is patently impossible in an open system, which is the perspective of small groups employed throughout this book.

Finally, observing only the group's outcomes is highly incomplete. At best, such an observational method answers only questions of *why* and *whether* group members achieve their outcomes. But it ignores the more important question of *how* groups achieve consensus. And only answers to the latter question can provide any insight into how we might increase the potential effectiveness of group decision making.

Sociometry

Sociometric methods are also commonly utilized for observing small groups. Sociometry, whose pictorial representations of social relationships are often known as sociograms, concerns itself solely with selected elements of the social dimension of a system. Essentially, sociometric methods seek to discover interpersonal attractions and repulsions among various members of the group, that is, the positive and negative feelings each group member has for each other member.

While valuable as an insight into a group's socioemotional dimension, sociometric methods afford at best only a partial view of the process of group development. By discovering the extent to which members are attracted to other members and are willing to work with them in other endeavors, the observer has some basis for assessing the degree of cohesiveness of that group. But in terms of any knowledge of a group's task dimension, sociometry is quite irrelevant.

Sociometric methods are also limited to the interpersonal attraction of group members at a specific point in time. That is, such methods can reveal the degree of cohesiveness only as it exists at the particular point in time at which the sociometric methods of observation are applied—usually as a self-report questionnaire distributed to the group members. Sociometry does not attempt to discover how the members developed their feelings, positive or negative, toward each other. In effect, sociometry's primary concern is with outcomes of group interaction in the social dimension of group development.

Not only do sociometric methods of group observation ignore totally the elements of the task dimension, but they also severely restrict the principle of interdependence inherent in a group process. Nearly every chapter in this book has emphasized the pervasive influence of interdependence, ranging from the global interdependence of the task and social dimensions to the specific interdependence of particular interacts which members perform during each successive phase of group decision making. Sociometry emphasizes the interdependence of group members only through their degree of internalized liking or attraction toward each other. That is, according to the inherent assumptions upon which sociometry is based, members of a group develop interdependent relationships only through reciprocating internalized feelings of attraction with each other. Thus, emotions, feelings, or other internalized phenomena are the basis for a group's interdependence rather than external communicative behaviors assumed by this book's perspective of communication and group process.

In summary, the three general types of observational methods used to analyze and describe small groups are generally unsatisfactory for our purposes. Certainly each of these methods provides highly valuable information about small groups, but that information is of a highly specialized and restricted scope. As far as communication and group process are concerned, these observational modes are only indirectly useful and only partially relevant.

First and foremost, all three methods—self-reports, outcome measures, and sociometry—ignore the interdependent structural and action aspects of any process. Each method is capable of observing the group at only a single instant in time and can therefore discover something about the group's structure at that time only. If the group is observed several times by using one of these methods, the observer can discover aspects of group structure as they exist at several different points in time. Comparing each observation with the others allows the observer to determine whether the group experienced any changes in its structure from one point in time to another. But how those changes occurred—the process of structural change—inherently escapes observation. If we are committed to the perspective of communication and group process, as we are, these methods cannot be considered satisfactory for our purposes.

All three types of observational methods discussed above also ignore the actual communicative behaviors of group members in preference to observing indirectly the internalized feelings within the members. The methods seek to discover what members "feel about" something rather than observing what they actually "do" about it. That is, the methods ask the group member to become introspective about his experiences, but not one of the methods seeks to discover what his experiences actually have been. The members' communicative behaviors escape the observer's eye as the observations emphasize the effects of those behaviors. The viewpoint of this book stipulates that the interstructured behaviors of members precipitate the effects or outcomes and are therefore the most important element of small groups to be observed.

Finally, the principle of interdependence employed by these methods is radically different from the principle as it has been discussed in preceding chapters of this book. Earlier chapters have consistently viewed interdependence as a relationship greater than the sum of its components, in which every component affects and is mutually affected by all other components. A leader leads because followers follow, which is precisely the same as saying that followers follow because leaders lead. Thus, leadership is an interdependent relationship between leader and follower and not a one-way linear influence exerted by one of the partners in the relationship. Both leader and follower interdependently comprise the social phenomenon of leadership.

The observational methods previously discussed, however, seek interpersonal relationships solely from the viewpoint of an individual member. Thus, the observer discovers what one group member feels or perhaps does vis-à-vis another member, but he forsakes the interdependent relationship which structures the behaviors of the two members and transcends the individual viewpoint of either. As these methods inherently focus on a single component or characteristic of a group, they deny the principle of interdependence and wholeness which requires that the observational viewpoint be the gestalt of the entire group taken as a whole, single entity.

It is again important to emphasize that self-reports, group outcomes, and sociometric methods of observing small groups are important and indeed valuable as techniques to observe selected structural aspects of decision-making groups. As a fundamental observational method from the viewpoint of communication and group process, however, each of these methods is too restricted in its scope and possesses too many inherent limitations to be highly useful.

OBSERVING COMMUNICATIVE BEHAVIOR

Obviously any method of group observation satisfactory for our purposes directly observes the communicative behaviors of all group members. Equally obvious is the fact that observing communicative behavior is extraordinarily difficult. There are no yardsticks, no microscopes with which to observe a communicative act. Communicative acts, first of all, are not physical objects which exist principally in space, such as a molecule of water. Rather, a communicative act exists only in the dimension of time. It is fleeting and transient. It ceases to exist immediately and is not permanently available for observation. And any relatively permanent record of communicative behavior, such as film or videotape, is inherently and vitally incomplete and distorted, which further compounds the problem of observation.

Of course, not all human behavior is necessarily communicative. Although any behavior may be communicative in a given situation, some behaviors performed during group interaction are not relevant in that they do not significantly affect the group process of interaction. Thus, any observation of communicative acts must judge which behaviors are significant or relevant and which are not. No concrete guidelines are available to enable an observer to make such judgments with unquestioned validity and reliability. And authorities in communication even disagree on what communication is.

The problems involved in observing communicative behaviors are not yet solved to everyone's satisfaction. This section emphasizes only a very few of those knotty problems encountered when attempting to describe and analyze human communicative behavior.

Verbal and Nonverbal

You may have heard Stan Freberg's rather famous recording of "John and Marcia," now several decades old. At the time it was first released, many radio stations banned the humorist's record from being played on the air on the grounds that it was too suggestive. Interestingly enough, this record includes only background organ music to a male and female voice (both by Freberg) repeating just two words over and over—"John" and "Marcia." But the full impact of the record is not available by reading a verbal transcript of the spoken words. Even without the visual medium, the nonverbal aspects of the record were sufficient for many people to consider the record obscene. Admittedly, most people thought the record was just humorous.

By comparison, the observation of verbal communicative acts is relatively simple. A written transcript provides a rather permanent record of verbal communication. The language employed by communicators embodies both a syntactical structure and semantic aspect which are generally clear to users of that language. Of course, meanings of words and phrases are typically developed throughout the interaction as McHugh (1968) has demonstrated. But all things considered, verbal communication is quite susceptible to observation when compared with nonverbal aspects of communicative behavior.

Scheflen (1969) firmly states that a complete observation of human communication should include both verbal and nonverbal aspects. But nonverbal communication—those elements of communication which do not involve an actual language or words, those elements of communication which do not appear in a stenographic transcript—is not easily observable. Nonverbal communication possesses no accepted rules of syntactical structure and no clear-cut meanings of nonverbal symbols. A brief survey of just a few of the varieties of nonverbal communication should highlight the difficulties inherent in observing it systematically or deriving any significant conclusions from its observation.

Perhaps the most familiar form of nonverbal communication is through the use of gestures and bodily movement. Commonly known as "kinesics," this form of nonverbal communication recently achieved a modicum of national popularity with the publication of a popularized, highly incomplete, and oversimplified treatment in a book called *Body Language* written by a free-lance writer, Julius Fast. *Body Language* was also the subject of a scathing and derisively frank book review (Huenergardt, 1971), which may be of interest to those who have read Fast's book as their only exposure to nonverbal communication.

As one might suspect, attempting to observe gestures and bodily movements as communicative acts is exceedingly difficult. What does a wave of the arm mean? How does one determine the difference between a nervous twitch and nonverbal communication? Do gestures differ in meaning and significance when used with spoken language? Attempts to answer such questions range from the unwieldy and cumbersome kinesic "alphabet" of Birdwhistell (1970, pp. 257–302) to the overly ambiguous and global analysis of Knapp (1972), discounting Fast's popularized version. The complexity of observing gestural communication is illustrated by Birdwhistell's notation system which includes ten symbols for different movements of the neck, thirteen symbols for different eye movements, and no fewer than twenty different positions of the mouth. Precisely what all those movements mean in a communicative situation remains highly speculative.

Communicators also use physical space as a medium for communication. The distance between communicators which, like kinesics, varies from one culture to another is a variety of nonverbal communication generally known as "proxemics." The study of proxemic communication and personal space has been confounded by the discovery of territorial behavior in nonhuman species. That is, a bird or other animal tends to lay claim to a particular geographical area and to defend that area against invaders. But despite numerous attempts to confirm territorial behavior in humans, territoriality has not been found to be a significant influence on human behavior (Weick, 1968, p. 90).

Applied to small group communication, proxemics has typically taken the form of determining whether the group leader tends to take a seat at the head of a rectangular table or whether most messages are exchanged between persons facing each other, sitting beside each other, or sitting diagonally from each other (Sommer, 1969). Such questions are probably only peripheral to the correct perspective of communication and small groups as a process because these questions assume a deterministic influence of the physical environment on the group's structure. Moreover, knowledge of a group process would lead us to believe that group members probably accustom themselves over a period of time to whatever spatial aspects of nonverbal communication are prevalent among the members. As group interaction progresses through time, group members tend to be less susceptible to the influence of the physical environment of their behavior.

Other nonverbal aspects of human communication appear to be significant in the observation of total communicative behavior. Williams (1970) and Lynch (1970) illustrate how stylistic features and syntactical structures of language employed by communicators may be observed, even though the observation may not be convenient or easy. Certainly vocal quality, emphasis, pitch, use of pauses, rate of speaking, pronunciation, word choice, and dialect contribute to the communicative act. "Anatomy of a Decision," included in Appendix One, hints at the potential significance of some of these nonverbal aspects of the language— specifically, pauses and word choice. These nonverbal aspects of verbal expression certainly are important to understanding the complete communicative situation.

Generally speaking, the methods used to observe nonverbal aspects of group communication are relatively unsophisticated at this early stage of development and unfortunately are of limited usefulness because of the limited extent of our knowledge. Until new and more convenient methods to observe nonverbal communication are devised and related to group process, the analytical method which will be proposed for the observation of group communication must reluctantly include only verbal aspects of communication.

The omission of nonverbal communication is particularly unfortunate. Scheflen (1965) has demonstrated that nonverbal communicative behavior is potentially quite significant to a process viewpoint of interdependent behaviors in group communication. Nevertheless, the system of interaction analysis to be discussed later excludes consideration of nonverbal communicative behaviors. It is hoped that such nonverbal aspects can be incorporated into an analytical system at some future date.

Effects of the Observer on Groups

Observing all the communicative behaviors, even just those verbal behaviors, of group members during group interaction requires that an observer be present in one form or another throughout the entire period of group interaction. The observation, of course, may not require the physical presence of an observing individual. But some observational device, such as a camera or a tape recorder, must be present in order to provide a semipermanent record of the group interaction. The question inevitably arises as to whether the presence of an observer or observational device significantly affects the behavior of group members during their interaction. That is, do members of a group behave differently because they are aware that they are being watched?

Sherif and Sherif (1964, p. 10) indicate that an observer unavoidably affects the behavior of persons who are aware of being observed. On the other hand, Herrold et al. (1953) indicate that the effect of an observer on group interaction is not significant. But Barker and Wright (1955) are more specific in their highly plausible explanation of the extent to which an observer affects group behavior. These authors indicate that the observer exerts significant effect on behaving individuals only during a brief period when the observation begins. As the individuals become accustomed to being observed, they essentially ignore the outside observer, considering him to be a part of the context, and behave normally.

Applied specifically to the process of small group decision making, the effect of the observer on the group process is probably negligible during most of their interaction. During the Orientation phase primary tension is at its peak, and the members are attempting to accustom themselves to the unfamiliarity of the group task and the social structure of the group. At this time of self-acclimation to the group task and the social structure of the group, the observer is just another unfamiliar phenomenon which must be considered along with all other aspects of the physical environment. It is reasonable to assume that after the members have alleviated their primary tension, the impact of an observer or observational device should be minimized.

Of course, the observer who is physically present with clipboard in hand and within sight of the "guinea pigs" may continue to develop "fish bowl" feelings among group members. Observational methods which require members to be wired to some electronic device which records their physiological responses would also hardly evoke normal behaviors from those individuals being so "observed." On the other hand, an unobtrusive tape recorder or camera should not reasonably evoke feelings among members that they are nothing more than guinea pigs in a laboratory. Indeed, classroom groups utilizing cassette tape recorders typically admit that they soon forget the tape recorder is there at all. On at least one occasion a classroom group demonstrated the minimal influence of the audiotape recorder on their interactive patterns. When the group failed to return the recorder after one of their group meetings, it was discovered that they had concluded their meeting and left the room with the tape recorder still running. There are also numerous examples of recorded dialogue from classroom groups which reflect their almost total lack of inhibitions due to the language they use and the subject matter they choose to discuss.

We can probably safely conclude that the observer of group communication may affect the communicative behavior of group members during their earliest and generally unstructured period of interaction. But the impact of the observer is probably localized within the initial period of observation and does not significantly affect the group process of decision making.

INTERACTION ANALYSIS

The method of observation most pertinent to communication and the group process is interaction analysis. Generally, interaction analysis may be considered a form of content analysis applied to human communicative behaviors. "Analysis" typically implies breaking down some "whole" into its component parts. For example, an analysis of the content of pure water would reveal the presence of two units of hydrogen and one unit of oxygen. In this example of content analysis, the content of water is analyzed into its compositional elements. The principle is the same for a content analysis of interaction—reducing the whole of interaction into its compositional factors and the relative quantity of each.

"Now is the time for all good men to come to the aid of their party" is a familiar sentence used for a variety of purposes. The sentence may also be submitted to various systems of content analysis. One system might analyze the sentence into categories of "parts of speech" and use "words" as the units to be measured or counted. Such an analysis would reveal sixteen words analyzed as four nouns, two verbs, four adjectives, one pronoun, one adverb, and four prepositions. (I surely hope my English grammar is correct.)

Often this sentence is used to test the functional operation of a typewriter in much the same way that the prospective automobile buyer kicks the tires of an automobile. But a second content analysis of that same sentence using "letters of the alphabet" as units of measurement as well as analytical categories reveals that eight letters are not included in that sentence. Thus, the typewriter inspector would fail to observe the function of eight different keys. A better sentence used for the purpose of testing typewriters would be, "The quick brown fox jumped over the lazy dog's back." A similar content analysis of this latter sentence reveals at least one instance of every letter of the alphabet. (Go ahead and check it!)

Interaction analysis, then, is a general method for analyzing the content of communicative behaviors by breaking down the whole of interaction into its component acts. While experts in many fields of study have employed numerous varieties and different methods of interaction analysis, the remainder of this section offers only a few of those varieties. This section will further emphasize one particular method of interaction analysis exemplified by one specific system. For a more complete description of the various methods of content analysis, many books are available which describe such procedures in much greater detail. One source book which describes various methods of content analysis and guidelines for developing new methods is Holsti (1969).

Characteristics

Perhaps the most important characteristic of any form of content analysis is developing the categories or "pigeonholes" to classify the units of the content which is to be analyzed. For example, the simple examples of content analysis, mentioned earlier, employed chemical elements, parts of speech, and letters of the alphabet as analytical categories. A postal employee is something of a content analyst, too, when he sorts mail into pigeonholes or mailbags. He uses the various destinations of mailed items as his analytical categories.

The categories used for all methods of content analysis also possess several essential characteristics. The list of categories used to analyze the content of group interaction, for our purposes, must be exhaustive, mutually exclusive, and context free. "Exhaustive" categories imply that every potential communicative act must be capable of being placed in one of the categories. If any communicative act does not "fit" into one of the categories, then the categories do not exhaust all possible communicative behaviors. Hence, some known communicative behaviors are not analyzed by the system.

"Mutually exclusive" categories stipulate that any communicative act can be placed in one and only one category. In other words, no two categories overlap each other. However, a complete list of analytical categories of any given system may include several dimensions or subcategories. In that case, all categories within each dimension must be mutually exclusive.

Categories are "context-free" to the extent that a communicative act is the same in all groups observed. That is, acts representing any category are the same in one group as they appear in any other group. For example, a group member expresses disagreement in one group in much the same manner that another group member expresses disagreement in any other group.

Methods of interaction analysis employed in the past have varied widely in terms of the categories used for the analysis of group interaction. For example, Fisher (1970a) and Longabaugh (1963) developed categories based on the various functions performed by communicative acts. Bales (1950a, 1950b) based his IPA categories on task and social problems which a group encounters during interaction. Berg's (1967) and Charles Larson's (1969) categories were themes discussed by members. Other category systems might include the intent of the communicator or the act's effect on the environment. It is obvious that there are no standard categories used in the interaction analyses of small groups—no list of categories upon which all or even most experts can even begin to agree. The reason for the absence of any standard list of categories of communicative behaviors should be apparent. Experts cannot even agree on a common theory of communication. Hence, they cannot agree on specific applications (that is, concrete acts) of a single theory. While Bales's system of Interaction Process

Analysis has enjoyed more popular usage than any other, it has probably outlived any further usefulness.

A second characteristic essential to a system of interaction analysis is the unit of measurement. In other words, what is the communicative act to be counted and placed into a category? Again there is no standardized unit of measurement. Hawes (1972a, 1972b), Berg (1967), and Amidon and Flanders (1967) counted as units of communicative behaviors time intervals ranging from three to five seconds. Bales (1950a, 1950b), along with Crowell and Scheidel (1961), preferred to use the expression of a single thought as a unit. Fisher (1970a) and Valentine (1972) employed function units reflected in group interaction.

But while the nature of the unit or the communicative act may differ, the more important characteristic of interaction analysis involves the process of how the sequences of acts are interstructured during group interaction. For the purpose of group process, then, it is more important that sequences of acts are treated as single units as well as each individual act by itself. Thus, interacts and double interacts become even more important than the nature of the individual act. Interacts (units of two contiguous acts) and double interacts (units of three contiguous acts) provide an insight into the process (both structure and action) of group communication which is missing from an analysis of just the quantity of single acts.

Many have advocated the use of multiple units of communicative acts in interaction analysis, including Weick (1968, p. 407, and 1969, p. 33), McGrath and Altman (1966, p. 74), Fisher and Hawes (1971), Scheflen (1969), and Gouran and Baird (1972). And some people have even utilized interacts (Fisher, 1970a; Amidon and Flanders, 1967) and double interacts (Barker and Wright, 1955, who used the term, "cycle") in actual applications of interaction analysis.

Contemporary methods of interaction analysis include two specific kinds which differ significantly in their relative emphases. In the absence of better terms, they shall be differentiated as "dimensional" interaction analysis and "dynamic" interaction analysis.

The type of interaction analysis discussed thus far has been the "dynamic" analysis which counts a specific communicative act as a unit and pigeonholes it into a single category. "Dynamic" analysis further emphasizes sequential clusters of acts in the form of interacts and double interacts. "Dynamic" analysis thus attempts to observe the process of group interaction by incorporating aspects of both the structure and action of group communication. Because this type of interaction analysis attempts to discover not only whether changes occur during group interaction but how those structural changes take place over time, it is called "dynamic" analysis. The specific system of interaction analysis which appears later in this section is a specific example of "dynamic" interaction analysis.

"Dimensional" interaction analysis, on the other hand, emphasizes specific qualitative dimensions of a single communicative act. Typically, observers judge qualitatively the degree to which certain dimensions of behavior (for example, assertiveness, objectivity, dominance, clarity) are reflected in a single communicative act. Systems of "dimensional" analysis, such as those developed by

Leathers (1971) and, to a great extent, Borgatta and Crowther (1965), emphasize specific characteristics of single acts rather than the broader view of sequences of acts embodied in a process. By observing dimensions of selected acts at various points in the discussion, of course, dimensional analysis can discover whether structural changes have occurred during group interaction but not the process of how the structure changed.

In short, "dynamic" interaction analysis sacrifices an in-depth analysis of specific communicative acts in favor of a process view. And "dimensional" interaction analysis sacrifices the process view in favor of an in-depth analysis of specific acts. Of course, these two types of interaction analysis are not antagonistic to each other and could easily be combined within a single system of interaction analysis. A rather comprehensive search during the writing of this book, however, failed to reveal even one instance of such a combined approach.

Any system of interaction analysis naturally does not attempt to observe all aspects of human communicative behaviors. Rather, any analysis inherently and necessarily focuses on those communicative aspects which are relevant to the categories. Hence, the categories selected for analysis are vitally important to the outcome of the analysis itself. Aspects of any behavior or act which are not reflected in the categories are implicitly considered irrelevant or insignificant and are ignored during observation and analysis. Interaction analysis, like any form of observation, is not reality itself but an abstraction of observed reality—incomplete and selective, and perhaps even somewhat distorted.

Unlike other forms of observing small groups and the process of communication, interaction analysis emphasizes what happens during group interaction, how it happens, and how changes in communicative structure occur over a period of time. Interaction analysis inherently observes communicative behavior directly. Aspects of why members behave as they do and what influence their behaviors have on determining the specific quality of eventual consensus decisions are not central to this mode of observation. Interdependent relationships, rather than their causes or effects, are considered infinitely more important and are at the core of the specific system of interaction analysis described in the following section.

A System of Interaction Analysis

Since the model of decision emergence discussed in Chapter 7 resulted from applied interaction analysis, the system which led to discovering that model of group decision making seems appropriate to illustrate how interaction analysis might function. This system is admittedly imperfect, as are all others. It includes only verbal communication and probably places undue emphasis on the task dimension of the group process. Despite its imperfections, however, the following system provides a general example of how interaction analysis might actually be utilized to observe group communication.

Central to this system of interaction analysis, you will recall from earlier chapters, is the concept of a decision proposal. As a member presents an issue for consideration by other group members, that issue is potentially an item which will achieve group consensus—that is, a proposed decision being considered by the group members. As each member comments on that proposal, he implicitly attempts to influence the group's perception of the proposal. Naturally he need not be aware of attempting to influence the other members. Thus, his comment "functions" on that proposal in some specific manner. The different functions which a member can possibly perform on a decision proposal through an act of communication comprise the list of categories used in the analysis.

Each member's uninterrupted comment is considered a unit or an act of communication. If his uninterrupted comment contains an instance of two functions (that is, if his single comment crosses function categories before it is interrupted by a comment from another member), it is considered two units. During actual observation of groups, nearly all uninterrupted comments were found to contain only a single act or unit of communication.

These functionally defined units are quite obviously not of uniform length in either number of words or number of seconds. A single individual performing a single function on the decision proposal in a single uninterrupted comment is considered to be a single act or communication unit regardless of its relative length.

The categories for this system of interaction analysis, slightly modified from their original form, are as follows:

1 Interpretation
    f   Favorable toward the decision proposal
    u   Unfavorable toward the decision proposal
    ab Ambiguous toward the decision proposal containing a bivalued (both favorable and unfavorable) evaluation
    an Ambiguous toward the decision proposal containing a neutral evaluation
2 Substantiation
    f   Favorable toward the decision proposal
    u   Unfavorable toward the decision proposal
    ab Ambiguous toward the decision proposal containing a bivalued (both favorable and unfavorable) evaluation
    an Ambiguous toward the decision proposal containing a neutral evaluation
3 Clarification
4 Modification
5 Agreement
6 Disagreement

Several additional symbols are employed to simplify the analysis of interaction in practice. One symbol O_n is used in addition to one of the categories above. It designates that act as the one which originates a new decision proposal (identified by a subscript number) by introducing that proposal into the group discussion for the first time. Another symbol D_n indicates the act which reintroduces into group discussion a decision proposal (identified by its original subscript number) which the group members had discussed previously. These two symbols do not represent categories of acts. Rather, they are used in addition to the actual analysis of interaction in order that the observer might keep track of which decision proposal is under consideration at all times.

A category, designated "Procedural," not included in the above list, specifies acts which do not actually discuss a decision proposal and are not substantive to the process of group decision making. Such acts coded into the "Procedural" category rarely occurred during group interaction and were excluded from the final results of interaction analysis.

While the categories are not difficult to understand, a brief explanation of each is probably necessary. The category of "Interpretation" (1) reflects a simple value judgment without evidence, reasons, or explanation offered to support the credibility of that judgment. "Substantiation" (2), on the other hand, refers to an act which does include supporting evidence and reasons to enhance the believability of the expressed value judgment. Thus, an act of "substantiation" is more argumentative than one of "interpretation."

Both "interpretation" and "substantiation" are subject to further classification in one of four subcategories or dimensions of the larger category. "Favorable" (f) and "unfavorable" (u) categories should be self-explanatory. The two varieties of "ambiguous" categories may be less clear. The comment, "That seems like a good idea, but we need to talk about it some more," is ambiguous because it includes both a favorable and an unfavorable evaluation of the proposal—hence, a bivalued evaluation and an instance of the "ab" category. The comment, "That is a very interesting suggestion," is unclear because it evaluates the idea without expressing clear approval or disapproval of the suggestion—hence a neutral evaluation and an instance of the "an" category. Both comments, of course, reflect interpretations rather than substantiation and would reflect both the general and the specific dimensions of the category—that is, "1ab" and "1an" respectively.

The category of "clarification" (3) indicates those acts which function to render an idea pertaining to the decision proposal more readily understandable. No evaluation is implied in such a comment. Rather, the act restates some previous act in more concrete language.

"Modification" (4) signifies an act functioning to amend the decision proposal under consideration by direct means. The section in Chapter 7 which discusses the group process of modifying decisions indicates that instances of this category rarely occur during group interaction.

"Agreement (5) and "disagreement" (6) express support or nonsupport of the immediately preceding act. A typical "5" comment, such as "Yes," "You're right," or "Okay," does not function directly on the decision proposal. But such a comment indirectly affects the members' perception of that proposal by adding weight to the act which precedes the agreement. Whatever the preceding function unit, the "5" unit assumes the functional meaning of that antecedent category and underscores it. If "5" follows a "2f" unit, for example, it reinforces by agreement the "substantiation favoring" the decision proposal.

If "6" or "disagreement" follows a "2f" act, it expresses disfavor through negatively reinforcing the "favorable substantiation." The "6" unit, then, indirectly functions as a negative evaluation of the decision proposal by disfavoring the specific preceding act which favored it. An excerpt from an actual group discussion might serve to clarify how one might apply this system of interaction analysis. The following excerpt is from a management training group discussing budget allocations for their hypothetical corporation. Decision proposal 1 might be phrased, "The corporation should seek to discover what its fixed costs will be after the proposed plant expansion has been completed." The first comment in the excerpt below initiates this proposal, and all other comments are directed toward that single proposal. The symbols which appear to the left of each communicative act indicate the classification of each unit according to the categories of the system. When in doubt, refer to the previous listing of the categories and their identifying symbols.

1an0$_1$	**A**	Would we want to spend $2,000 this first quarter to find out what the cost of our plant expansion is going to be?
3 (asks for)	**D**	The cost of what?
3	**A**	Our fixed expenses. Would we like to know how much they are going to be?
1u	**B**	No. I'm not really worried about that.
1u	**D**	No. I'm not concerned about that.
2f	**A**	But if we are concerned about production and profit, that's a factor. That is a fixed operating cost we are going to have to live with. We should know in advance what it is going to cost us.
6	**B**	No.
2u	**C**	But knowing it won't influence our decision to expand or not.
2u	**D**	Why pay $2,000 to get it if we are going to have to pay it anyway!
2f	**A**	Until we do it the first time, we've got no idea if this is going to be another $6,000 or whether it's going to be as high as $30,000. That might influence us considerably on our long-range goals.
2u	**B**	We are going to have to expand in spite of that, though.
2u	**D**	I don't think we are ever going to refuse to expand. So the first time that we do expand, we are going to find out the fixed operating cost.
5	**G**	Yeah.
2u	**D**	By rights, it shouldn't be more. By normal operating procedures, it shouldn't be more than we pay right now. It should be less because our main plant has already been built.
3 (asks for)	**A**	Do you mean less than $6,000?
3 (restates)	**D**	Yes, I do.
2u	**A**	Well, if it is anything less than $6,000, it would really be silly to spend $2,000 to find it out.

2u   **D** By just using common business sense, you have to say it is $6,000 or less. It can't be more unless they have to blast a hillside out of the way to get the addition to the main plant in.

5   **C** Yeah, I think you're right.

  The above excerpt should explain by example how this system of interaction analysis may be utilized in actual practice. Note the several comments which ask for clarification. In both cases, the comment immediately following the request provides the clarification. Member D's "Yes, I do" might appear, outside the context of the interaction, to be agreement. But it is really a clarification of his preceding comment in direct response to A's request for clarification of his intended meaning. The other coded acts appear to need no further explanation.

  After the group interaction has been analyzed into acts, the interaction is then divided into interacts. Figure 11 illustrates the interacts included in the brief excerpt coded above. The rows of the matrix in Figure 11 are the categories of the interaction analysis system which include the first or "antecedent" comment of each interact. The columns across the top of the matrix are the categories of the second or "subsequent" act of each interact. Thus, each cell in the matrix represents an interact. The first act is the row across, and the second act is the column down.

  Nineteen acts appear in the excerpt above which translates into eighteen interacts. The first act "1an" is the antecedent of the second act "3" and comprises the first interact in the excerpt. The second act "3" is also the antecedent of the third act in the excerpt, also "3" which together comprise the second interact in the excerpt. Thus, a sequence of three acts includes two interacts, and the entire excerpt of nineteen single acts contains a total of eighteen interacts.

  Figure 11 indicates during even this brief excerpt that a trend develops regarding the group's treatment of decision proposal 1 in their interactive patterns. Note that the only acts expressing favor of the proposal, two "2f" units, are immediately followed by acts which conflict with the favoring function. One of the subsequent acts is outright disagreement, "6", and the other argues the opposing side, "2u." Once the argument started, the other members "piled it on" by positively reinforcing the seven "2u" units with additional "2u" units a total of three times, and twice with agreement, "5."

  Scheidel and Crowell (1964) named a matrix with interacts, such as that in Figure 11, "contiguity analysis." Such an analysis provides the basis for analyzing possible phases of group decision making. A single matrix could be used to summarize all the interacts during a specified time period, for example, five minutes, so that a sixty-minute group discussion would require twelve matrices such as that illustrated in Figure 11. Each matrix could then be compared with the next, and any changes in interact patterns could be easily discerned. In this way, phase progressions during group decision making were discovered.

  Statistical treatment confirmed that differences between phases of group

Figure 11 Interacts contained in interaction analysis.

	Subsequent acts											
Antecedent acts	1f	1u	1ab	1an	2f	2u	2ab	2an	3	4	5	6
1f												
1u		1			1							
1ab												
1an									1			
2f						1						1
2u					1	3			1		2	
2ab												
2an												
3		1			1				2			
4												
5						1						
6						1						

decision making were indeed statistically significant differences. Scheidel (1969) has also demonstrated how such a matrix could be converted to indicate the probability of occurrence of double interacts during group interaction. But our purposes do not include explaining the various statistical manipulations employed in any observational system of interaction analysis. It is sufficient that we are able to perceive how interaction analysis can work and how it is possible to observe an honest-to-goodness decision-making group in action.

POSTSCRIPT

This system of interaction analysis, illustrated and explained above, is by no means ideal or standardized. But it does provide some explanation of the difficulties involved in observing the process of group communication. It should also indicate that despite these difficulties, group communication can be observed and observed validly and reliably with just a little practice. In fact, this system could be employed by classroom groups to analyze their own or another group's interaction patterns. Everyone should be encouraged to try this or another system of interaction analysis. The important point is not to tout any one method of interaction analysis (at least, not yet) but to realize that interaction analysis does provide a method, however imperfect, for observing and understanding group communication as a process during group decision making.

A Reader's Guide to Jargon

AN INTRODUCTORY NOTE

One complaint frequently expressed by students involves the use of unfamiliar and often incomprehensible terms peculiar to a specific area of study. Contrary to the firm convictions of most students, nearly everyone deplores the unwarranted use of jargon. Nevertheless, it sometimes appears that alleged experts speak to each other in their own specialized foreign language, familiar only to other experts within that field, just so they can "snow" those of us who are unaware.

Jargon has become infamous as a term commonly applied to all meaningless gibberish. In all frankness, much jargon seems to be little more than mere gibberish. But jargon, in and of itself, is not inherently evil. In fact, jargon is vitally important to any specialized field in order to add precision to an otherwise deplorably vague language. Distinctions in any specialized field are often so precise that no word or phrase in the common English vocabulary can adequately describe these distinctions. Hence, a new word is coined in order to describe specifically an event or phenomenon that would otherwise be inadequately described. Descriptions without jargon are, at best, awkward, lengthy, and abstract. Jargon allows specialists to make further advances in their study. Unfortunately, nonspecialists often find the jargon confusing.

Jargon is not only unavoidable and even desirable but absolutely essential to the progress of any specialized field of study. But jargon can also create unnecessary problems for a student who is new to that field. Problems most often arise when jargon proliferates beyond the bounds of rational explanation. Unnecessarily picayune distinctions aid the proliferation of jargon in many areas. Unfortunately the field of communication, particularly group communication, possesses more than its share of superfluous jargon. The reason for this undesirable state of affairs is probably the fact that no unifying theory exists to guide specialists in their study of communication. As a result, new "discoveries" often create new terms and new distinctions which seem uncommonly similar to other distinctions made earlier by other specialists. It is ironic but probably true that specialists in the study of communication don't communicate with each other very well. And in the meantime, the jargon of communication proliferates.

This book was written by a person who possesses an intense personal dislike of superfluous jargon and who is aware of his students' even greater distaste for apparent gibberish. As a result, much of the jargon related to communication and group decision making does not appear in these pages. For example, the following jargonistic terms do not appear on any other page in this volume: synergy, syntality, comparison level of alternatives, satisficing, propinquity, parmia, propathy, dynamogenics, cyclothymia, entropy, and equifinality. Some of these terms, obviously jargon, do symbolize extremely important distinctions. But none of the terms was considered essential to our present purpose. Therefore, they were all omitted. Of course, some of the terms in the brief list above also seem, personally, to be absolutely superfluous.

This section is intended as a handy reference to jargon used recurrently in this volume and recognized for what it is—jargon. But these distinctions are considered vital to the understanding of communication and group process. While all terms are not completely defined below, most of the key definitions are included.

One word of caution for the reader who uses this section of the Appendix! Do not be misled by simple and, in most cases, oversimplified definitions. To repeat, definitions are easy; understanding is more difficult. Do not use a brief definition as a substitute for understanding the concept. Every definition is admittedly general and incomplete. But each definition also includes the chapter or chapters in which the term is discussed in more detail. Memorize definitions if you must, but don't confuse your ability to define with genuine understanding and knowledge.

THE JARGON

Affective conflict   Emotional clashes between members of a social system typically on procedural issues. (Chapter 6)

Assembly effect   The ability of a group to achieve collectively a level of productivity greater than the sum of the individuals working by themselves. (Chapter 3)

Barrier or Breakdown A cessation or blockage of communication based on the fallacious assumption that communication embodies only the structural aspects of sending and receiving messages along a channel. (Chapter 8)

Centrality A characteristic of a communication network indicating the position in the network requiring the fewest linkages to transmit a message to every other member of the group. (Chapter 8)

Channel capacity The number of items of information which an individual can effectively process at one time. (Chapter 8)

Coalition A temporary alliance among two or more members of a social system typically oriented toward a difference of opinion on means to achieve the group goal. (Chapters 6, 7, and 8)

Cohesiveness The output of a group's socioemotional dimension; essentially, the degree to which members are attracted to each other and personally committed to the group. (Chapter 3)

Conformity Uniform behaviors exhibited by members of a social system due to the members' choosing among conflicting alternatives of behavior that alternative least subject to negative social influences. (Chapter 6)

Consensus The degree of personal commitment the members feel toward the group decision after it has been reached. (Chapter 7)

Contingency model A model of group leadership developed by Fiedler which incorporates general predictions of leader effectiveness in selected situations. Predictions are based on ASo/LPC scores of group leaders. (Chapter 5)

Decision In a group, a choice from among available alternatives which is validated by achieving consensus among members. (Chapter 7)

Decision making As a group task, the process of choosing among alternatives for which no "best" or "correct" answer can be validated by any means other than group consensus. (Chapter 7)

Deviance Behavior of members not in conformity with group norms or expectations. (Chapter 6)

Distance, communication A characteristic of a communication network indicating the number of links required for one position in the network to transmit a message to another position. (Chapter 8)

Double interact A sequence of three contiguous acts performed by group members. (Chapters 2, 7, and 8)

Emergence A gradual process describing how groups develop their roles, including leader, and decisions in the LGD. (Chapters 5 and 7)

Encapsulation A method used for controlling social conflict through regulating conflict by a set of rules agreed upon by all parties to the conflict. (Chapter 6)

Evolution The characteristic of a system embodying its history, that is, the enduring changes in the system's structure and function over an extended period of time. (Chapter 2)

Feedback   A mutually causal sequence of events or acts which, self-reflexively, exerts influence on the original act or event in the sequence. Feedback, as a response to a deviant act or event, serves to counteract that deviance (negative feedback) or amplify the deviance (positive feedback). (Chapters 6, 7, 8, and 10)

Flight   The behavioral tendency of a group to cease considering their task as a means of avoiding some unpleasant stimulus, commonly social conflict. (Chapters 6 and 7)

Formal   A term used to describe the norms, status hierarchy, communication networks, etc., of a social system sanctioned or prescribed by legitimate sources of power or authority. (Chapters 5 and 10)

Formula answer   An oversimplified and unrealistic solution to a complex problem; typically so general that it is incapable of being implemented. (Chapters 6 and 9)

Function   The characteristic of a system denoted by the relationships among components in time and which serves to regulate the ongoing action of the system. (Chapter 2)

Group   A collection of three or more individuals whose behaviors are interstructured so that members exert on each other a mutual reciprocal influence. (Chapter 2)

Group mind   An outmoded belief in the independence of a group's manner of thinking and feeling apart from its members. (Chapters 2 and 10)

Idiosyncrasy credits   An economic model which explains the leader as both a deviant and a conformist and which illustrates the ability of a group leader to innovate after having conformed to the group norms for a period of time. (Chapter 6)

Informal   A term used to describe the norms, status hierarchy, communication networks, etc., developed through the emergent "natural process" and not necessarily sanctioned by legitimate sources of authority or power. (Chapters 5 and 10)

Interact   A sequence of two contiguous acts performed by group members. (Chapters 2, 7, and 8)

Interaction Process Analysis (IPA)   The system of interaction analysis developed by Robert F. Bales. (Chapter 7)

Interdependence   A relationship between two or more elements so that each influences and is influenced by the other. (Chapters 2 through 10)

Leaderless group discussion (LGD)   A task-oriented group whose members possess the capacity to determine for themselves the group's structure, function, and behavior. (Chapter 2)

Leadership   A high-status position achieved in an LGD by performing leadership acts recognized by other group members as helping the group perform its task; defined interdependently with followership. (Chapter 5)

Legitimacy   The principle of prescription or prior approval of norms, values, roles, or other standards imposed on a group by some person or source outside the group whose authority over them is recognized by the group members. (Chapters 5 and 10)

Message A single communicative act. (Chapter 8)

Natural process A process of group development, nearly universal, which is based on "rules" governing behavior. Group members need not be aware of these "rules." (Chapter 10)

Network The structure of channel linkages among group members which illustrates the pattern of transmitting and receiving messages. (Chapter 8)

Nonsummativity A principle inherent in any system which stipulates that the whole is greater than or different from the sum of its parts due to the interdependent relationships among the parts. (Chapter 10)

Norm A standard which regulates the behavior of all members of a group through negative feedback directed at members whose behaviors are contrary to that standard. (Chapter 4)

Primary tension The inhibitions of group members during the early period of group development; similar to the individual's phenomenon of "stage fright." (Chapter 4)

Process A sequence of events or actions continuously changing over time in progress toward some goal. (Chapter 2)

Productivity The output of a group's task dimension; the quality or quantity of work performed by a group. (Chapter 3)

Punctuation In a system, the process of organizing the sequence of acts or events in order to discover meaning and significance in the sequence. (Chapter 10)

Reach-testing The process of introducing a new idea from an anchored position of group agreement in the spiral model. Other group members test that idea through discussion and may accept it, reject it, extend it, or revise it. (Chapter 7)

Reciprocity A norm typical of most social systems which encourages members to respond to the behaviors of others with similar behaviors. (Chapter 4)

Risky shift The tendency of a group to make decisions involving greater risk, that is, with a bigger payoff but a lower probability of attainment, when compared with decisions made by individuals. (Chapter 3)

Role A position occupied by a group member in an interlocking network including all group members; defined in terms of the behaviors performed by the member. (Chapter 4)

Secondary tension Social discomfort typified by abrupt and abnormal departures from the routine functioning of a group; induced by interpersonal conflict, environmental pressures, feeling of frustration, etc. (Chapter 4)

Self-disclosure Statements made to another person which reveal one's feelings, thoughts, beliefs, desires, or needs in the social situation. (Chapter 4)

Spiral model The process of decision making involving constant backtracking and reach-testing of ideas until the idea develops during group interaction to represent the consensus of the group members. (Chapter 7)

Status A social class or division rank ordered in a hierarchy from high to low. Status may be ascribed, that is, given the position by some higher authority. Status may also be achieved, as in the LGD, through behaviors recognized by other group members as beneficial to the group. (Chapter 5)

Structure   The characteristic of a system denoted by the physical or spatial arrangement of the components at any given point in time. (Chapter 2)

Substantive conflict   Intellectual clashes among members of a social system on issues pertaining to the group task. (Chapter 6)

System   An entity which behaves as an entity because of the interdependence of its component elements. (Chapters 2 and 10)

Tolerance threshold   The maximum degree of tension which will not prohibit a group from functioning normally. Social tension at a level above the threshold disrupts the ability of the group to function as a group. (Chapter 4)

Verbal innovative deviance (VID)   The behavior of a group member reflecting his agreement with the group goal but his disagreement with the group majority on the appropriate means for achieving that goal. (Chapter 6)

Wholeness   A principle inherent in a system which stipulates that every component of the system affects and is affected by every other component and that a change in any one component inherently effects change in all other components. (Chapter 10)

References

Allen, Vernor, and J. Levine. (1969) "Consensus and Conformity," *Journal of Experimental Social Psychology,* **5**:389–399.

Allport, Floyd H. (1927) *The Group Fallacy.* Minneapolis: Sociological Press.

Allport, Gordon W. (1968) "The Historical Background of Modern Social Psychology," in Gardner Lindzey and Elliot Aronson (eds.), *The Handbook of Social Psychology,* 2nd ed., Vol. I. Reading, Massachusetts: Addison-Wesley, pp. 1–80.

Amidon, Edmund, and Ned Flanders. (1967) "Interaction Analysis as a Feedback System," in Edmund J. Amidon and John B. Hough (eds.), *Interaction Analysis: Theory, Research, and Application.* Reading, Massachusetts: Addison-Wesley, pp. 121–140.

Asch, Solomon E. (1951) "Effects of Group Pressure upon the Modification and Distortion of Judgments," in Harold Guetzkow (ed.), *Groups, Leadership, and Men.* Pittsburgh: Carnegie, pp. 171–190.

Asch, Solomon E. (1955) "Opinions and Social Pressure," *Scientific American.* **193**:31–55.

Asch, Solomon E. (1956) "Studies of Independence and Conformity: I. A Minority of One against a Unanimous Majority," *Psychological Monographs.* **70**:1–70.

Bales, Robert F. (1950a) *Interaction Process Analysis: A Method for the Study of Small Groups.* Cambridge, Massachusetts: Addison-Wesley.

Bales, Robert F. (1950b) "A Set of Categories for the Analysis of Small Group Interaction," *American Sociological Review,* **15**:257–263.

Bales, Robert F. (1953) "The Equilibrium Problem in Small Groups," in Talcott Parsons, Robert F. Bales, and Edward A. Shils (eds.), *Working Papers in the Theory of Action.* New York: Free Press, pp. 111–161.

Bales, Robert F. (1955) "Adaptive and Integrative Changes as Sources of Strain in Social Systems," in A. Paul Hare, Edgar F. Borgatta, and Robert F. Bales (eds.), *Small Groups: Studies in Social Interaction.* New York: Knopf, pp. 127–131.

Bales, Robert Freed. (1970) *Personality and Interpersonal Behavior.* New York: Holt, Rinehart and Winston.

Bales, Robert F., and Philip E. Slater. (1955) "Role Differentiation in Small Decision-making Groups," in Talcott Parsons et al. (eds.), *The Family, Socialization, and Interaction Process.* Glencoe, Illinois: Free Press, pp. 259–306.

Bales, Robert F., and Fred L. Strodtbeck. (1951) "Phases in Group Problem-Solving," *Journal of Abnormal and Social Psychology,* **46:**485–495.

Barker, R. G., and H. F. Wright. (1955) *Midwest and Its Children.* Evanston, Illinois: Row Peterson.

Bass, Bernard M. (1949) "An Analysis of the Leaderless Group Discussion," *Journal of Applied Psychology,* **33:**527–533.

Bass, Bernard M., C. R. McGehee, W. C. Hawkins, P. C. Young, and A. S. Gebel. (1953) "Personality Variables Related to Leaderless Group Discussion," *Journal of Abnormal and Social Psychology,* **48:**120–128.

Bayless, Ovid L. (1967) "An Alternate Pattern for Problem-Solving Discussion," *Journal of Communication,* **17:**188–197.

Beisecker, Thomas. (1969) "Communication and Conflict in Interpersonal Negotiations." A paper presented to the Speech Communication Association.

Benne, Kenneth D., and Paul Sheats. (1948) "Functional Roles of Group Members," *Journal of Social Issues,* **4:**41–49.

Bennis, Warren G., and Herbert A. Shepard. (1956) "A Theory of Group Development," *Human Relations,* **9:**415–437.

Bennis, Warren G., and Herbert A. Shepard. (1961) "Group Observation," in Warren G. Bennis, Kenneth D. Benne, and Robert Chin (eds.), *The Planning of Change,* 1st ed. New York: Holt, Rinehart and Winston, pp. 743–756.

Berg, David M. (1967) "A Descriptive Analysis of the Distribution and Duration of Themes Discussed by Task-Oriented Small Groups," *Speech Monographs,* **34:**172–175.

Berlo, David K. (1960) *The Process of Communication.* New York: Holt, Rinehart and Winston.

Birdwhistell, Ray L. (1970) *Kinesics and Context: Essays on Body Motion Communication.* Philadelphia: University of Pennsylvania Press.

Black, Edwin B. (1955) "Rhetorical Breakdown in Discussion," *Speech Monographs,* **22:**15–19.

Blau, Peter M. (1960) "A Theory of Social Integration," *American Journal of Sociology,* **65:**545–556.

Borgatta, Edgar F., and Betty Crowther. (1965) *A Workbook for the Study of Social Interaction Processes.* Chicago: Rand McNally.

Bormann, Ernest G. (1969) *Discussion and Group Methods.* New York: Harper and Row.

Bossman, Larry J., Jr. (1968) "An Analysis of Inter-Agent Residual-Influence Effects upon Members of Small Decision-Making Groups," *Behavioral Science,* **13**:220–233.

Brilhart, John K. (1967) *Effective Group Discussion.* Dubuque, Iowa: William C. Brown.

Cartwright, Dorwin, and Alvin Zander. (1968) "Leadership and Performance of Group Functions: Introduction," in Dorwin Cartwright and Alvin Zander (eds.), *Group Dynamics: Research and Theory,* 3rd ed. New York: Harper and Row, pp. 301–317.

Cattell, Raymond B. (1955) "Concepts and Methods in the Measurement of Group Syntality," in A. Paul Hare, Edgar F. Borgatta, and Robert F. Bales (eds.), *Small Groups: Studies in Social Interaction.* New York: Knopf, pp. 107–126.

Coch, Lester, and John R. P. French, Jr. (1948) "Overcoming Resistance to Change," *Human Relations,* **1**:512–533.

Cohen, A., W. Bennis, and G. Wolkon. (1961) "The Effects of Continued Practice on the Behavior of Problem-Solving Groups," *Sociometry,* **24**:416–431.

Collins, Barry E., and Harold Guetzkow. (1964) *A Social Psychology of Group Processes for Decision-Making.* New York: Wiley.

Coser, Lewis. (1956) *The Functions of Social Conflict.* New York: Free Press.

Crowell, Laura, and Thomas M. Scheidel. (1961) "Categories for Analysis of Idea Development in Discussion Groups," *Journal of Social Psychology,* **54**:155–268.

Dance, Frank E. X. (1970) "The 'Concept' of Communication," *Journal of Communication,* **20**:201–210.

Davis, James H. (1969) *Group Performance.* Reading, Massachusetts: Addison-Wesley.

Dentler, Robert A., and Kai T. Erikson. (1959) "The Functions of Deviance in Groups," *Social Problems,* **7**:98–107.

Dewey, John. (1910) *How We Think.* New York: Heath.

Fiedler, Fred E. (1964) "A Contingency Model of Leadership Effectiveness," in Leonard Berkowitz (ed.), *Advances in Experimental Social Psychology,* Vol. I. New York: Academic Press, pp. 149–190.

Fisher, B. Aubrey. (1970a) "Decision Emergence: Phases in Group Decision Making," *Speech Monographs,* **37**:53–66.

Fisher, B. Aubrey. (1970b) "The Process of Decision Modification in Small Discussion Groups," *Journal of Communication,* **20**:51–64.

Fisher, B. Aubrey. (1971) "Communication Research and the Task-Oriented Group," *Journal of Communication,* **21**:136–149.

Fisher, B. Aubrey, and Leonard C. Hawes. (1971) "An Interact System Model: Generating a Grounded Theory of Small Group Decision Making," *Quarterly Journal of Speech,* **58**:444–453.

Geier, John G. (1967) "A Trait Approach to the Study of Leadership in Small Groups," *Journal of Communication,* **17**:316–323.

Gerard, Harold B. (1964) "Conformity and Commitment to the Group," *Journal of Abnormal and Social Psychology,* **68:**209–211.

Gibbs, Jack P. (1965) "Norms: The Problem of Definition and Classification," *American Journal of Sociology,* **70:**586–594.

Goffman, Erving. (1959) *The Presentation of Self in Everyday Life.* Garden City, New York: Doubleday.

Goffman, Erving. (1963) *Behavior in Public Places: Notes on the Social Organization of Gatherings.* New York: Free Press.

Goffman, Erving. (1967) *Interaction Ritual: Essays on Face-to-Face Behavior.* Garden City, New York: Doubleday.

Gouran, Dennis S. (1969) "Variables Related to Consensus in Group Discussions of Questions of Policy," *Speech Monographs,* **36:**387–391.

Gouran, Dennis S., and John E. Baird, Jr. (1972) "An Analysis of Distributional and Sequential Structure in Problem-Solving and Informal Group Discussions," *Speech Monographs,* **39:**16–22.

Gruenfeld, Leopold W., David E. Rance, and Peter Weissenberg. (1969) "The Behavior of Task-Oriented and Socially-Oriented Leaders under Several Conditions of Social Support," *Journal of Social Psychology,* **79:**99–107.

Grunig, J. E. (1969) "Information and Decision Making in Economic Development," *Journalism Quarterly,* **46:**565–575.

Hall, Jay, and W. H. Watson. (1970) "The Effects of a Normative Intervention on Group Decision-Making Performance," *Human Relations,* **23:**299–317.

Hall, Jay, and Martha S. Williams. (1970) "Group Dynamics Training and Improved Decision Making," *Journal of Applied Behavioral Science,* **6:**39–68.

Hancock, Brenda Robinson. (1972) "An Interaction Analysis of Self-Disclosure." A paper presented to the Western Speech Communication Association.

Hawes, Leonard C. (1969) "Ambivalence and Productivity in Experimental Triads." A paper presented to the Speech Communication Association.

Hawes, Leonard C. (1972a) "Can a Seeker of a Process Methodology Find Happiness with a Markov Model?" A paper presented to the University of Minnesota Symposium on Communication Theory and Practice.

Hawes, Leonard C. (1972b) "The Effects of Interviewer Style on Patterns of Dyadic Communication," *Speech Monographs,* **39:**114–123.

Herrold, K. F. et al. (1953) "Difficulties Encountered in Group Decision-Making," *Personnel and Guidance Journal,* **31:**516–523.

Heslin, Richard, and Dexter Dunphy. (1964) "Three Dimensions of Member Satisfaction in Small Groups," *Human Relations,* **17:**99–112.

Hill, Walter. (1969) "A Situational Approach to Leadership Effectiveness," *Journal of Applied Psychology,* **53:**513–517.

Hoffman, L. Richard, Ernest Harburg, and Norman R. F. Maier. (1962) "Differences and Disagreement as Factors in Creative Group Problem-Solving," *Journal of Abnormal and Social Psychology,* **64:**206–214.

Holder, Harold, and William P. Ehling. (1967) "Construction and Simulation of an Information-Decision Model," *Journal of Communication,* **17:**302–315.

Hollander, Edwin P. (1958) "Conformity, Status, and Idiosyncrasy Credit," *Psychological Review,* **65:**117–127.

Hollander, Edwin P., and James W. Julian. (1969) "Contemporary Trends in the Analysis of Leadership Processes," *Psychological Bulletin,* **71:**387–397.

Holsti, Ole R. (1969) *Content Analysis for the Social Sciences and Humanities.* Reading, Massachusetts: Addison-Wesley.

Homans, George C. (1950) *The Human Group.* New York: Harcourt, Brace.

Homans, George C. (1961) *Social Behavior: Its Elementary Forms.* New York: Harcourt, Brace.

Huenergardt, Douglas W. (1971) "Books in Review: Body Language," *Quarterly Journal of Speech,* **57:**110.

Kelley, Harold H., and John W. Thibaut. (1954) "Experimental Studies of Group Problem Solving and Process," in Gardner Lindzey (ed.), *Handbook of Social Psychology,* Vol. II, 1st ed. Reading, Massachusetts: Addison-Wesley, pp. 735–785.

Kent, R. N., and Joseph E. McGrath. (1969) "Task and Group Characteristics as Factors Influencing Group Performance," *Journal of Experimental Social Psychology,* **5:**429–440.

Knapp, Mark L. (1972) *Nonverbal Communication in Human Interaction.* New York: Holt, Rinehart and Winston.

Lanzetta, John T., and Thornton B. Roby. (1957) "Group Learning and Communication as a Function of Task and Structure 'Demands,'" *Journal of Abnormal and Social Psychology,* **55:**121–131.

Lanzetta, John T., and Thornton B. Roby. (1960) "The Relationship between Certain Group Process Variables and Group Problem-Solving Efficiency," *Journal of Social Psychology,* **7:**135–148.

Larson, Carl E. (1969) "Forms of Analysis and Small Group Problem Solving," *Speech Monographs,* **36:**452–455.

Larson, Charles U. (1969) "Attention Span and the Leader." A paper presented to the Central States Speech Association.

Larson, Charles U. (1971) "The Verbal Responses of Groups to the Absence or Presence of Leadership," *Speech Monographs,* **38:**177–181.

Leathers, Dale G. (1971) "The Feedback Rating Instrument: A New Means of Evaluating Discussion," *Central States Speech Journal,* **22:**32–42.

Lewin, Kurt. (1951) *Field Theory in Social Science.* New York: Harper.

Longabaugh, R. (1963) "A Category System for Coding Interpersonal Behavior as Social Exchange," *Sociometry,* **26:**319–344.

Lucas, Richard L., and Cabot L. Jaffee. (1969) "Effects of High-Rate Talkers on Group Voting Behavior in the Leaderless-Group Problem-Solving Situation," *Psychological Reports,* **25:**471–477.

Lynch, Mervin D. (1970) "Stylistic Analysis," in Philip Emmert and William D. Brooks (eds.), *Methods of Research in Communication.* Boston: Houghton Mifflin, pp. 315–342.

Maier, Norman R. F. (1963) *Problem-Solving Discussions and Conferences.* New York: McGraw-Hill.

Maier, Norman R. F., and James A. Thurber. (1969) "Limitations of Procedures for Improving Group Problem Solving," *Psychological Reports,* **25:**639–656.

Martin, Howard, and Kenneth Andersen (eds.). (1968) *Speech Communication.* Boston: Allyn and Bacon.

McGrath, Joseph E., and Irwin Altman. (1966) *Small Group Research: A Synthesis and Critique of the Field.* New York: Holt, Rinehart and Winston.

McHugh, Peter. (1968) *Defining the Situation: The Organization of Meaning in Social Interaction.* New York: Bobbs-Merrill.

Merton, Robert K. (1957) *Social Theory and Social Structure.* New York: Free Press.

Miller, George A. (1956) "The Magical Number Seven, Plus or Minus Two: Some Limits on Our Capacity for Processing Information," *Psychological Review,* **63:**81–97.

Morris, Charles G., and J. Richard Hackman. (1969) "Behavioral Correlates of Perceived Leadership." *Journal of Personality and Social Psychology,* **13:**350–361.

Mortensen, Calvin D. (1966) "Should the Discussion Group Have an Assigned Leader?" *Speech Teacher,* **15:**34–41.

Newcomb, Theodore M. (1953) "An Approach to the Study of Communicative Acts," *Psychological Review,* **60:**393–404.

North, R. C., H. E. Koch, and Dina A. Zinnes. (1960) "The Integrative Functions of Conflict," *Journal of Conflict, Resolution,* **4:**355–374.

Parsons, Talcott. (1951) *The Social System.* New York: Free Press.

Phillips, Gerald M. (1966) *Communication and the Small Group,* 1st ed. New York: Bobbs-Merrill.

Phillips, Gerald M., and Eugene C. Erickson. (1970) *Interpersonal Dynamics in the Small Group.* New York: Random House.

Pollay, Richard W. (1969) "Intrafamily Communication and Consensus," *Journal of Communication,* **19:**181–201.

Pruitt, Dean G. (1961) "Informational Requirements in Making Decisions," *American Journal of Psychology,* **74:**433–439.

Pyke, Sandra W., and Cathie A. Neely. (1970) "Evaluation of a Group Training Program," *Journal of Communication,* **20:**291–304.

Riecken, Henry W. (1952) "Some Problems of Consensus Development," *Rural Sociology,* **17:**245–252.

Russell, Hugh C. (1970) "Dimensions of the Communication Behavior of Discussion Leaders." A paper presented to the Central States Speech Association.

Sampson, Edward E., and Arlene C. Brandon. (1964) "The Effects of Role and Opinion Deviation on Small Group Behavior," *Sociometry,* **27:**261–281.

Scheflen, Albert E. (1965) "Quasi-Courtship Behavior in Psychotherapy," *Psychiatry,* **28:**245–255.

Scheflen, Albert E. (1969) "Behavioral Programs in Human Communication," in William Gray, Frederick J. Duhl, and Nicholas D. Rizzo (eds.), *General Systems Theory and Psychiatry.* Boston: Little, Brown, pp. 209–228.

Scheidel, Thomas M. (1969) "Idea Development in Problem-Solving Group Discussion." A paper presented to the Central States Speech Association.

Scheidel, Thomas M., and Laura Crowell. (1964) "Idea Development in Small Discussion Groups," *Quarterly Journal of Speech,* **50:**140–145.

Scheidel, Thomas M., and Laura Crowell. (1966) "Feedback in Small Group Communication," *Quarterly Journal of Speech,* **52:**273–278.

Schein, Edgar H., and Warren G. Bennis. (1967) *Personal and Organizational Change Through Group Methods: The Laboratory Approach.* New York: Wiley.

Sharp, Harry, Jr., and Joyce Milliken. (1964) "The Reflective Thinking Ability and the Product of Problem-Solving Discussion," *Speech Monographs,* **31:**124–127.

Shaw, Marvin E. (1971) *Group Dynamics: The Psychology of Small Group Behavior.* New York: McGraw-Hill.

Shepherd, Clovis R. (1964) *Small Groups: Some Sociological Perspectives.* San Francisco: Chandler.

Sherif, Muzafer, and Carolyn W. Sherif. (1964) *Reference Groups.* New York: Harper.

Simmel, Georg. (1955) *Conflict.* New York: Free Press.

Smith, Alexander B., Alexander Bassin, and Abraham Froelich. (1962) "Interaction Process and Equilibrium in a Therapy Group of Adult Offenders," *Journal of Social Psychology,* **56:**141–147.

Smith, Dennis R. (1970) "The Fallacy of the Communication Breakdown," *Quarterly Journal of Speech,* **16:**343–346.

Smith, Ewart E., and Stanford S. Knight. (1959) "Effects of Feedback on Insight and Problem Solving Efficiency in Training Groups," *Journal of Applied Psychology,* **43:**209–211.

Sommer, Robert. (1969) *Personal Space: The Behavioral Basis of Design.* Englewood Cliffs, New Jersey: Prentice-Hall.

Streufert, Siegfried. (1969) "Increasing Failure and Response Rate in Complex Decision Making," *Journal of Experimental Social Psychology,* **5:**310–323.

Talland, George A. (1955) "Task and Interaction Process: Some Characteristics of Therapeutic Group Discussion," *Journal of Abnormal and Social Psychology,* **50:**105–109.

Tallman, Irving. (1970) "The Family as a Small Problem Solving Group," *Journal of Marriage and the Family,* **32:**94–104.

Theodorson, George A. (1962) "The Function of Hostility in Small Groups," *Journal of Social Psychology,* **56:**57–66.

Thibaut, John W., and Harold H. Kelley. (1959) *The Social Psychology of Groups.* New York: Wiley.

Tuckman, Bruce W. (1965) "Developmental Sequence in Small Groups," *Psychological Bulletin,* **63:**384–399.

Turk, H. (1961) "Instrumental and Expressive Ratings Reconsidered," *Sociometry,* **24:**76–81.

Valentine, Kristin B. (1972) "The Analysis of Verbal Innovative Deviance in Small Group Interaction." A paper presented to the Speech Communication Association.

Verba, Sydney. (1961) *Small Groups and Political Behavior.* Princeton, New Jersey: Princeton University Press.

Weick, Karl E. (1969) *The Social Psychology of Organizing.* Reading, Massachusetts: Addison-Wesley.

Weick, Karl E. (1968) "Systematic Observational Methods," in Gardner Lindzey and Elliot Aronson (eds.), *The Handbook of Social Psychology,* Vol. II, 2nd ed. Reading, Massachusetts, pp. 357–451.

Williams, Frederick. (1970) "Analysis of Verbal Behavior," in Philip Emmert and William D. Brooks (eds.), *Methods of Research in Communication.* Boston: Houghton Mifflin, pp. 237–290.

Wilson, Stephen R. (1970) "Some Factors Influencing Instrumental and Expressive Ratings in Task-Oriented Groups," *Pacific Sociological Review,* **13:**127–131.

Zaleznik, Abraham, and David Moment. (1964) *The Dynamics of Interpersonal Behavior.* New York: Wiley.

Index